Hawaii: A History

Other Books by the Authors

By Ralph S. Kuykendall

A HISTORY OF HAWAII
HAWAII IN WORLD WAR I
CONSTITUTIONS OF THE HAWAIIAN KINGDOM
THE HAWAIIAN KINGDOM
Vol. I. FOUNDATION AND TRANSFORMATION
Vol. II. TWENTY CRITICAL YEARS
Vol. III. THE KALAKAUA DYNASTY (in press)

By A. Grove Day

CORONADO'S QUEST
THE SPELL OF THE PACIFIC (*with Carl Stroven*)
RASCALS IN PARADISE (*with James A. Michener*)
A HAWAIIAN READER (*with Carl Stroven*)
HAWAII, FIFTIETH STAR
HAWAII AND ITS PEOPLE
THE STORY OF AUSTRALIA

Hawaii: A History

From Polynesian Kingdom to American
State

Revised Edition

by

Ralph S. Kuykendall

and

A. Grove Day

Prentice-Hall, Inc.
Englewood Cliffs, N. J.

Hawaii: A History *by Ralph S. Kuykendall
and A. Grove Day*

*Copyright © 1948, 1961 by Ralph S. Kuykendall
and A. Grove Day
Renewal © 1976 by Gloria H. Kuykendall,
Delman L. Kuykendall and A. Grove Day*

Printed in the United States of America

*Prentice-Hall International, Inc., London
Prentice-Hall of Australia, Pty. Ltd., Sydney
Prentice-Hall of Canada, Ltd., Toronto
Prentice-Hall of India Private Ltd., New Delhi
Prentice-Hall of Japan, Inc., Tokyo
Prentice-Hall of Southeast Asia Pte. Ltd., Singapore
Whitehall Books Limited, Wellington, New Zealand*

10   9   8

Library of Congress Catalog Card Number: 61-8894

*38429—T
0-13-384305-X pbk.*

Foreword to First Edition

THE people of the Hawaiian Islands have passed, during the span of one hundred and seventy years, from the Stone Age into the Atomic Age. The United States had not yet won its independence when, in 1778, the vessels of Captain James Cook, manned by the first Europeans ever to view these charming Polynesian islands, brought Hawaii within the ken of the great world powers. After the atom bomb brought to a close the greatest war that the Pacific has ever seen, Hawaii was on the threshold of becoming a new state of the U.S.A.

It was an accident that Hawaii was the last important Pacific island group to be discovered by voyagers from the outer world; but it was no accident that Hawaii, because of its strategic position, was the first to achieve modernity. Only through a study of the past can we hope to imagine what the future may be; and it is believed that a reading of Hawaii's eventful history will give many clues to the future of America's role in the Pacific Era. The present volume is designed to give the general reader the main narrative of Hawaii's history, from the days of the ancient feather-cloaked warriors to the present time, when Hawaii's fight for statehood has made its history an issue of national importance.

Many are the books that evoke the romantic side of life in the Hawaiian Islands. One can find in this subtropical archipelago a wealth of glamor, and the romance of swaying palm trees and hula skirts has not passed away. But a careful analysis of the facts of history that have created the life of modern Hawaii will reveal a deeper romance at work here—the romance of reality. Throughout its life—as a native monarchy, as a polyracial republic, and as an American territory—the mainsprings of Hawaii's prosperity have been trade, industry, and agriculture. Tourists can still find in these islands the picturesque languor of flowery Polynesia. But no one should overlook the forces by which, through economic initiative and under democratic ideals, a group of Pacific islands have been transformed, within a few lifetimes, into a thriving commonwealth of almost half a million Americans of many ancestral stocks, all working together to erect an American state at the "Crossroads of the Pacific." Honolulu, one of the great ports of the world, is an American metropolis. The true story of the creation of this commonwealth in the midst of the world's greatest ocean is one that should bring inspiration to all believers in progress.

There has long been a need for an authoritative one-volume work that would give in straight narrative form the consecutive events of Hawaii's history to date. This book is based upon many years of research on this subject by the senior author. Much new material, derived from documentary sources, has been included in this fresh presentation of Hawaiian history for the reader of today. The style has been aimed toward the ordinary well-informed reader. With the index is combined a pronunciation key and a glossary of Hawaiian words. It is hoped that the book will be of special interest not only to the residents of Hawaii and to students of its history, but likewise to the many visitors—in uniform or out—who have come to its shores in the past and who may come in future. Those who are concerned about the fitness of Hawaii's people to become citizens of a new state should be interested particularly in the later chapters, which give a review of Hawaii's position in the post-war world.

R. S. K.
A. G. D.

University of Hawaii
August, 1948

Contents

List of Illustrations

Book 1

Ancient Hawaii

(*to* 1779)

CHAPTER ONE

Before the "Haole" Came

THE vast Pacific Ocean is the most prominent geographical feature of our earth. Scattered in this ocean, which occupies a third of the surface of the globe, lie the Hawaiian Islands, the "Crossroads of the Pacific."

The Hawaiian Islands are not located, as many persons imagine, in the middle of the Pacific. Nor are they in the South Pacific, but in the eastern half of the North Pacific. On the modern world map, shrunken to small size by airplanes and radio, Hawaii lies just off the coast of North America. But even before such modern devices came in, these islands were closer to America than to any other important body of land. They are only a little farther from that continent than from the nearest other groups of Polynesians, the race to which the Hawaiians belong. Honolulu, a little more than two thousand nautical miles from San Francisco, is considerably closer to San Francisco than San Francisco is to Washington, D.C. There are geographical as well as historical reasons for Hawaii's evolution into an American state.

The Hawaiian group includes seven major inhabited islands, Hawaii, Maui, Oahu, Kauai, Molokai, Lanai, and Niihau; the first four are by far the most important. Another island, Kahoolawe, is sometimes listed as an eighth major island but hardly deserves the honor. Extending toward the northwest is a chain of uninhabited islets which include Nihoa, Necker, French Frigate Shoal, Gardner, Laysan, Lisiansky, and Ocean. Total area of the group is about 6,500 square miles. Nearly two-thirds of this land is on the island of Hawaii, which for that rea-

3

son is locally called the "Big Island." The Big Island is also the highest, having two mountains nearly 14,000 feet high. The only active volcanoes, Mauna Loa and Kilauea, rise on that island. One of the world's largest extinct volcanoes, Haleakala (elevation, 10,000 feet), is on the neighboring island of Maui. The only good natural harbors are found in the island of Oahu. Kauai, northwesternmost of the main islands, boasts of having one of the wettest spots on the globe, the summit of Mount Waialeale, where the average annual rainfall is about forty feet. At another place fifteen miles away the annual rainfall is twenty inches.

At the present time more than three-fourths of the total population live on Oahu. More than half are in the city of Honolulu, which is the political capital and economic metropolis of the group. But in olden times the Big Island had the largest population and was politically most important. History will explain these changes.

The islands lie just below the Tropic of Cancer, but the climate is not torrid or tropical. Within a few miles on one island, Hawaii, one may descend from snowy slopes to sandy deserts. For the populated areas, the words "mild" and "equable" best describe the climate, but a government meteorologist says: "It seems doubtful that one could find anywhere else, within such short distances, such wide diversity of climate as in the Hawaiian Islands." This diversity results from the presence of the mountains which dominate the landscape on all the islands. The same writer notes as the outstanding features of the climate "the remarkable differences in rainfall over adjacent areas; the tenaciousness of the trade winds through practically all seasons and over all islands of the group; and the persistently equable temperature."

The Hawaiians, who lived on these islands for fourteen centuries before the coming of the *haoles* (foreigners), are a part of the great Polynesian family. When Europe's Age of Discovery began, the Polynesians had already discovered and populated the widely scattered islands in the central and southern parts of the

Pacific Ocean included in what is called the "Polynesian triangle." At the points of this triangle are Hawaii, Easter Island, and New Zealand. The early Polynesians were the world's most venturesome explorers, and in the course of their migrations, while discovering and occupying what came to be their island homes, they performed feats of navigation that have not been equaled by any other primitive people.

The Polynesian sailors, at a time when our European ancestors knew little more than the shores of the narrow Mediterranean Sea, were making voyages of thousands of miles in the world's mightiest ocean. How, without the compass, could they hope to find another island in that expanse? The answer is that they guided their craft by the sun, clouds, birds, currents, and waves, and at night by the stars. The native navigator knew more than a hundred and fifty stars by name, knew what ones were in the same latitude, and knew their changes in position from month to month. Many voyagers never reached land, but others always followed.

From southeastern Asia, the ancestors of the Polynesians are supposed to have migrated into the western islands of Indonesia before the beginning of the Christian Era. In successive stages over the course of centuries their descendants moved on—or were driven on—toward the east, and by 100 or 200 A.D. had reached Tahiti and the islands in the center of the Polynesian triangle.

What route did they follow? According to the older view, it ran eastward through Indonesia, along the coast of New Guinea, and through Melanesia into Central Polynesia, from which the race spread to the outlying groups of islands. More recent research, however, points very strongly to a different route, a northern one through Micronesia. Along this route, from the eastern Carolines one group may have gone northeastward and found the Hawaiian Islands, while the main body made its way southeastward into Central Polynesia. There is much uncertainty about the details, and it is possible that the discoveries and earliest inhabitants of Hawaii went there from Central Polynesia.

From whatever direction they came, these first Hawaiians and their descendants lived isolated in their little island world for several hundred years. They increased in number and adapted their rude culture to the limited resources which they found on the islands. They were the *Menehunes*, whom the makers of legends in following centuries transformed into dwarfs or brownies having magical powers that enabled them to perform with incredible speed marvelous feats of engineering in the construction of fish ponds, water courses, and temples for their gods.

After some centuries of isolation, there followed a period of perhaps two hundred years, between the beginning of the eleventh and the close of the fourteenth centuries, when there was a great migration movement throughout Polynesia and many voyages were made among the different island groups. During this time, Hawaii was visited by adventurous travelers from Central Polynesia and some Hawaiians made the long journey to the southern lands. Many of those who came to Hawaii in this period remained as permanent dwellers on these northern islands. They brought with them almost all the cultivated Polynesian food plants, dogs, pigs, chickens, and the paper-mulberry tree. The newcomers possessed a culture more highly developed than that previously existing in Hawaii, and they became the dominant element in the population. Their chiefs (*alii*) became the ruling class and their priests took over the direction of the religious observances and introduced some new temple forms and practices and some new gods. "To the Hawaiian people," wrote Fornander, this was "an era of activity and enterprise, an awakening from a sleep of fifteen generations. . . . It modified the ancient customs, creed, and polity. It even affected the speech of the people."

Hawaiian legends and genealogies preserve the names and adventures of many of the travelers and immigrants of this period of the "long voyages." There is, for example, the story of Paao, a member of the priestly order in Tahiti, who quarreled with his brother and then left his home, journeying northward to Hawaii, where he became a high priest; to him is credited the introduction of some of the new religious practices mentioned above. Finding the island of Hawaii oppressed by a cruel and wicked king, Paao sent a messenger to Tahiti, or went back himself, and brought from there a chief named Pili. The wicked king was deposed and Pili took over the reins of government. Pili was the ancestor of Kamehameha, who founded the modern Hawaiian kingdom, and in the reign of Kamehameha a descendant of Paao was the high priest of Hawaii.

The epoch of the long voyages came to an end and communication ceased between Hawaii and the rest of Polynesia. Again for several centuries the Hawaiian people lived in isolation, with only traditions to tell them of the world beyond the encircling waters of the great ocean. Generation followed generation while the population grew and rival chieftains struggled to enlarge their petty feudal holdings. The history of these centuries is full of the adventures of the *alii*, male and female, and the details of battles that were fought in their quest for supremacy. The entire group had a natural tendency to fall into four kingdoms dominated by great families of chiefs on the larger islands—Hawaii, Maui, Oahu, Kauai. The smaller islands sometimes maintained a precarious independence, but more commonly belonged, as prizes of war, to one or another of their more powerful neighbors. There was little stability or permanence in any of these political arrangements, since they depended mainly upon the rise and fall of individual *alii*. Occasionally some ambitious chieftain set out on a career of conquest, hoping to bring all the islands under his rule, but none succeeded before the time of Kamehameha.

In the Hawaiian way of life as developed in these early centuries, government, social organization, the economic system, and religion all were closely interwoven. The general pattern, except in religion, was quite similar to the feudal system of medieval Europe. At the top were the chiefs of various grades, at the bottom the common people who did the rough work and were subject to the will of the chiefs. There was no middle class in the modern sense, but the *kahunas* (priests, doctors, sorcerers, navigators, and experts in various other lines) comprised a class closely associated with the chiefs.

Thus, in the Hawaii of old, the entire group of islands was not united under a single king, but there were little kingdoms whose size and boundaries were continually changing, varying with the power of the chiefs who governed them. Because of the clashing ambitions of rival chieftains, wars were frequent. The land belonged to the ruling chief and he, after taking such parts as he wanted for his own use, divided the rest among the lesser chiefs who were loyal to him. There was no permanence or security of possession, since the chief above could take the land away from the one below, and such dispossession was not uncommon. The people at the bottom were attached to the soil, though they could change from one chief to another. They cultivated not only the little plots on which they lived but also the land of the chief, and they also gave him part of the produce of their own holdings; and when they went fishing the chief got part of the catch. When the chief went to war, the common people were called up for military service.

The people lived, for the most part, near the seashore or within sight of it. From the sea they obtained a large part of their food. Fishing was important not only as work but also as recreation. The Hawaiians were expert fishermen, expert also in the making of canoes and in fashioning fishlines, nets, hooks, and various kinds of lures with which to carry on fishing operations. The commonest type of vessel used by the Hawaiians was the simple outrigger canoe, but they also constructed large double canoes which were quite seaworthy and capable of carrying many people and a substantial amount of cargo. Some canoes were equipped with "crab-claw" sails of woven coconut or pandanus leaves.

On land a frequent activity was the building of houses, since each family normally required several of them. The grass-covered house was a simple structure and not too durable, but the expression "grass shack" so common in recent songs hardly does justice to the skill required in erecting the Hawaiian house in olden days, before the Hawaiians ever saw nails or metal tools.

Fire was precious to the Hawaiians. When fire had to be made, they used a Polynesian invention, the "fire plow." A pointed stick was firmly and swiftly rubbed in a groove in a plank until smoke rose from the heap of wood dust that accumulated in the groove. Then this tinder was nursed into flame.

Providing food for the household was the man's job. Fish and poi were the two most important articles of the Hawaiian diet. Poi is made from taro, and the growing of taro and its manufacture into poi required skill and a great amount of hard work. For wet-land taro, the kind most extensively used, special beds with raised borders like rice fields had to be prepared, so that the growing crop could be kept well supplied with water. To bring to the taro beds the large amount of water that was required, the Hawaiians devised elaborate irrigation systems. The sharing of water was carefully regulated in accordance with well-recognized water rights. After the taro was harvested it was steamed in an underground oven (*imu*) and pounded into a thick paste with heavy stone pounders on the poi board; it was then mixed with water to the desired consistency. Other vegetable foods used less extensively were sweet potatoes, breadfruit, yams, coconuts, arrowroot, sugar cane, and seaweeds. Pigs, dogs, and chickens were raised and eaten in large numbers.

Women attended to the care of children, the plaiting of mats, and the preparation of clothing from *kapa*, sometimes called bark cloth. The manufacture of *kapa* from the inner bark of the paper mulberry was a laborious task requiring no small skill. The cloth was dyed in shades of gray, brown, blue, red, and yellow, and on it were imprinted lovely decorative patterns.

Little clothing was needed in the islands, and a short skirt for women and a loin cloth (*malo*) for men often sufficed. The instinct for adornment, however, led to the fashioning of lengthy robes of *kapa*. Matting was worn in rainy weather. Woven pandanus leaves were used for many purposes. Ornaments of great charm were made of wood, stone, shells, and the bones and pelts of animals. Tattooing of the body was a characteristic form of personal adornment. Most typical, however, was the featherwork of the Hawaiians, in which they excelled all other peoples. The feather helmets and cloaks of ancient Hawaii, woven from the plumage of thousands of small birds, are still treasured.

The life of the Hawaiians was not all hard work. They had actually many hours of leisure and a great variety of sports, games, and entertainment. Everyone enjoyed the healthful and invigorating sports of swimming and of surf-riding on carved boards, at which the Hawaiians became amazingly skillful. Coasting down steep hill courses on narrow sleds was a daring sport practiced by the chiefs; children in similar fashion slid down hills on *ti* leaves and coconut fronds, a game still common among the youth of the islands. Boxing, wrestling, and foot-racing were popular sports. The Hawaiians had a form of bowling, several kinds of dart and throwing games, guessing games, and one called *konane* that was something like checkers. Many of these sports and games furnished entertainment for spectators, as did military exercises, sham battles, and hula exhibitions. The hula had a threefold value: it was a religious exercise, a system of physical training, and a form of entertainment.

The ancient Hawaiians loved to travel about their islands, and strangers were traditionally greeted with courtesy and offered full hospitality. Whoever violated the ideals of hospitality might be shamed and punished. Welcoming a visitor was ingrained in the Hawaiian nature, as white voyagers were to discover.

Religion played a great part in the life of the people. Every important activity, from making a house or a canoe to planning a battle, had to be started with an appropriate religious ceremony. Their religion was a kind of nature worship. The Hawaiians were impressed by the manifestations in the world about them of a mysterious power, unseen and little understood. Their ceremonies aimed to establish and preserve proper relationships between man and this unseen power. The gods were personifications of natural objects and the forces of nature. Hence there were many gods, but there were three that stood out above all the rest: Kane, god of light and life; Lono, god of the harvest; Ku, god of war. These gods were common to all Polynesia, but it is said of Ku that he attained his greatest glory in Hawaii. Regarded from all points of view he was the dominating figure of the pantheon in these islands. The special name of the war god of Kamehameha was Kukailimoku. The *heiau* was the place dedicated to the public worship of the gods. It was a stone-paved platform or terrace enclosed by stone walls and containing various objects and structures needed for the religious services. There were some *heiaus* in which human sacrifices were offered.

Closely related to the religious practices was the *kapu* system, which has been spoken of as a "system of religious law." Visitors to the Hawaiian Islands soon become familiar with the word *kapu*, which appears on warning signs in many places. The system of *kapu* originated from the distinction between that which was sacred or divine and that which was common or earthly, between male and female. In practice the system consisted mainly of a multitude of prohibitions, things that must not be done, and set up severe penalties for violation of the rules. A common person could not stand in the presence of the sacred chief or, even inadvertently, touch his clothing. Women could not eat with men, and there were some foods—pork, bananas, coconuts, certain kinds of fish—which they could not eat. Since the highest chief was thought to be sacred or divine, and lesser chiefs had varying amounts of this quality, the *kapu* system worked to their advantage. If they did not play the game honestly, cruel abuses could develop.

The Hawaiian language, which is a local variant of the tongue spoken by the Polynesian race, is soft and musical, since every syllable ends in a vowel, and there are only seven consonants, none of them harsh in sound. Its vocabulary contains more than twenty thousand words, and is capable of expressing rather fine shades of meaning—particularly in symbolic or poetic style.

Because their language had not been reduced to written form, the Hawaiians had no libraries. Their books were the memories of men. They had an extensive literature recorded in that way and handed down by word of mouth from generation to generation. It consisted of songs (*meles*), genealogies, stories, ritualistic and honorific chants, and traditions embodying fragments of history and biography. A large part of this lore was given in the form of poetry, much of which shows high literary power. Since the time when the language was reduced to writing, much of the old Hawaiian literature has been recorded in written or printed form and some of it has been translated. This literature is the source material from which our knowledge of the early history and ancient culture is derived.

This, then, was the native race that first found the Hawaiian Islands. These were the people who, for centuries unaware of the world beyond the sea's rim, in the latter eighteenth century greeted the first European explorers to break in upon their island solitudes.

CHAPTER TWO

Captain Cook, the Discoverer

THE discovery of the Hawaiian Islands by men from the outer world comes on a late page in the book of exploration. Magellan, Villalobos, Legaspi, Mendaña, Drake, Quiros, Tasman, and others had ranged through the expanses of the Pacific. For more than two centuries, the Manila galleon had yearly navigated the scurvy-haunted sea leagues between the Philippines and Mexico, but its routes across the Pacific ran to the north and south of Hawaii, and Spain knew no more of these islands than did the Portuguese or the Dutch. The old idea of an early Spanish discovery has been thoroughly disproved. The first European to find the Hawaiian Islands was an English navigator who was seeking something that did not exist—the fabled Strait of Anian, a passage through North America that would shorten the voyage from Europe to Asia. Captain Cook, who first broke in upon the seclusion of Hawaii and brought the seeds of a transforming culture, was greeted as a god, and left his bones—very human ones—on its volcanic shores.

James Cook was born in 1728 in a humble cottage. At an early age the smell of the sea lured him to the deck of a ship. By hard work and strict application he learned navigation and quickly gained the rank of mate in the merchant service. He volunteered in 1755 as ordinary seaman in the British navy, was soon promoted to master's mate, and for the next few years served in America in the French and Indian War. He conducted a detailed survey of the coast of Newfoundland from 1763 to 1767. A year later he was given command of an expedition sent to Tahiti to observe the transit of the planet Venus across the sun, and to engage in explorations in the little-known South Pacific. This voyage in the *Endeavour*, during which he explored the coasts of Australia and New Zealand and circumnavigated the globe, was the first of three voyages during ten years which made him the foremost man of his time in Pacific discovery.

On his third voyage Cook, in command of the *Resolution* and the *Discovery*, was instructed to go first to the Society Islands, thence to the coast of America at about 45 degrees north latitude, and from there to follow the coast northward in search of the supposed passage through the continent. He left Borabora in the Society group in December, 1777. At dawn on January 18, 1778, his little squadron sighted an island to the northeast, and shortly afterward another island was seen to the west of it. These islands were Oahu and Kauai.

The first meeting of discoverer and native, which took place next day when the ships drew near the shores of Kauai and were met by a number of canoes, is described in the words of Cook himself:

> They had from three to six men each; and, on their approach, we were agreeably surprised to find that they spoke the language of Otaheite and of the other islands we had lately visited. It required but very little address to get them to come alongside; but no entreaties could prevail upon any of them to come on board. I tied some brass medals to a rope and gave them to those in one of the canoes, who, in return, tied some small mackerel to the rope, as an equivalent. This was repeated; and some small nails, or bits of iron, which they valued more than any other article, were given them. For these they exchanged more fish and a sweet potato, a sure sign that they had some notion of bartering or, at least, of returning one present for another.

The hunger of the Hawaiians for the precious iron (which they had possessed only as fragments probably salvaged from drift

logs) was increasingly shown in the next few days, when the
two vessels came to anchor off the village of Waimea on Kauai.
Their desire for iron is reflected in the native account of the
coming of the white god:

It is at Waimea, on Kauai, that Lono first arrived. . . .
He arrived in the night at Waimea, and when daylight came
the natives ashore perceived this wonderful thing that had
arrived, and they expressed their astonishment with great
exclamations.

One said to another, "What is that great thing with
branches?" Others said, "It is a forest that has slid down into
the sea," and the gabble and noise was great. Then the chiefs
ordered some natives to go in a canoe and observe and
examine well that wonderful thing. They went, and when
they came to the ship they saw the iron that was attached
to the outside of the ship, and they were greatly rejoiced at
the quantity of iron.

A moderate-sized nail, wrote Captain Clerke of the *Discovery*,
supplied his ship's company with enough excellent pork for the
day, with potatoes and taro thrown in. Cook seized the opportunity
to load his ships with fresh water and to barter old iron for pigs,
fowls, yams, plantains, and taro.

Trading was conducted fairly, but even before the ships landed
the Hawaiians had a taste of the power of firearms. Small boats
were sent by Cook toward land to discover a watering place, and
the leading boat was surrounded by eager natives intent upon
pulling it ashore. One native who attempted to grab the boat hook
was shot and killed by Lieutenant Williamson, the officer in
command.

Captain Cook went ashore three times at Waimea, and wherever he passed, the common people prostrated themselves before
him just as they did before their own chiefs of highest rank. The
Discovery was visited by a handsome young couple who were

understood to be the king and queen of the island, and with whom gifts were exchanged.

The ships next visited the small island of Niihau, where they obtained salt and many fine yams. Here Cook left a ram goat and two ewes, a British boar and sow pig, and seeds of melons, pumpkins, and onions. A party sent ashore to trade was forced to remain on Niihau for two days and nights because of the high surf. Cook had given orders aimed to prevent the introduction of venereal disease among the natives, but could not keep the two races apart, and it is only too certain that this scourge was introduced in the islands by his sailors.

Cook remained a fortnight in the group, without seeing the islands to the southeast. He then sailed to the northwest coast of America to carry on his explorations there, having christened his discovery the Sandwich Islands, in honor of his friend and patron the Earl of Sandwich, then First Lord of the British Admiralty.

During the eight months that passed before Cook returned with the intention of wintering in the Sandwich Islands, the news of his visit spread to the windward islands, and the natives decided that he should be worshiped as an incarnation of Lono, god of the *makahiki* season. The manner in which Cook's squadron sailed along the coasts twice during the *makahiki* months, their sails resembling Lono's banner of *kapa*, may have suggested to the native mind the progress of the god during that festival. At any rate, Cook was greeted as Lono when he again appeared in the islands.

On November 26, the ships raised the north coast of Maui, and later in the day gained a distant view of Molokai. The next day Kahekili, king of Maui, visited the *Discovery* and gave Captain Clerke a red feather cloak. Three days later, off the east end of Maui, Kalaniopuu, king of the island of Hawaii, who was at war with Kahekili, visited the *Resolution* with a retinue of chiefs, some of whom spent the night aboard.

One of these observers was the chief Kamehameha, whose intelligent curiosity about the ways of white men in war and peace was to help him pull together in the islands a kingdom that would endure for more than a century despite foreign encroachments. This casual meeting of the two main figures of eighteenth century Hawaiian history is not even mentioned by Cook in his journal.

A leisurely tour of the eastern end of Maui and the eastern and southern sides of Hawaii occupied the weeks until January 17, 1779, when the two ships came to anchor in Kealakekua Bay on the Kona coast of Hawaii. An excited throng estimated at ten thousand people greeted their arrival, most of them afloat in canoes or on surf boards, or swimming in the waters of the bay. As soon as Cook went on shore, he was led to the *heiau* of Hikiau, where he underwent a ceremony by which the priests acknowledged him as Lono. It is doubtful if the foreigners understood the religious significance of this act; but to the last day of his life Cook was treated with adoring respect.

The next two weeks and a half were devoted to refitting and provisioning the ships for a return to the Arctic and to getting further information about the people of Hawaii. Astronomical instruments were landed and set up in a sweet potato patch over which the priests had placed a *kapu*. Every day the Hawaiians sent aboard large quantities of hogs and vegetables. On January 25 King Kalaniopuu again visited Cook, exchanged names with him, and presented him with several feather cloaks. Cook in return gave the king a linen shirt, a sword, and later a "complete tool chest." During the visit, the natives entertained with boxing and wrestling matches, and the visitors gave a display of fireworks.

Farewells were said on February 4 and the two ships headed north along the Kona coast. A few incidents of highhandedness on the part of the Europeans and the natural tendency of the natives to take what they fancied had not been permitted to mar their amicable relations. All would have gone well with Cook had not a severe storm unluckily arisen off the coast of Kohala which damaged the foremast of the *Resolution,* so that the squadron had to turn back to Kealakekua.

The time between February 11 and February 13 was spent in

setting up the astronomical instruments beside the *heiau* and
working on the injured mast near by. On the afternoon of the
13th, several altercations with the natives arose. Next morning
it was found that the large cutter of the *Discovery* had been stolen
in the night. Cook himself, since Clerke was unwell, took charge,
and with three small boats and a marine guard went ashore to the
village of Kaawaloa. His plan—one that had always worked before
in his dealings with Pacific Islanders—was to take King Kalaniopuu
on board the flagship and hold him as hostage for the stolen boat.

At first the king agreed and started to walk to the shore; then
he stopped to listen to the suspicions voiced by his wife and several
chiefs, who were alarmed at the seemingly hostile conduct of Lono
and his armed guard. Meanwhile a great crowd had gathered.
News came that a chief crossing the bay in a canoe had been killed
by a shot from one of the cordon of boats which had been stationed
there. Some of the bolder natives, now armed with daggers, clubs,
spears, and stones, made threatening gestures.

Cook gave up the attempt to take the king aboard, and with his
marines withdrew and formed in line on the rocks by the shore.
One Hawaiian aimed a dagger at the captain, who fired one barrel
of his gun, loaded either with a blank or a charge of small shot,
which did no damage and only emboldened the natives. Cook fired
the other barrel, loaded with ball, and killed a man. Lieutenant
Phillips, the marines on shore, and the sailors in the boats also
began shooting. Cook ordered the boats to cease firing and to come
in closer. In the melee that followed, Cook was struck down with
a club and stabbed in the back with a dagger. He fell into the
water and either died of his wounds or was drowned.

One chief, according to the native story, had "seized Captain
Cook with a strong hand, designing merely to hold him, and not
to take his life; for he supposed him to be a god, and that he could
not die. Captain Cook struggled to free himself from the grasp,
and as he was about to fall uttered a groan. The people immediately exclaimed, 'He groans—he is not a god,' and instantly slew
him."

About a score of natives were killed in the fray. Most of the marines swam off to the pinnace, but four were slain, and their bodies, along with Cook's, were carried off by the natives. The bones of Captain Cook were divided among the high chiefs and priests.

The anger aroused by this fight did not soon cool, in spite of the conciliatory policies of the leaders on both sides. Many natives were killed and a number of houses were burned in the week that followed. Finally peace was restored. Most of the bones of Cook were given up and were buried in the waters of the bay on February 21.

Late in the evening of February 22 the two English vessels weighed anchor and left the bay where tragedy had taken their leader. For three weeks they lingered among the main islands of the group, taking on water and provisions. On March 15, 1779, the expedition left for the north to continue its explorations on the coasts of America and Asia, and did not return to the Sandwich Islands.

Book 2

Evolution of a Constitutional Kingdom

(1778–1854)

CHAPTER THREE

Kamehameha Founds the Kingdom

KAMEHAMEHA is the hero of the Hawaiian people because it was he who first united the islands under a strong rulership—strong enough to maintain independence during the critical years when the islands were first opened to the enterprise of traders and explorers from Europe and America.

The last quarter of the eighteenth century is a period of Hawaiian history marked by the emergence of Kamehameha as the victor in a running series of civil wars. The period of peace that followed 1796 enabled him by the power of his personality to make firm the foundations of the Hawaiian kingdom.

Kamehameha ("The Lonely One") was born in Kohala, Hawaii, on a stormy winter night soon after the middle of the century (1758 is a probable date). Although his father and mother were of high rank, Kamehameha was not in the direct line of kingly succession. At this time, the islands were divided into four kingdoms, each ruled by a leading chief (*alii-aimoku*). The most prominent of these were Kahekili of Maui and Kalaniopuu of Hawaii, uncle of Kamehameha. The young warrior grew up at the court on Hawaii, and in 1775, in one of the battles between Kalaniopuu and Kahekili on Maui, saved the life of his instructor in warfare, Kekuhaupio. In 1778 Kamehameha spent many hours on the ships of Captain Cook, where Lieutenant King remarked of him that he had "the most savage face" he had ever beheld.

A year or two later, Kalaniopuu, now an old man, proclaimed his son Kiwalao his successor, and gave to Kamehameha the guardianship of the war god. In this capacity Kamehameha soon aroused the anger of Kiwalao by summarily sacrificing a captured rebel chief while Kiwalao was preparing to perform this rite. He therefore retired to his lands at Kohala until after the death of Kalaniopuu in 1782.

Five chiefs of the Kona district, fearing that they would be unfairly treated in the distribution of lands by the new king, formed a cabal and asked Kamehameha to be their leader. Their fears were justified, and soon an open war broke out, in which the forces of Kamehameha won a victory at Mokuohai. Kiwalao was killed, and as a result the island of Hawaii was divided into three regions, with Kamehameha in control of Kohala, Kona, and Hamakua.

Ten years of civil war followed, in which Kamehameha was pitted against Keawemauhili of Puna; Keoua, brother of Kiwalao, of Kau; and Kahekili, king of the neighboring island of Maui.

An incident in the early part of this period will always be remembered by the Hawaiians. During a raid on Puna, Kamehameha saw some fishermen on the beach and leaped ashore alone to attack them. As he pursued the fleeing men, he slipped and caught his foot in a crevice of the lava. A bold fisherman returned and struck the chief on the head with a canoe paddle, which broke in pieces. The fishermen then escaped and Kamehameha freed himself and returned to his canoe.

The fishermen were later caught, however, and brought to judgment. Kamehameha then admitted his fault in attacking the innocent, and set them free with a gift of lands. In after years he gave the name *Mamalahoe Kanawai* (the law of the splintered paddle) to one of his decrees, which ran: "Let the aged, men and women, and little children lie down in safety in the road."

Another prophetic incident occurred during the civil war period. Kamehameha, now allied with Keawemauhili, was waging a campaign against Maui and Oahu. Keoua, taking advantage of this diversion, invaded the Hilo district, killed Keawemauhili, and ravaged Waipio and Waimea. Kamehameha returned and soon drove the invaders back toward their homes in Kau. While

Keoua's army was passing Kilauea, the volcano erupted and about a third of the soldiers, with their wives and children, were killed by the ashes and fumes (1790). This event was taken as proof that the fire goddess Pele was on the side of Kamehameha.

As the warfare continued, with Keoua master of half the island, Kamehameha sought the advice of a renowned soothsayer of Kauai. The oracle reported that, if the king wished to conquer Hawaii, he must build a large *heiau* at Puukohola, Kawaihae, in honor of the war god. When this great undertaking was finished, Keoua was induced to go to the sacred spot to be reconciled with Kamehameha. He agreed, although he might have guessed the fate that awaited him. When the visitor's canoe approached the shore, Kamehameha hailed him: "Rise and come here, that we may know each other." As Keoua stepped ashore, he was slain by the spear of Keeaumoku, one of Kamehameha's loyal band of chiefs. The companions of Keoua were slaughtered, and in the smoke from the sacrificial altar vanished all opposition to the control by Kamehameha of the Big Island.

The death of Keoua in 1791 left Kamehameha free to carry on his war with Kahekili, who by this time had emerged as overlord not only of Maui, but of Molokai, Oahu, and Kauai as well. Kamehameha had already invaded Maui in 1790 and had nearly destroyed the enemy army at Iao Valley, where the stream beneath the famous needle was red with their blood. But when he had to return to the island of Hawaii to deal with Keoua, Kahekili and his brother Kaeo had retaliated by ravaging northern Hawaii.

Kamehameha's success in getting foreign arms and foreign recruits now gave him the upper hand over chiefs visited less often by the traders who followed in the wake of the discovery. In the winter of 1789–1790 the first American vessels had visited the islands. The earliest was the *Columbia*, under Captain Robert Gray, the first American ship to circumnavigate the globe. Another was the *Lady Washington*, whose captain, John Kendrick, sold guns and ammunition to the chiefs.

Two other vessels in these waters at the same time played a

celebrated role. These were the *Eleanora* and the *Fair American*. Commanded by Captain Simon Metcalfe and his son, who was about eighteen years old, these two ships were wintering in the islands after trading for furs on the northwest coast of America. While the *Eleanora* was stopping on the coast of Maui about the first of February, 1790, an attack on the ship was punished by Metcalfe, who fired on the natives and burned their village. Trading was resumed, but one day, when many natives had come out in canoes to barter, the vengeful captain fired on them with guns loaded with grapeshot and nails. More than a hundred Hawaiians, it is reported, were slaughtered and many others were wounded in this Olowalu massacre.

The small vessel *Fair American* some days later arrived off Hawaii. A chief who had been whipped by Metcalfe plotted to capture the ship. All the six members of the crew were killed except one, Isaac Davis, who barely escaped death. The boatswain of the *Eleanora*, John Young, was visiting other white men on the island at the time. Kamehameha, although he took no part in the capture of the *Fair American*, kept Young and Davis on shore, and Metcalfe sailed away without learning of the loss of his schooner and the death of his son.

Kindly treatment soon enabled the king to enlist the loyalty and advice of Young and Davis, who were made chiefs and served the kingdom faithfully. These two men gave signal service in the sea battle off the north coast of Hawaii, when the canoes of Kamehameha's fleet defeated those of the invading Kahekili. Both sides were armed with small cannon obtained from fur traders, but Davis and Young directed their fire with better effect. Probably the *Fair American* formed part of the fleet at this battle, which was fought in the spring of 1791, only a few months before Keoua died and left Kamehameha sole ruler of the island of Hawaii.

The next four years passed in an uneasy truce, while both sides tried to build up their forces by the aid of foreign traders. During this time Captain George Vancouver made his three visits to the islands, but was unable to bring about an end to the civil wars.

The aged Kahekili, who died in the summer of 1794, divided his kingdom between his brother Kaeo and his son Kalanikupule, and foolishly they were soon engaged in a struggle between themselves. With the aid of two trading vessels under Captain William Brown, the *Jackal* and the *Prince Lee Boo*, which had put in at Honolulu, the forces of Kalanikupule overcame Kaeo and killed him. As an aftermath, Brown was murdered and his two ships, with guns and ammunition, were added to the Oahu fleet. The English sailors, who had been forced to work the ships under guard, turned the tables and escaped to sea in the two ships. They then informed Kamehameha at Hawaii of the events at Oahu.

The time seemed ripe for conquest. Kamehameha collected the largest army ever seen in the islands and embarked in an immense fleet of war canoes. Maui was captured, then Molokai. The army landed at Waikiki and marched to the Nuuanu Valley, where Kalanikupule's army was arrayed for the final battle. Hundreds of the vanquished defenders were killed, and many were driven over the brow of the Nuuanu *Pali* (precipice) and dashed to pieces on the rocks below.

Kamehameha was master now of all the islands except Kauai and Niihau. During the spring of 1796 he attempted an invasion of Kauai, but his fleet was shattered by a storm. Moreover, a last revolt flared on the island of Hawaii. In the autumn the king returned there and quickly crushed the rebellion. This was the end of the wars of Kamehameha, for eventually Kauai and Niihau were ceded to him without a fight. He was now the unquestioned monarch of the archipelago, and could turn his talents to the government of the new kingdom during the more than two decades that still remained to him.

Kamehameha's first efforts were directed toward putting his realm under a firm and permanent system of government. As conqueror, everything belonged to him, land and people alike. His rule was feudal. According to Hawaiian custom, he divided the lands and their inhabitants among his chiefs as a reward for their services—retaining, however, a number of valuable districts as his own private estate. The chiefs in turn subdivided their grants among their own followers. The greatest areas were given to the four chiefs of Kona, who had been his stanch allies during the wars, and these chiefs also formed a council of advisers. When these men died, their sons succeeded them. A capable and faithful younger chief, Kalanimoku ("Billy Pitt"), was made prime minister and treasurer, the most important person in the kingdom next to Kamehameha. The various islands were ruled by governors chosen for their wisdom and loyalty. Keeaumoku, one of the Kona chieftains, was governor of Maui, and John Young was for a long time governor of the island of Hawaii.

The country was in a ruined condition at the end of the long period of civil war. Thousands of men, women, and children had been killed or had died of starvation. Famine was widespread. Before leaving for Kauai in 1796, Kamehameha had caused all the hogs on Oahu to be destroyed so that the people might not be able to rise against him in his absence. The land was untilled and the plight of the Hawaiians was desperate.

Kamehameha showed his statesmanship by quickly restoring the islands to prosperity. He urged the chiefs and commoners to raise food, and took the lead by laboring with his own hands. The people said of him: "He is a farmer, a fisherman, a maker of cloth, a provider for the needy, and a father to the fatherless." Disorder and crime were put down, and industry flourished during the first years of peace. In 1798 a trader remarked of Oahu: "The lands are in the highest state of cultivation . . . you here see the breadfruit, coconut, plantain, sweet potatoes, taro, yams, banana, which are native productions, and watermelons, muskmelons, pumpkins, cabbages, and most of our garden vegetables, introduced by foreigners."

All the people were called upon to pay taxes in kind, the results of their labor: pigs, chickens, dogs, vegetables, mats, calabashes, birds and rare feathers, and fish. In the last decade of the reign, sandalwood was an important source of revenue. Kamehameha's policy of fairness in dealing with the traders from foreign lands who had begun to come to the ports of the kingdom further added to its wealth and prosperity.

After his return to the island of Hawaii, the king made his court at Kailua for some years. His thoughts still turned toward the conquest of Kauai, and his people spent several years in building the famous *peleleu* fleet, consisting of large double canoes, each with a sail and a platform. More than eight hundred of these were said to have been built. The fleet sailed first to Maui, where the king stayed for a year, and then passed on to Oahu. The further voyage was postponed because of the great plague called *mai okuu* (probably either the cholera or the bubonic plague) which struck the islands in 1804 and killed numerous people. Kamehameha barely escaped death by the disease, and all the other great chiefs perished.

He persisted in his preparations, however, and by the end of 1809 the fleet consisted of more than forty sailing vessels, built at Waikiki with the aid of the many foreigners in his service. After some negotiations, Kaumualii, the young king of Kauai, realized that he could not hope to resist the coming conquest. In 1810 he went to Honolulu and acknowledged himself a subject of Kamehameha, and was allowed to retain the government of Kauai on condition that he pay a yearly tribute of goods.

King Kamehameha throughout his life maintained the ancient religion of the Hawaiians with great strictness. As official guardian of the war god that had brought him success in battle, he performed the necessary acts of worship, and appointed priests to carry on the ceremonies for the other gods. He kept the *heiau* temples in repair and built new ones. The *kapu* custom was observed, and as late as 1817 several persons were executed for violations of these religious bans. His gods had brought him to power and guarded him for years on the throne of a growing kingdom, and he would not forsake them. No missionaries of Christianity arrived during his lifetime, and the example of the foreigners that came in increasing numbers to trade with and settle in his realm did not give him a high respect for the religion of the world beyond his borders.

CHAPTER FOUR

Traders, Explorers, and Settlers

THE islands of Hawaii were visited, a few years after the death of Captain Cook, by ships from all the leading seafaring nations of the world, intent upon trade and exploration. Some men from these ships stayed behind in the islands, and formed the nucleus of a group of residents of foreign origin. This immigration soon led to international complications and eventually the "foreigners" came to outnumber the Hawaiian natives.

A few skins of the sea otter carried from the northwest coast of America by the ships of Cook's squadron were sold for high prices in the China market. In a few years, this coast was the goal of Russian, English, Spanish, and American ships, eager to build up the fur trade with China. Many of these traders and explorers began the custom of wintering in the Sandwich Islands or stopping there on the way to the Orient. A member of Vancouver's party that stopped in the islands in 1792 wrote: "What a happy discovery these islands were! What would the American fur trade be, without these to winter at and get every refreshment? A vessel going on that trade will need only sufficient provisions to carry her to these islands, where there is plenty of pork and salt to cure it, and yams as a substitute for bread."

As time went on, the Hawaiians learned to make a close bargain, and would no longer exchange for a few bits of iron the products of their soil and their skill at handicraft. The chiefs were eager to obtain the firearms possessed by the trading ships, and bartered for muskets, cannons, and ammunition which were used to intensify the bitter civil wars.

The first trading ship to stop at the islands was an unnamed 60-ton brig under Captain James Hanna which, returning to China with a valuable cargo of sea otter pelts, touched at the group in the autumn of 1785. In the spring of 1786 two English fur traders, Captains Nathaniel Portlock and George Dixon of the *King George* and *Queen Charlotte*, stopped for twenty days on the passage via Cape Horn to Nootka. During their stay, the ill-fated French expedition under Captain J. F. G. de la Pérouse, in the ships *La Boussole* and *L'Astrolabe*, touched at Lahaina, Maui. Portlock and Dixon returned later in the year to winter in the islands.

In 1787 another fur trader, *Imperial Eagle*, under the flag of the Austrian East India Company, stopped at the islands. A young Hawaiian woman was taken aboard as personal servant to Mrs. Barclay, wife of the captain; she was the first native to leave the islands. A certain Irish surgeon, John Mackay, who had just spent a year living among the Nootka Indians, left the *Imperial Eagle* and remained on Hawaii.

In September, 1787, Kaiana, a large-bodied Hawaiian chief, sailed in the fur trader *Nootka* to China with Captain John Meares. Kaiana was given many presents by the admiring Chinese before voyaging with Meares to the American northwest coast; after seeing these shores from Alaska to Vancouver Island he returned in the *Iphigenia*, with Captain Douglas, to his native land in December, 1788. He then joined Kamehameha and was a prominent adherent of that chieftain for several years. Kaiana was the first of many Hawaiians to join trading ships that took them to many parts of the world. It was soon discovered that Hawaiians made excellent sailors, and in later years the number of natives who left their homes to follow the sea reached alarming proportions.

During 1787 at least six vessels, all connected with the fur trade, were in Hawaiian waters. With the exception of the La Pérouse expedition, all vessels known to have visited the islands before the autumn of 1789 were commanded by British subjects. Although the Americans were not represented until Gray came in the *Columbia* that autumn, within ten years the transpacific fur trade was to be almost a monopoly of New England vessels. The American sloop *Lady Washington*, Captain John Kendrick, and the American brig *Hancock*, Captain Crowell, both came in 1791. The American brigantine *Hope*, with Joseph Ingraham as master, paid two visits in that year. The French ship *Solide*, commanded by Etienne Marchand, made Hawaii in October, 1791. The Spanish flag was first flown in a Hawaiian port in 1791, by Lieutenant Manuel Quimper of the *Princess Royal*, a ship which had been captured during the Nootka controversy from the British explorer James Colnett. Colnett was in the islands during this same year as master of the trader *Argonaut*.

The capture of the *Fair American*, which has already been described, took place in 1790. In that year, when Davis and Young joined the court of Kamehameha, three foreigners were already living on Hawaii: S. I. Thomas, John Mackay of Nootka fame, and Isaac Ridler, a deserter from the *Columbia*. This year also marks the discovery of sandalwood on the islands, but the first shipments of this fragrant wood were considered inferior by the Chinese, and for twenty years this potential wealth was overlooked.

The most important visitor to the islands during the next three years was the English explorer Captain George Vancouver. This able commander had been with Cook on that tragic final voyage. Now he was being sent by the British government to carry out the terms of a treaty made with Spain over a dispute arising out of the fur trade on the western coast of America. He was also instructed to make a careful exploration of that coast from Alaska to California, and to report as well on the Sandwich Islands. Two ships, the *Discovery* and the *Chatham*, were placed under his command, and another, the *Daedalus*, was later sent out to him with supplies.

Vancouver arrived off the coast of Hawaii on March 1, 1792. He got in touch with the natives through a Hawaiian sailor who had been brought from England. Leaving after a few days without having been visited by Kamehameha, the ships made a brief stop at Waikiki, Oahu, and a longer one at Waimea, Kauai. The captain made many friendly overtures and gave seeds and plants to the various chiefs, but refused their requests for firearms. He then departed for the coast of America.

Some six weeks later, Vancouver's store ship *Daedalus* arrived off Waimea, Oahu. While ashore obtaining a supply of water, a party was attacked by natives, and Lieutenant Hergest, the commanding officer, and three other men were killed. The *Daedalus* then went on its way.

On its second visit, Vancouver's squadron sighted Hawaii on February 12, 1793. The *Chatham* skirted the south coast of the island while the *Discovery* sailed around the north. Before the flagship arrived at Kealakekua, Kamehameha came on board, and Vancouver, who had met him in Cook's day, remarked that he was "agreeably surprised in finding that his riper years had softened that stern ferocity which his younger days had exhibited, and had changed his general deportment to an address characteristic of an open, cheerful, and sensible mind, combined with great generosity and goodness of disposition."

Vancouver had three aims in mind during this visit to the Sandwich Islands. One was accomplished when he landed a number of cattle brought from California, thus introducing a cattle-raising industry that would grow in importance. The second was to obtain the punishment of the murderers of Lieutenant Hergest; and on visiting Maui and Oahu, Vancouver obtained satisfaction from Kahekili when three natives (who may or may not have been the guilty ones) were executed. The third and most difficult task was to arrange a permanent peace among the various island chiefs. In this Vancouver was not successful, but he had high praise for the ability of Kamehameha and his *haole* advisers Young and Davis.

During Vancouver's third and last visit, in the spring of 1794, he did accomplish something on the political side. In a ceremony shortly before his departure, Kamehameha and his chiefs came aboard the *Discovery* on February 25 and ceded the island of

Hawaii to Great Britain, with the understanding that the land would be protected from foreign enemies but that the native religion, government, and customs would not be interfered with. This cession was never accepted by Vancouver's government, but it led to a tradition of English supremacy in the islands for some years.

Vancouver's other efforts on his final visit led to more practical results. Additional cattle were brought from California, and the king placed a *kapu* upon their slaughter for a period of ten years. The carpenters of the British ships constructed the framework of the *Britannia,* the first foreign-style vessel ever built in Hawaii. Kamehameha watched the proceedings with interest, and James Boyd, a carpenter in his service, promised to complete the vessel. When Vancouver sailed away in March, he left behind a memory of fair dealing and efforts toward peace, and the attention he had given to Kamehameha heightened the prestige of that chief and undoubtedly made it easier for him to pacify the entire group.

In November, 1794, two English fur-trading vessels, the *Jackal* and the *Prince Lee Boo,* under command of Captain William Brown, entered the harbor of Honolulu, which had been recently discovered. A few days later the American ship *Lady Washington,* Captain John Kendrick, also entered the harbor. Both these captains were enlisted by Kalanikupule in his war against Kaeo, and their aid helped to win the battle at Ewa on December 12. In celebrating this victory the next day, Kendrick was killed by a shot from a loaded gun firing a salute, and his ship soon sailed for China. When some difficulty arose over payment to Brown for his services, the followers of Kalanikupule captured the two ships while most of the crew was ashore killing and salting hogs. Captains Brown and Gardner were killed and the sailors were made prisoners. The tale of their recapture of the vessels and flight to join Kamehameha's fleet has already been told.

A prominent visitor in 1796 was Captain William Robert Broughton in the British sloop of war *Providence,* which touched at Kealakekua in January and brought the first grape vines to the islands. This benefit was ill repaid when, on a return visit in July, the *Providence* stopped at Niihau and two of its marines were slain by the natives. This was the last of such attacks on visiting ships by the Hawaiians.

Notable later visits of trading vessels include those of the *Lelia Byrd* and the *Tonquin*. The *Lelia Byrd,* in the summer of 1803, at Kawaihae, landed the first horses to be seen in Hawaii; William Shaler was listed as master and Richard J. Cleveland as supercargo. This vessel came again in 1805; as she leaked badly, Shaler exchanged her for the *Tamana,* a ship built at Oahu in that year, and the *Lelia Byrd* was added to Kamehameha's growing fleet. The *Tonquin,* Captain Jonathan Thorn, touched at the islands in 1811. She was the first of the supply ships of John Jacob Astor sent to the fur posts of the Columbia River country. On her departure, she carried twelve Hawaiians to work in Oregon.

The war of 1812 caused a flurry among the merchantmen in the Pacific, but only one incident aroused much concern in the Hawaiian group. The *Sir Andrew Hammond,* a British letter-of-marque ship captured by the Americans, arrived at Honolulu on May 23, 1814, commanded by Lieutenant John Gamble of the Marine Corps. It was the first war vessel flying the United States flag to enter Honolulu Harbor. It departed June 11 and two days later was retaken by the British ship *Cherub* and brought back to Honolulu. Gamble was taken away on the *Cherub* as a prisoner of war.

The latter years of Kamehameha's reign were troubled by the threats of an adventurer who sought to seize a part of the islands and make it Russian territory. The Russian American Company at the beginning of the nineteenth century had secured a monopoly of the fur trade in Alaska, and sought to establish trading posts in California and the Hawaiian Islands as sources of supplies. In June, 1804, two ships in the Russian Imperial service, the *Nadeshda* under Adam John von Krusenstern and the *Neva* under Urey Lisiansky, visited the islands, and in 1809 the *Neva,* under Captain Hagemeister, spent three months there, but obtained only a cargo of salt. In 1812 a Russian settlement was founded on the California coast at Fort Ross ("Russ") north of San Francisco. Two years later Baranoff, governor of the Russian company, sent the *Bering* (formerly well known in the islands as the *Atahualpa*, a Boston trading vessel) to purchase supplies. The *Bering* was wrecked on the shores of Kauai, but the natives of that island salvaged much of the cargo.

Toward the end of 1815, Baranoff sent Georg Anton Scheffer, a German physician, to the islands, ostensibly to recover the salvaged goods, but actually to obtain a foothold and try to establish a strong Russian post. Scheffer was well received by Kamehameha and allowed to travel about. During his stay on Kauai, he won the favor of Kaumualii by his medical skill.

Reinforced in the spring of 1816 by two additional ships, Scheffer went to Honolulu, landed his men, and started to build a fort there. Informed by John Young of these bold acts, Kamehameha ordered that the Russians be sent away. The fort, which was completed by the Hawaiians under Young, is remembered in the name of Fort Street in Honolulu.

Scheffer returned to Kauai and by promises and presents sought to lead Kaumualii to declare his independence and grant monopolies to the Russians. The Russians, aided by native labor, threw up breastworks at Hanalei, and early in 1817 built a strong fort at Waimea, over which the Russian flag was raised. At last, Kaumualii was convinced by American traders that the Russians were in truth enemies to him. He obeyed the strict orders of Kamehameha that Scheffer and his men be expelled, and after some fighting this was done. The Russians were taken to California, and Scheffer made his way to St. Petersburg via Canton, to present to the czar his dream of Hawaiian annexation. But his actions were repudiated by Baranoff and by the Russian government. The first attempt at foreign interference with Hawaiian affairs thus collapsed.

At the end of 1816, while Scheffer was on Kauai, a Russian Navy exploring ship, the *Rurick*, under Lieutenant Otto von

Kotzebue, spent a few weeks in the islands. Kotzebue's report probably confirmed the feeling of the czar that Great Britain's influence in the Hawaiian Islands was too strong to be easily shaken. Aboard the *Rurick* was Louis Choris, an artist who made some notable drawings of the islands in Kamehameha's day. This ship returned to Hawaii in 1817, and in the following year a Russian sloop of war, *Kamschatka,* Captain Golovnin, spent some time in Hawaiian waters.

At the end of Kamehameha's reign, the islands had already taken on some of the color of a melting pot. As early as 1794, the foreigners on the island of Hawaii numbered at least eleven, including English, American, Irish, Portuguese, Genoese, and Chinese. In 1818, visitors estimated that from one hundred to more than two hundred foreigners lived there. The charm of the islands and the generous policies of the king were so great that hardly a ship touched without leaving one or more sailors behind. The hills concealed escaped convicts from the Australian penal settlements. Many foreigners, however, were among the trusted advisers of Kamehameha. Among these may be mentioned Oliver Holmes of Massachusetts, Captain Harbottle, James Boyd, George Beckley, Alexander Adams, William Davis, Anthony Allen (a Negro), and the Spaniard, Francisco de Paula Marin ("Manini"), whose interest in horticulture led to the introduction of many useful plants.

The predominant trading interests of the Americans and the British were reflected in the combination of Union Jack and red, white, and blue stripes appearing in the Hawaiian flag, which as early as 1816 flew over the fort in Honolulu.

Honolulu began to be important as a trading center after 1795, and its importance was increased when in 1804 the king took up residence at Waikiki. Storehouses of stone were built near the harbor to hold the royal goods. Honolulu was a place where produce from the other islands was transshipped. After some time traders stored goods in houses on shore, from which they would sell to the natives; but permanent trading houses were not established until after the death of Kamehameha. The king learned the foreign custom of charging pilotage and wharfage fees to visiting vessels, and in the latter part of his reign these charges swelled the royal treasury, which was filled with foreign specie.

Kamehameha died on May 8, 1819, at Kailua, Hawaii, where he had retired in 1811. All the powers of the native *kahunas* were exerted during his final illness; a *heiau* was built and the priests told him that a human sacrifice was demanded. Kamehameha refused, saying, "The men are *kapu* for the king"—meaning his son Liholiho, who was to succeed to the throne. Nor after his death was the customary sacrifice of human life offered, although the other funeral ceremonies were carried out. Then the bones of the great king were taken and concealed in a secret cave. "Only the stars of the heavens know the resting place of Kamehameha."

CHAPTER FIVE

The Reign of Kamehameha II

THE year 1819, in which Kamehameha the Great died, was a critical year in Hawaiian history. Many pressing questions had to be answered. Could the kingdom that Kamehameha had held together by feudal force be kept united after the accession of a prince who lacked his father's strength of character? Could the ancient religious practices which had begun to decay during the old king's last years be cast off, and could the religious war that would follow such an act be won in battles against the opponents of change? Could the lively commerce that had grown up—particularly the booming trade in sandalwood—be controlled for the benefit of the people of Hawaii, or would the foreign traders introduce further complications into the problems of government?

The most urgent of these questions were dealt with before the year ended. The throne held firm. The *kapu* system was broken, though the ancient beliefs were not all obliterated. But British and American vessels still thronged to Hawaii, bringing many new problems in their wake. This year 1819 was one of financial crisis in the United States; specie was scarce, and the New England traders desperately needed other media of exchange for the China market. Sandalwood was very acceptable there, and hence the traders swarmed about the Hawaiian chiefs, intent upon selling them everything from pins and kitchen utensils to billiard tables, houses, and sailing ships, in exchange for the coveted sandalwood. Two other New England types—the whaler and the missionary— were about to descend in growing numbers upon this fresh field of endeavor. In September, 1819, the crews of two whale ships, the

Balaena of New Bedford and the *Equator* of Nantucket, killed a whale off Kealakekua Bay; these were the first of hundreds of such vessels to make use of the ports of the islands. At this very time, the first shipload of Christian missionaries was at sea, bound for these new pastures, unaware that a religious revolution had taken place that would immeasurably lighten their task of bringing the Bible to the heathen of Hawaii. What would be the changes in the life of the islands that would follow in the train of these invading merchants, whale hunters, and mission workers?

The reign of Liholiho, who took the name of Kamehameha II, was brief (1819–1824), and the young ruler suffered by comparison with the two strong monarchs that preceded and followed him. Yet in these critical years many events of note influenced the stream of history.

Liholiho, who was about twenty-three at the time of his accession, was an amiable prince with some shrewdness, but there were serious elements of weakness in his character. Fortunately, he had sound advisers. To strengthen the throne, his father had appointed his favorite queen Kaahumanu as *kuhina nui,* an office of such great importance that she was virtually a co-ruler. The capable Kalanimoku remained as prime minister, and Keopuolani, mother of Liholiho, was likewise an important member of the advisory group.

Kekuaokalani, a strong chief, had been made guardian of the war god by Kamehameha I, and this chief, as head of the conservative faction, was soon to lead an open revolt.

Meanwhile, disaffection among the nobles was somewhat allayed when they were allowed to share in the sandalwood monopoly. In August, 1819, a French warship, *L'Uranie,* visited Hawaii, and Liholiho's position was strengthened when Captain Louis de Freycinet made it known that he supported the king.

Liholiho and his advisers soon took the decisive step that they had been contemplating. The ancient *kapu* system was abolished. One very important part of this system was restriction of eating; men and women were forbidden to eat together, and women were not allowed to eat pork, bananas, coconuts, and certain kinds of fish. Many Hawaiians had secretly fallen away from these practices, owing to the example of the foreign population and to the news that idolatry and tabu had been abolished by the Polynesians of Tahiti. Before Kamehameha died, some of his people had begun to have doubts about the gods of old Hawaii.

The young king, persuaded by his advisers—among them the high priest Hewahewa—courageously performed the symbolic act of *ai noa* (free eating) by eating with the women at a feast he had called at Kailua, Hawaii, in the first week of November. This act broke the old law. When the meal was ended, he ordered that the *heiaus* and the idols should all be destroyed.

A number of Hawaiians, however, refused to accept this religious revolution, and many idols were hidden and worshiped secretly. Kekuaokalani, angered by his cousin's act and perhaps remembering that Kamehameha the Great rose to power as a defender of the war god, was the center of an insurrection against the breaking of the *kapu*. He refused to listen to an embassy of peace, and in the ensuing battle in December, 1819, at Kuamoo, the king's army, led by Kalanimoku, ended the rebellion when Kekuaokalani was killed as he bravely defended the old gods.

The prime endeavor of many of the chiefs in the year 1819 was the effort to show the outward signs of wealth in foreign goods. The booming trade in sandalwood, which had been a monopoly of the old king, was now shared by some of the chiefs.

The active trade in sandalwood had been begun in 1811 by three Bostonians, Nathan Winship, Jonathan Winship, and William Heath Davis, masters of the ships *Albatross, O'Cain,* and *Isabella.* On their way to China with furs, they picked up a cargo of sandalwood, and were able to make a good payment to Kamehameha from the proceeds. These men on July 12, 1812, signed a contract with the king which gave them a ten-year monopoly of this article of export. The War of 1812 abrogated this contract, but soon thereafter, sandalwood became the main article of Hawaiian commerce. The king stored up a heap of Spanish dollars and foreign trade-goods, and in the years 1816–1818 added six foreign ships to his fleet, all of them paid for with sandalwood. The royal monopoly did prevent abuses of the trade, and Kamehameha I is said to have placed a *kapu* on the young trees to conserve this resource.

When Liholiho shared the sandalwood trade with his chiefs, a buying mania struck them. The best silks, liquors, tableware, and foreign clothing were none too good for the *alii*, one of whom paid $800 for a single mirror. In 1819–1821, Liholiho and the chiefs bought eight sailing ships—some completely unseaworthy—for more than $300,000. Some American trading houses sent out special cargoes solely for the Hawaiian chiefs. These merchants, if payment in sandalwood was not forthcoming, would accept promissory notes which added up to a burdensome debt that caused much trouble a few years later. Moreover, the demand for tax payments in sandalwood led to pitiless exploitation of the common people, who were forced to toil in the cold, wet mountains without reward, piling up the fragrant wood into shiploads that sold for a fortune in the Orient.

Early visitors have given many pictures of sandalwood gathering. One traveler in 1822 wrote that the sandalwood "is brought from the woods in logs three or four feet long, and from two to seven or eight inches in diameter. There being no carriages on the island, these logs are carried down to the seaside on the heads and shoulders of men, women, and children (for all bear a part in the busy scene) and lodged in large storehouses, to be ready for shipment. . . . For conveying their sandalwood from the distant parts of Woahoo [Oahu] and the other Sandwich Islands to the port of Hannah-rourah [Honolulu], about twelve small brigs and schooners are now employed." Another observer, while stopping at Kohala, was awakened at dawn by vast throngs of people bringing sandalwood down from Waimea. "There were between two and three thousand men, carrying each from one to six pieces of sandalwood, according to their size and weight. It was generally tied on their backs by bands of *ti* leaves, passed over the shoulders and under the arms, and fastened across their breasts." Growing of food was neglected as men, women, and children chopped and carried wood all day and sometimes at night; this forced labor and the resulting famine weakened the people and was a cause of decline in the native population.

The traders paid $7 to $10 a picul (133⅓ pounds) for sandalwood which they sold in Canton at a profit of $3 or $4 a picul; in later years this price declined. Since the traders paid not in cash but in merchandise on which they placed an exorbitant price, they made two profits on the trade, both at the expense of the Hawaiians.

The reckless exploitation of the forests diminished the supply of sandalwood so that in a few years the quality degenerated and the trade almost disappeared. Although today some surviving groves of sandalwood can be found on the less accessible slopes of the mountains, the trade collapsed about 1830, and this source of revenue was replaced by the selling of merchandise to the whaling fleets—a trade in which the Hawaiians had only a small share.

The coming of the "Pilgrims of Hawaii" in 1820—exactly two hundred years after the *Mayflower* landed in New England—was likewise to have a profound effect upon life in the islands.

The beginnings of the Sandwich Islands Mission movement can be traced to the story of a young Hawaiian named Opukahaia (called Obookiah in New England), who was brought to the United States by a Captain Brintnall in 1809 and who lived with the captain's family in New Haven, Connecticut. The boy was one day found on the steps of Yale College, weeping because of his ignorance. He eagerly welcomed the offer of several students to teach him, and his inquiring and friendly spirit soon made him well known in the region. He became an ardent Christian, and desired to return to the islands as a missionary.

Several other Hawaiian youths then in the United States were also discovered to have aptitude for learning, and in 1816 Opukahaia and three others were enrolled in a school established in that year by the American Board of Commissioners for Foreign Missions, with the intention of training them to be sent back to their native land to be "preachers or teachers." Although Opukahaia died in 1818, while still a student, his ambition to Christianize the islands was at last realized when the Sandwich Islands Mission was organized at Boston on October 15, 1819.

Four days later the new church group sailed from Boston on the brig *Thaddeus*. On board were the Reverend Hiram Bingham and the Reverend Asa Thurston; Daniel Chamberlain, farmer, and his five children; Dr. Thomas Holman, physician; Samuel Whitney and Samuel Ruggles, schoolmasters; Elisha Loomis, printer; the wives of these men; and four Hawaiian youths, Thomas Hopu, William Kanui, John Honolii, and George P. Kaumualii. The last of these was not properly a member of the mission, but it was thought that he might be useful because of his unique background. He was the son of the king of Kauai and had been sent to the United States to receive an education. When his funds vanished, he became a laborer and later a seaman in the American Navy, and was wounded in the War of 1812. He was destined to become a thorn in the side of the Kamehameha dynasty a few years after his return to Hawaii.

The *Thaddeus* company first viewed the land of their labors when they raised the island of Hawaii on March 30, 1820. Messengers sent ashore soon brought back the stirring news that old Kamehameha was dead, and that young King Liholiho had abolished the *kapu* and destroyed the idols. The pagan forces had been overthrown in battle. The Christians could not have come at a more opportune moment, for the religious vacuum that had been created could be filled at once by appeals to the yearnings of the strongly religious-minded Hawaiian people.

The ship anchored at Kailua, site of the royal residence, on April 4, and the members of the Mission paid their respects to Liholiho and his chiefs. They told of their desire to start a Christian mission at Kailua and a branch at Honolulu, and asked permission to begin at once. After much argument, the king agreed to the plan.

Mr. Thurston, one of the two ordained ministers, was chosen by ballot to stay at Kailua, and on April 12 he and his wife took up residence. Dr. Holman and two of the Hawaiian youths, at the king's request, also stayed there. The remainder of the group landed a week later at Honolulu and began their work, finding shelter in several small houses. Mr. Whitney and Mr. Ruggles, with their wives, went on to Kauai to witness the reunion of George Kaumualii and his father. King Kaumualii joyfully received the newcomers and begged them to settle on his island; after consideration, they agreed and set up at Waimea the first mission station on Kauai. Mr. Loomis at the strong request of Kalanimoku went to Kawaihae, Hawaii, to teach the chief and his family the message of the Gospels.

From the first, the native chiefs showed strong interest in the work of the missionaries, particularly the establishment of schools for the noble families. By the end of 1820, the various missions had about one hundred pupils of both sexes and all ages. The wives of the missionaries rendered great service in the teaching work. At first it was necessary to talk through interpreters, but soon the teachers acquired a knowledge of Hawaiian, and within a few years, when books were printed in that language and native teachers had been trained, the pupils numbered thousands.

The Hawaiian language had never been reduced to a practical written form. One of the first tasks of the missionaries was to learn the language, to invent a system of transcribing it in roman characters, and then to translate the Bible and textbooks to this form and print them for use in churches and schools. Not until January 7, 1822, was the first printing done in the Hawaiian islands—a pamphlet containing the Hawaiian alphabet and some short lessons in spelling and reading. Thereafter the mission press was busy turning out school books, religious tracts, and translations of parts of the Bible.

The first Christian house of worship was dedicated in August, 1821, on the site in Honolulu now occupied by the Kawaiahao Church. The first Christian marriage in the islands was not performed until August 11, 1822. The growing missionary work was strengthened in April, 1822, when a committee from the London Missionary Society, including Daniel Tyerman and George Bennett, reached the islands. Among this English group was the Reverend William Ellis, who had worked for six years in Tahiti. His knowledge of the Tahitian tongue enabled Ellis within a few weeks to master Hawaiian, and he was the first person to preach a sermon in that language. He was urged to remain in the islands to assist the Americans; he did so, and his help was widely appreciated.

In 1823 a large number of workers sent out by the American Board reinforced the efforts of the pioneers. The station at Kailua, abandoned when the king moved to Honolulu at the end of 1820, was reopened. A station was set up on the island of Maui at the village of Lahaina, a popular port of call for foreign ships, and in 1824 a second station on Hawaii was founded at Hilo.

Conversion of the natives was not a hurried process. Those who had taken the lead in breaking the *kapu* were among the first to be received into the fold. Keopuolani, the queen mother, was baptized one hour before her death on September 16, 1823. Kapiolani, an important chiefess, testified in public to her faith by descending into the volcano of Kilauea in December, 1824, and defying the wrath of the fire goddess Pele. Kaahumanu had been friendly with the missionaries from the first, but about the beginning of 1824 she became quite interested in promoting the movement, and thereafter the native congregations were to grow rapidly. The sacrament of baptism was not lightly given, but after lengthy training in Christian principles, a celebrated blind convert, Puaaiki, was baptized on July 10, 1825, under the name of Bartimeus and admitted to the church at Lahaina, and on December 5, eight Hawaiians, most of them of high rank, were taken into the church at Honolulu.

Two other main events of the reign of Liholiho arose from the demands of his restless spirit: his trip to Kauai and his voyage to England. In 1822 he began practicing an old custom of making royal progresses about his kingdom; more than a thousand persons of the court visited many parts of the islands. On July 21, 1821, Liholiho set out from Waialua, Oahu, in a small sailing vessel crowded with more than thirty persons. His purpose was to test the allegiance of his vassal Kaumualii. Through the day and far into the night the craft wallowed across the dangerous Kauai channel, unable to turn back because of the king's determination. The king survived to carry out successfully his political visit, and Kaumualii renewed his submission. When after some weeks Liholiho returned to Oahu, he took the Kauai king with him as a sort of state prisoner. When Kaumualii was taken as husband to Kaahumanu, the *kuhina nui,* the power of the Kamehameha dynasty was further confirmed.

In his foreign relations, Liholiho continued his father's policy of considering himself under the protection of Great Britain. In fulfillment of Vancouver's promise to Kamehameha I, a small schooner built at Sydney, Australia, the *Prince Regent,* armed with six guns, was delivered at Honolulu in May, 1822, by Captain J. R. Kent of the cutter *Mermaid.* Liholiho, in addressing his thanks to the British monarch, stated: "The whole of these islands having been conquered by my father, I have succeeded to the government of them, and beg leave to place them all under the protection of your most excellent Majesty."

Liholiho's voyage to England was an outgrowth of his long-cherished wish to increase his power and his knowledge of the world by visiting the kingdom under which he had placed himself. In the English whaleship *L'Aigle* the king departed on November 27, 1823, accompanied by his favorite wife Kamamalu, Governor Boki of Oahu and his wife Liliha, Kekuanaoa, the priest Kapihe, a chief named Manuia, James Young Kanehoa, some servants, and his secretary, John Rives, a Frenchman. The king's nine-year-old brother Kauikeaouli was named heir to the throne, and during the king's absence the kingdom was under the regency of the queen dowager Kaahumanu.

The ship *L'Aigle* arrived at Portsmouth, England, about May

18, 1824, and its captain, Valentine Starbuck, conducted the group to London. Here they were lodged in a luxurious hotel by the government, and a lengthy program of truly royal entertainment was offered to do them honor. Before an audience with King George IV could be carried out, however, the king and queen, as well as several members of their party, were stricken with measles. Despite every care, Kamamalu died of the disease on July 8. Liholiho, smitten with grief, thereafter succumbed rapidly and died on July 14, a royal victim of his desire to know the world beyond his home islands.

CHAPTER SIX

Kamehameha III and the First Constitution

THE reign of Kamehameha III (1825–1854) was the longest in Hawaiian history, and during this thirty-year period the government and the people made marked progress in domestic affairs, in foreign relations, in social, educational, and cultural achievement, and in the growth of commerce and industry.

It is interesting to note how the ruling chiefs, faced with new ideas and the demands of foreigners for rights in the community, slowly evolved a government of laws, and under continual threats of foreign intervention won an independent status for this small kingdom in the circle of nations. The story of political happenings previous to the proclamation of Hawaii's first written constitution (1840) must first be told.

The older chiefs, just after Liholiho departed for England, held a council and decided upon a policy which maintained peace and order. Six months later Kaahumanu, the regent, proclaimed a brief code of civil laws, clearly based on missionary teachings, which prohibited murder, theft, fighting, and Sabbath-breaking.

Civil war challenged the stability of the kingdom in the summer of 1824. In May of that year, Kaumualii had died in Honolulu, leaving the island of Kauai to Liholiho; but malcontents led by his son George Kaumualii, who had not lived up to the hopes of his missionary friends, began an insurrection on August 8 with an attack on the fort at Waimea. The island was pacified after some months, and a chief of high rank was appointed as governor. When news arrived in the islands on March 9, 1825, of the death of Liholiho and his queen in London, there was grief and wailing, but none of the civil commotion that formerly could have been expected in such case.

In mid-April, Captain Richard Charlton, who had been appointed British consul, returned to Honolulu with the news that the 46-gun frigate *Blonde* would soon arrive, bearing home in state the survivors of the royal party and the bodies of the king and queen. The vessel reached Honolulu on May 6, and on May 11 the royal dead were brought ashore and given a temporary burial until a suitable mausoleum could be built.

The commander of the *Blonde*, Captain the Right Honorable (George Anson) Lord Byron, R.N., a cousin of the poet, was a highly capable and tactful man. He was well able to carry out his secret instructions to cultivate a good understanding with the native people and to assert British authority only if dire necessity demanded the protection of British subjects or the prevention of seizure of the islands by some other power. He did offer a number of suggestions to the national council of chiefs on June 6, at which the accession of Kauikeaouli as Kamehameha III was confirmed. Trial by jury was introduced after 1825 as a result of one of these suggestions. But Lord Byron made it clear that the natives themselves must take up the burden of making their own laws and enforcing them. Thereafter the business of lawmaking did receive much attention from the chiefs.

After leaving Oahu, the *Blonde* sailed to Hilo, where the harbor was surveyed and came to be known as "Byron's Bay." Scientific observations were made of the volcano at Kilauea, and before his return to England Lord Byron raised a monument at Kealakekua Bay in honor of Captain James Cook.

American interests in the islands also created a need for new laws. The sandalwood trade was almost wholly in the hands of Americans, and the chiefs were heavily in debt to firms which were pressing for payment. American whaling ships were more and more often calling at Hawaiian ports, and deserting sailors caused much trouble not only to the ship captains but also to the native authorities. During three months in the spring of 1826 nearly forty American whaling vessels stopped at Honolulu. In response to appeals from the whaling interests, the United States ship-of-war *Dolphin* arrived early in that year and remained about three months. Lieutenant John Percival, its commander, obtained from the king and chiefs an acknowledgement that the debts due to American citizens would be recognized as government obligations; here may be found the origin of the Hawaiian national debt.

In the fall a second vessel, the United States sloop-of-war *Peacock*, stayed for another three months. Captain Thomas ap Catesby Jones obtained a renewed pledge of payment of the debts, and to raise the money the rulers passed on December 27, 1826, the earliest written tax law of Hawaii, which required every able-bodied man in the kingdom to deliver half a picul of good sandalwood or to pay four Spanish dollars, and every woman to furnish a woven mat, piece of tapa, or one Spanish dollar. The privilege given to each man of cutting half a picul of sandalwood for himself hastened the decline of the forests, and much wood was cut; but the debts lingered on. In 1829 the commander of the United States ship *Vincennes* obtained renewed notes, but all these claims were not paid off until 1843.

Captain Jones also made, on behalf of his government, certain "articles of arrangement" which formed a rough treaty providing for peace between the Americans and the Hawaiians, and for the protection of American interests. This was the first treaty ever negotiated between Hawaii and a foreign country, and although it was never ratified by the United States, it was respected for many years.

Revealingly, the first laws printed in the kingdom (1822) had been designed to control the misdeeds of deserters and rioting sailors ashore. In August, 1825, the chiefs met and placed a *kapu* upon gambling, vice, drunkenness, theft, and violation of the Sabbath. A similar ban was soon put upon immorality on the ships in the harbors, a ban that was fiercely resented by foreign sailors, who on several occasions demonstrated against it with armed riots. Their rage was directed not against the natives but against the missionaries, particularly the Reverend Hiram Bingham at Honolulu and the Reverend William Richards at the port of Lahaina, into whose house in 1827 several cannon shots were fired.

At a council in December, 1827, the chiefs attempted to further the fight for law and order by recommending a brief code directed against six offenses. Before these could be proclaimed, Boki, governor of Oahu, objected that no laws could be issued without the approval of the British government, but this idea was repudiated by the chiefs. It was finally decided that only three laws would be passed at this time, to go into effect in March, 1828; these prohibited murder, theft, and adultery. Three others, against rum selling, prostitution, and gambling, were drawn up, to be explained to the people before final action was taken on them. This was the beginning of legislation by the Hawaiian chiefs, who groped their way from arbitrary rule by custom and *kapu* to a realization of the need for uniform law enforcement. Their efforts at enforcement were hampered not so much by the natives as by the foreigners, who clamored when their interests or their pleasure seemed to be in danger.

There was distinct progress in law enforcement during the regency of Kaahumanu, but when she died on June 5, 1832, her strong ruling hand was lost to the side of order. Her successor as *kuhina nui* was Kinau, a daughter of Kamehameha I, who was considerably older than the eighteen-year-old king. The two ruled jointly for a year, but in 1833 the king, resentful of his half-sister's control, threw off all restraints and began a two-year course of license and dissipation. In March a crier proclaimed through the streets the abrogation by the king of all laws except those relating to theft and murder. The hula and other ancient sports were revived, and many of the people indulged in gambling, drunkenness, and other vices in a reaction against what they felt to have been a puritanical rule.

The king dared not assume too autocratic a power, however, and after two years of confusion, he was reconciled to Kinau and left the responsibility of government largely in her hands. She

KAMEHAMEHA III AND THE FIRST CONSTITUTION

yielded up the regency but remained as *kuhina nui*, and the council of chiefs held as much power as before.

The need for a new code of laws having become evident, on January 5, 1835, the king proclaimed a penal code which was the result of much consultation among the chiefs. The first chapter dealt with homicide and its penalties. The second dealt with theft, and called for a fine of twice the amount stolen, or imprisonment, or a number of lashes on the bare back. The third related to adultery and divorce; the fourth to fraud; and the fifth to drunkenness.

The main sources of trouble in applying laws in the islands came in cases having to do with foreigners and foreign governments. Questions about the right of foreigners to enter the country, to reside there, to engage in business, to acquire house lots and other land, to build on this land, and to transfer their property were frequent. In course of time it came to be understood that such rights could be acquired only by treaties with the foreign governments involved. After 1820 many foreigners came who did not understand the native system, or who disdained it and dealt with their property as they would have done in their own countries. Some *haoles* began to deny the right of the native government to restrict their acts, and appealed to their own governments for protection and redress.

The repeated criticisms of the Hawaiian government made by foreigners living in the islands or visiting them in ships convinced the ruling chiefs that agreements concerning the rights of foreigners should be put into written form as treaties. These experiences likewise convinced the chiefs that they should become better informed about the polity of civilized nations.

As early as 1836 they attempted to obtain the services of an American teacher of economics and political science. After their first efforts failed, William Richards, an American missionary in Hawaii, entered the employ of the king on July 3, 1838, as a teacher of political economy and government, and embarked upon a series of lectures before an eager group of chieftain pupils. The result was a rapid series of constitutional changes.

The council of chiefs, which included the king and the *kuhina nui,* had by this time evolved into a body having actual legislative power. A law of 1838 begins: "Be it enacted by the King and Chiefs of the Sandwich Islands, in council assembled." The higher chiefs formed an advisory group. The common people were still completely subjected to the nobles, without any rights except that of moving to the land of another feudal chief. Nor had there been any formal organization of the government such as that found among the countries of Europe and America.

The chiefs were anxious to learn, and the first product of their study was the declaration of rights and laws of June 7, 1839. The laws comprised something like a civil code, and included sections on taxation, public welfare, enactment of laws, and inheritance of property. The declaration, which has been justly termed the Hawaiian Magna Charta, was a voluntary concession of rights granted by the monarch to his people. Its preamble begins: "God hath made of one blood all nations of men, to dwell on the face of the earth in unity and blessedness. God has also bestowed certain rights alike on all men, and all chiefs, and all people of all lands. These are some of the rights which he has given alike to every man and every chief: life, limb, liberty, the labor of his hands, and productions of his mind."

The rights defined in this declaration were repeated in substance in the Constitution of 1840. This first written constitution for Hawaii was signed by Kamehameha III and the *kuhina nui,* Kekauluohi, on October 8, with the approval of the council of chiefs. The document was in large part descriptive of existing political institutions in the land, but there were several innovations. The most sweeping of these created a "representative body" of legislators elected by the people; for the first time, the common man had a share of political power. Another innovation was the creation of a supreme court, to consist of the king, the *kuhina nui,* and four other judges appointed by the Hawaiian house of representatives. Executive authority remained in the hands of the king, the *kuhina nui*, and the four island governors, who were appointed by the king. The king and *kuhina nui* were members of the council of chiefs, which together with the lower house met annually. New laws had to be approved by a majority in both legislative houses and by the king and *kuhina nui* as well.

Now that the Hawaiian rulers had set their house in order, the fight for freedom from threats of foreign intervention, and for recognition of Hawaii's independence, could begin. But this position had been achieved in the midst of international jostling for special favors and interests in the islands. The needs of trade and the impact of foreign customs and ideas, both political and religious, were changing Hawaii's position in the world. The rivalry of American and British interests in the kingdom has already been suggested. The entrance of France into this contest for privileges came about through the efforts of Catholic missionaries to establish themselves in Hawaii, an effort which had the active support of the French government. The challenge to Hawaiian independence raised by the Catholic missionaries was therefore a political as well as a religious problem.

CHAPTER SEVEN

France and the Catholic Missionaries

THE origin of the Catholic mission in the Hawaiian Islands goes back to the death of Liholiho in London. His secretary, John Rives, a Frenchman, left the deathbed of the king and went to France to present a scheme of commercial and religious expansion in the islands. The time could not have been more favorable to his plan, and as a result of his talks to merchants, government officials, and Catholic missionary authorities, two commercial expeditions and a religious mission were organized.

The first vessel to leave sailed from Le Havre in April, 1826, with Rives aboard. It was planned that this ship, *Le Héros*, would trade along the coast of California and thence go to Hawaii, where Rives would prepare the way for a French agricultural settlement on land which he claimed to own. But Rives had never possessed much property and was now out of favor with Kaahumanu. He therefore did not return to Hawaii, and for lack of his promised support, the settlement of French colonists was abandoned and the missionary enterprise was badly handicapped.

The second expedition sailed from Bordeaux in November, 1826, in the ship *Comète*. It contained a few agricultural settlers, a young lawyer, Auguste de Morineau, and a missionary party consisting of three priests of the Order of the Sacred Hearts of Jesus and Mary, Fathers Alexis Bachelot (head of the group), Abraham Armand, and Patrick Short; a choir brother; and two lay brothers. They landed at Honolulu on July 7, 1827, and without obtaining a formal permit settled in the village. Kaahumanu ordered the captain of the *Comète* to take the priests away, but he sailed off without them. In August, Morineau obtained a piece of land from the king for the use of the lay brothers, and in January, 1828, a chapel was opened.

Although a number of natives were baptized during the first two years of Catholic residence, there was no open disturbance. Boki, the governor of Oahu and personal guardian of the king, was a political malcontent whose dislike of Kaahumanu led him to side with any opposition, and he made no move to eject the priests. At first the Protestant missionaries believed that the Hawaiians would recognize Catholic doctrines as clearly erroneous, but later, although they frowned upon persecution, they made efforts to have the priests removed from the islands.

To the Hawaiian chiefs, who had made Protestant Christianity virtually a state religion, the embracing of Catholicism by their native subjects seemed to be insubordination. In August, 1829, natives were forbidden to attend Catholic services. In spite of this prohibition, some natives continued to go to the chapel, and during the following decade a number were punished for their religious beliefs and practices.

The support of Boki was soon withdrawn. Early in 1828 he had gathered a group of supporters at Waikiki and seemed about to lead a revolt against Kaahumanu, but abandoned his plan. He had sunk into debt through the failure of trading enterprises in which he had engaged, and when toward the end of 1829 an Australian ship brought the report of a South Pacific island that was rich in sandalwood trees, he seized the idea of recouping his fortunes. He fitted out two vessels, the *Kamehameha* and the *Becket,* put on board nearly five hundred of his followers, and sailed in search of the wonderful island. The *Kamehameha* was never heard of again; it was probably lost at sea with Boki and his people. Eight months later the *Becket* returned from the south with twenty survivors aboard; the rest had died of hunger and disease.

In 1831, Boki's wife Liliha, who had become governor in his place, was removed. On April 2 of that year, a formal decree of banishment composed by the chiefs was read to Fathers Bachelot and Short. In spite of stated penalties if they did not comply within three months, the priests soon showed that they had no intention of leaving voluntarily. The chiefs then abandoned the idea of penalties, and fitted out one of their own ships, the brig *Waverley*. The two priests were placed aboard the ship and sailed from Honolulu on December 24, 1831. They were landed in California, where they remained, laboring at various missions, until 1837, always hoping for a favorable time to return to Hawaii. One of the lay brothers, Melchior Bondu, was left in sole charge in Hawaii until October, 1834, when a second brother joined him.

The U.S. frigate *Potomac* visited Honolulu in the summer of 1832, and partly as a result of Commodore John Downes's plea for religious tolerance, the persecution of native Catholics was discontinued for several years.

A second attempt to found a mission in Hawaii was made in 1835. The Vicariate Apostolic of Eastern Oceania had been created by the Church, with Father Bachelot as prefect of the area north of the Equator. From Mangareva, in the southern prefecture, Bishop Rouchouze sent Brother Columba Murphy to Honolulu in the fall of 1835. Murphy made a brief investigation and then went on to Valparaiso. There it was decided to send to Hawaii a young priest, Father Arsenius (Robert A.) Walsh, a worker under the missions guided by the Order of the Sacred Hearts. It was thought that Walsh, a British subject, would have better success than a French priest.

Father Walsh arrived on September 30, 1836. He was ordered to depart, but the timely arrival of a French warship, *La Bonite*, enabled him to stay because of the efforts of the French commander, who persuaded the chiefs that the priest should remain and teach foreigners but not natives.

As *La Bonite* was leaving, the British war vessel *Acteon* arrived. The commander, Lord Edward Russell, negotiated on November 16 a treaty between the Hawaiian government and Great

Britain, which gave British subjects the right to trade, to reside, and to build houses and warehouses in Hawaii with the consent of the king. Russell made an unsuccessful effort to have Father Walsh permitted to teach and baptize the natives. Nevertheless, in the next four years the priest did baptize a few Hawaiians.

Considering the time a favorable one, Fathers Bachelot and Short returned to Honolulu from California on April 17, 1837, in the ship *Clementine*. As the king and Kinau were at Lahaina at the time, the governor of Oahu at first ordered the priests to go back on the ship, but later permitted them to stay ashore until the return of the king. On April 30, Kinau brought forth a royal decree that the banished priests should go away on the same vessel that had brought them.

The *Clementine*, as it happened, was owned by a Frenchman of Honolulu, Jules Dudoit, but was sailing under the British flag. Moreover, during the passage from California it had been chartered by an American merchant. Now that the ship was returned to its owner, Dudoit stated that he was not responsible for bringing the priests and would not take them back on the *Clementine* unless their passage was paid and they went voluntarily. In the warm discussion that followed, the British and American consuls took the part of the priests and of Dudoit against the chiefs.

When, in May, the priests were compelled to go aboard the ship, Dudoit hauled down the British flag and left the ship. The flag was given to Consul Charlton, who publicly burned it, declaring that it had been insulted by the Hawaiian government.

The British warship *Sulphur*, commanded by Captain Edward Belcher, and the French warship *Venus*, commanded by Captain A. du Petit-Thouars, arrived early in July. After an argument with Kinau, Captain Belcher sent a company of marines to "recapture" the ship. He and Captain du Petit-Thouars then escorted the priests to their former residence ashore.

The king arrived a few days later and conferred with the two commanders, but insisted upon his right of decision. Belcher then signed a promise that Father Short would leave at the first opportunity, and Du Petit-Thouars made a similar pledge for Father Bachelot. A few days later the French captain signed an agreement with the king giving French subjects all rights enjoyed in the Hawaiian Islands by subjects of any other nation.

Two other priests had been sent by the Bishop of Eastern Oceania to attempt a landing in Honolulu. They were the Rev. Columba Murphy, who now returned to the scene, and the Rev. L. D. Maigret. They arrived November 2, 1837, but were at once forbidden to land. Father Murphy had just recently been ordained as a priest, but the fact was kept secret, and when the British consul stated to Kinau that Murphy was not a priest, he was permitted to reside ashore.

Father Maigret was absolutely forbidden to remain, and since Father Bachelot was still waiting for a ship, the priests bought a schooner from Dudoit. On this vessel the two priests sailed from Honolulu on November 23. Father Bachelot, who was in poor health, died at sea on December 5 and was buried near Ponape in the Caroline Islands.

Soon after the departure of the priests, Kamehameha III proclaimed a ban against the teaching or practice of Catholicism. Persecution of native Catholics was renewed, but despite this ban, certain forces were at work to promote greater tolerance. Among these were the advice of foreign visitors, the death of Kinau on April 4, 1839, and the fear of reprisals by the French government. As a result the king, in June, 1839, issued an oral order which amounted to an edict of toleration, stating that Catholics should no longer be subject to punishment because of their religion.

The French government considered itself the protector of all Catholic missionaries in the Pacific area. Captain du Petit-Thouars in the fall of 1838 had obtained reparation from the queen of the Society Islands (Tahiti) for having expelled French Catholic priests. Another French ship, the frigate *Artemise,* Captain C. P. T. Laplace, was also in the Pacific, on a voyage around the world to promote French commerce. The *Artemise* arrived at

Honolulu on July 9, 1839. Laplace had been given instructions from Paris to use force if necessary to exact reparations, and to make the chiefs understand that they should "conduct themselves in such a manner as not to incur the wrath of France." With no other grasp of the facts than that gained in an interview with Dudoit, the French consul, Captain Laplace sent the king a "manifesto," accusing the chiefs of having violated the treaty made with Du Petit-Thouars. Under threat of immediate war, Laplace demanded a new treaty providing that the Catholic religion be allowed, that land be given for a Catholic church at Honolulu, that $20,000 be deposited with him as a guarantee of good conduct by the Hawaiian government, and that the French flag be saluted with twenty-one guns.

These demands were made while the king was at Lahaina. In order to avert war, the treaty was immediately signed by the *kuhina nui*, Kekauluohi, and the governor of Oahu. The money was borrowed from foreign merchants and all the demands were fulfilled.

The king approved the act when he returned a few days later, but Laplace was now demanding still another treaty. This agreement contained two articles which were highly arbitrary. One gave to Frenchmen accused of crime in the islands the right to be tried by a jury of foreigners named by the French consul. The other provided that French merchandise, "especially wines and brandies, shall not be prohibited, nor pay a higher duty than five per cent ad valorem." This article virtually repealed a law of 1838 which had prohibited the importation of strong liquors. The king had no alternative but to sign.

Bishop Rouchouze himself arrived in Honolulu on May 15, 1840, to take charge of the Catholic mission. With him he brought three priests, one of whom was Father Maigret, who had figured in the events of 1837. The cornerstone of a stone church was laid on July 9, 1840; and schools were built to advance the mission's work, which extended to other islands. Early in 1841 the bishop left for France to seek additional support and to reinforce his staff of workers. Fatefully, the party of six priests, one subdeacon, seven lay brothers, and ten sisters was lost at sea with the bishop after this company sailed from St. Malo in the brig *Marie-Joseph*.

Meanwhile, many legal difficulties had arisen in the mission work at Honolulu, and the French consul asked the Catholics to submit their grievances to him, to be forwarded to France for enforcement of their views. Some of the Hawaiians felt that this policy was designed to stir up pretexts for seizure of the islands by France.

A French naval squadron under Admiral du Petit-Thouars took possession of the Marquesas Islands in July, 1842, and the admiral ordered a ship sent to Hawaii. This sloop of war, *Embuscade*, arrived on August 24, and Captain S. Mallet presented a letter to the king, making demands and charging violations of the treaty made with Laplace. To yield to the demands of Mallet would have given to the Catholic priests the right to appoint certain officers of the Hawaiian government, and would have placed the Catholics in a more favored status than the Protestants. The king made a dignified reply stating that the laws were designed to maintain tolerance and impartiality, and that he had faithfully observed all treaties. He could not accept these demands without giving up his sovereignty. The king added that he had sent ministers to the king of France to request a new treaty. Mallet took no further action, and the problem of French domination became part of the larger problem of securing recognition of Hawaii's independence among the nations of the world.

CHAPTER EIGHT

Hawaii in the Family of Nations

THE Constitution of 1840 laid the foundations for political reforms inside the Hawaiian kingdom, and smoothed the way for a number of other improvements in dealing with domestic affairs—particularly the land problem—in the reign of Kamehameha III. This period likewise brought new treaties with Great Britain, France, the United States, and other nations, and saw also the beginnings of the movement for annexation that was to draw Hawaii ever closer to union with the United States of America.

There were times when it seemed likely that Hawaii might become a colonial possession of France, a fate which befell the Marquesas and Society Islands. Other influences were at work that might have thrown the little country into the possession of Great Britain, which had annexed the Polynesian islands of New Zealand in 1840. The British consul, Richard Charlton, seemed bent upon getting his government to interfere in Hawaiian affairs. In particular, he set up in 1840 a claim for a piece of land in Honolulu which he said had been given to him by Kalanimoku, the former prime minister. This lease was probably fraudulent, but the claim caused trouble for some years; in 1847 Charlton finally got possession.

The need for recognition of Hawaii's independence was made more urgent by the desires of foreign capitalists who wished to develop the agriculture of the islands, but who held back because of the unsettled future of the Hawaiian government. The achievement of this recognition was to come during the exciting years 1840 to 1843.

First efforts toward independence were made in 1840 through a visiting American lawyer, Thomas J. Farnham, who was commissioned as minister plenipotentiary to the three foreign governments concerned, but he accomplished nothing. The next step was made by Peter A. Brinsmade, who was promoting the development of a land concession which had been granted by the Hawaiians to the American firm of Ladd & Company on condition that independence be recognized. Brinsmade on a trip to Washington delivered a letter to the secretary of state, Daniel Webster, and urged favorable consideration.

A more influential helper now appeared on the scene, Sir George Simpson, governor of the Hudson's Bay Company in North America, who came to Hawaii on a world tour. He advised that commissioners should be sent out with authority to negotiate treaties with Great Britain, France, and the United States; and he offered, if so requested, to be one of them. His offer was accepted, and he agreed to meet in London the other two members of the commission, who would visit Washington on their way to Europe. These men were William Richards, political mentor to the chiefs and the king, and Timothy Haalilio, a young native who was private secretary to the king and a member of his treasury board.

The two envoys departed on July 18, 1842, on their mission to gain recognition of independence, to secure better treaties, and to have better men appointed to represent the great powers in Hawaii. They arrived in Washington on December 5, and at once began to present their arguments to Secretary of State Webster. They appeared before President John Tyler and his cabinet on the 27th, and their persistence was rewarded when on the 30th Webster gave them a document which constitutes the first formal recognition of the Hawaiian kingdom's independence.

This paper stated that the United States was more interested in Hawaii than any other nation could be, and declared that "no power ought either to take possession of the islands as a conquest, or for the purpose of colonization, and that no power ought to seek for any undue control over the existing Government, or any exclusive privileges or preferences in matters of commerce."

The declaration was officially sent to the governments of Great Britain and France, and soon afterward Richards and Haalilio left for England. They arrived in London on February 18, 1843, and began negotiations with the able and sympathetic head of the British Foreign Office, the Earl of Aberdeen. Their path was made rough, however, by the arrival in London of Richard Charlton, who had heard of the commission's departure and had hurried from Honolulu to London to deliver complaints in person against the Hawaiian government.

The envoys were able to secure the backing of influential Europeans, such as King Leopold of Belgium, and in Paris obtained from the foreign minister, François Guizot, a verbal promise of recognition of independence. When they got back to London, Sir George Simpson's support enabled them to settle remaining questions with the Earl of Aberdeen, and his promise of recognition was confirmed in an official letter of April 1. Before a written acknowledgement could be obtained from Guizot, however, word came from Hawaii that a British naval officer had seized the islands. Instantly it became clear that the independence of Hawaii was a matter that must be settled by the three great powers.

British prestige in the islands had begun to decline about 1825, and some British subjects there felt that the administration was too much under the influence of American missionaries. When Charlton left for London he appointed as acting consul Alexander Simpson, a man unacceptable to the Hawaiian government. Simpson, although a cousin of Sir George, disliked him and his ideas. In the hands of Alexander Simpson, a lover of intrigue, the claims of British subjects could be made the excuse for adding the islands to the British Empire.

In Mexico, on his way to Europe, Charlton had made complaints to British authorities. As a result, Rear Admiral Richard Thomas, commander of the British squadron in the Pacific, sent Lord George Paulet in the frigate *Carysfort* to Honolulu to protect British interests, and in particular to demand restoration of property which Simpson alleged to have been illegally taken from Charlton. Thomas had not yet been informed by Aberdeen of the policy of his government toward Hawaii; otherwise he would have been more careful in giving instructions to Paulet, and the latter would have acted differently.

The *Carysfort* arrived on February 10, 1843, and Alexander Simpson immediately went aboard and told his prejudiced story. Captain Paulet followed his advice throughout. When the king was summoned from Lahaina, he was met with a demand from Paulet for an interview. The king replied that he would name as his negotiator Dr. Gerrit P. Judd, a medical missionary who had taken the place of William Richards as "translator and recorder." The same evening, Paulet sent a second letter, declining to meet Dr. Judd and enclosing certain demands inspired by Simpson's complaints. These must be complied with by four o'clock the next afternoon; otherwise the guns of the *Carysfort* would fire on the town.

The king stated that he had sent ministers to England to settle all difficulties, but since he was helpless to resist, he agreed to comply with the ultimatum under protest. Simpson, relishing his triumph, added other claims and demands, including an indemnity of more than $100,000. It soon became clear to the king and Dr. Judd that the British officers were determined to seize the islands. Believing in the ultimate fairness of the government these men represented, Kamehameha III on February 25 made a provisional cession of the islands. The Hawaiian flag was lowered, to be replaced by the British flag, a twenty-one gun salute was fired, and the ship's band played "God Save the Queen."

Three government schooners were taken by Paulet to serve the new regime, and their native names were changed to *Albert, Victoria,* and *Adelaide.* On March 11 Alexander Simpson left in the *Albert* to carry Paulet's report to Mexico, to be forwarded to London. Since this vessel had been previously chartered to Ladd & Company, the company agreed to surrender their charter only if their agent might go on the trip. The company confidentially suggested to the king that their agent might carry dispatches to Washington and London to protest against the seizure of the islands. A young American merchant, James F. B. Marshall, was chosen and commissioned as envoy extraordinary and minister plenipotentiary. His credentials and the documents he was to carry were drafted with great secrecy by Dr. Judd in the royal tombs, using the coffin of Kaahumanu as a writing desk. The two opposing messengers of state, Simpson and Marshall, thus traveled on the same ship, and the documents that they guarded were finally placed together on the same desk in the British Foreign Office.

From February 25 until the end of July, the Hawaiian Islands were under the British flag. The cession deed provided that in all native matters no changes would be made, but that the government should be in the hands of a commission consisting of the king or his deputy, Captain Paulet, Major Duncan Forbes Mackay (a British subject), and Lieutenant Frere, R.N. The king appointed Dr. Judd as his deputy. Mackay resigned on March 4 because of ill health. Dr. Judd did his best to maintain good feeling. Soon, however, the commission began to overstep its powers, and to meddle in all sorts of internal affairs, even assuming judicial functions. Laws on liquor control and other matters were changed. A new police force and a body of native soldiers called the "Queen's Regiment" were formed, and were paid from the king's treasury. On May 10 Dr. Judd protested against the actions of the commission and next day resigned as king's deputy. The remaining members, Paulet and Frere, became more and more arbitrary in their rule. Dr. Judd secretly removed the public archives to the royal mausoleum to prevent their seizure by the naval officers. On July 11, Commodore Lawrence Kearney, commander of an American squadron, issued from his flagship, *Con-*

stellation, a protest against the cession. Conditions were fast approaching an open break.

Fortunately, on July 26 Admiral Thomas arrived at Honolulu in his flagship, the frigate *Dublin.* He had come at once to remedy the harm done by the cession. He immediately held an interview with the king, in which it was soon clear that the admiral intended to restore Hawaii's independence. Before doing so, however, he obtained the king's agreement to certain articles in the nature of a treaty which closely guarded the interests of British subjects. The king gave his consent, conditional upon final arrangements in London.

At a colorful ceremony on July 31, the Hawaiian flag was again raised over the islands in recognition of Kamehameha III as an independent sovereign. In the afternoon, at a thanksgiving service at the Stone Church (Kawaiahao), the king stated that, as he had hoped, the life of the land had been restored. He is said to have then used the words which have become the motto of Hawaii: *"Ua mau ke ea o ka aina i ka pono* (The life of the land is preserved by righteousness)."

The British government, which had already disavowed Paulet's act to the governments of the United States and France—although Britain later refused, on a technicality, to pay the Hawaiians any indemnity for the consequences of that act—confirmed the restoration by Thomas. The admiral resided in Honolulu for the following six months, until the arrival of General William Miller, the new British consul general, in February, 1844. The friendly naval officer won the hearts of the people, who named for him Thomas Square in Honolulu, site of the restoration ceremony.

The mission of Richards, Haalilio, and Sir George Simpson was triumphantly completed when on November 28, 1843, a joint declaration was signed in London through which the independence of the Sandwich Islands was recognized by the Queen of Great Britain and the King of the French. The United States, whose special interests in Hawaii were obvious to everyone, was invited to join in this declaration; but the invitation was declined on the ground that such a declaration would be contrary to the American policy of avoiding entangling alliances. To Richards and Haalilio, Secretary of State John C. Calhoun in the summer of 1844 reaffirmed the recognition of Hawaii's independence by the United States, but no treaty was made at this time.

The new British consul general, Miller, brought with him a "convention" or treaty to replace the articles signed in 1836. This convention was almost identical with that forced upon the king by the Frenchman Laplace in 1839, and contained both the objectionable points which limited the sovereignty of Kamehameha III. The Hawaiian government had no choice but to accept or reject the convention *in toto*, and it was signed at Lahaina on February 12, 1844.

The hard work and patience of Richards and Haalilio, who had successfully refuted all the complaints of Charlton and Simpson except Charlton's old land claim, had resulted in recognition of Hawaiian independence. The envoys were not able, however, to secure a new treaty with France. In the spring of 1844 they returned to the United States, and in November sailed for Hawaii. Haalilio died at sea on December 3, his health undermined by his travels far from home. Richards arrived in Honolulu in March, 1845, having been away for almost three years.

Meanwhile, Kamehameha III, assisted by competent advisers, was carrying forward his constitutional reforms. The king, who was earning the title of most wise and beloved of all Hawaiian monarchs, took the lead in putting the finances of the kingdom on a sounder basis. He appointed a treasury board on May 10, 1842, consisting of his right-hand man Dr. Judd, Timothy Haalilio, and John Ii. The private property of the king was separated from government property, and the board was given control of government income and taxes. Within a few years the system brought many economies, and by 1846 the national debt had been paid off.

The need for a capable legal adviser to aid the government in handling lawsuits—especially those brought into court by foreigners—had long been apparent. On March 9, 1844, the king appointed as attorney general a young American lawyer named John Ricord. Well trained and highly energetic, and not afraid of making enemies, Ricord loyally defended and advised the king, and in his spare time worked out a modernized plan of government which, approved by the legislature, was codified in a series of Organic Acts.

The first of these acts went into effect in March, 1846. It provided that the executive branch should be divided into five departments—interior, foreign relations, finance, public instruction, and law—with a minister in charge of each. The *kuhina nui* was to be minister of the interior. The privy council, which was to become a very important body, was to be composed of the five ministers, the four governors, and other members appointed by the king. The first formal ministry consisted of John Young (son of the old adviser to Kamehameha I), as premier and minister of the interior; Robert C. Wyllie, an extremely able Scotsman who had taken over Dr. Judd's department of foreign affairs in 1845, as minister of foreign relations; Dr. Judd as minister of finance; William Richards as minister of public instruction; and John Ricord as attorney general. According to law, those ministers who were foreign born became naturalized Hawaiian subjects.

The second Organic Act also went into effect in 1846, and gave details for operation of the executive departments. The most important part of the act was the creation of a Board of Commissioners to Quiet Land Titles. This "Land Commission," as it was called, was part of the scheme for placing all land tenures in the kingdom on a more satisfactory basis. Consideration of this problem resulted in doing away completely with the old feudal system of landholding, and in putting all land holdings under fee-simple title.

As a first step in the process, all the land in the kingdom was divided between the king and the chiefs, and this division (*mahele*) was recorded in the *Mahele* Book. According to the accepted theory, the government had an interest, amounting to about one third, in the lands of both king and chiefs. This government claim was satisfied in the following way. The king divided his lands into two parts, retaining one (the "Crown Lands") for his own use, and turning over the other, the larger one, to the government as a public domain ("Government Lands"). This division also was recorded in the *Mahele* Book. Many of the chiefs surrendered portions of their land to the government and thus obtained clear titles to the rest. All others had to pay a "commutation" to the government. As a further step in the land revolution, the lands occupied and cultivated by the common people were given to them as outright possessions. These grants, called *kuleanas,* came out of the holdings of the king, chiefs, and government; they varied in size from one to forty acres. A law was passed under which government lands could be sold to commoners at a low price. Finally, after a great deal of discussion, foreigners were given the same rights as natives in the holding of land. With the exception of the king, everyone had to present a claim for his land to the Land Commission, which, after investigation, gave an "award," and these Land Commission Awards are the firm basis of the titles to all lands covered by them.

The third Organic Act, which went into operation early in 1848, made badly needed improvements in the judiciary branch of the government. Attorney General Ricord had begun to prepare such a law, but when he resigned his position and left the islands, the law was completed by William L. Lee, a young American lawyer with an excellent legal education. The most important court created by the act was the Superior Court of Law and Equity, consisting of a chief justice and two associate justices. This was virtually the supreme court of the kingdom. Below this were four circuit courts, taking the place of the old governors' courts, and below these were twenty-four district courts, including the police courts at Honolulu and Lahaina. The act prescribed the manner in which trials and lawsuits should be conducted. Judge Lee was appointed chief justice of the Superior Court, and his associates were Lorrin Andrews and John Ii, a native Hawaiian who had been educated in the mission schools. All these men served with great distinction and contributed wisely to the new and growing body of Hawaiian law in this stormy, formative period.

Although Hawaiian independence had been recognized by the three great powers in 1843, the fight for equitable treaties had to be carried on by the Hawaiian government for ten years thereafter. The burden fell upon Robert C. Wyllie, whose character made him fully equal to the task.

A fair treaty was signed with the kingdom of Denmark in 1846. In the same year the British and French governments sent the king new treaties, exactly alike, which were an improvement on earlier agreements but which still contained two objectionable articles. The king signed these in the hope of getting them replaced by more favorable treaties. This aim was accomplished in 1851 with Great Britain, but with France it took a little longer.

Relations with France improved for a while after 1843, when Dudoit learned of the London declaration. The $20,000 taken away by Captain Laplace in 1839 was restored to the Hawaiian government by a French admiral in 1846; the money was still packed, unopened, in the original boxes.

Early in 1848, however, Dudoit was replaced by a new French consul, Guillaume Patrice Dillon, who proved to be a trouble maker. A crisis in relations came in April, 1849, when the king asked the French government to recall Dillon. In the middle of August, at the latter's request, the French commander in the Pacific, Rear Admiral Legoarant de Tromelin, arrived in Honolulu with two warships, *La Poursuivante* and *Gassendi*. Again a French seizure seemed imminent. The admiral, after consulting with Dillon, sent the king a set of ten demands, accompanied by threats of force. The king courteously denied the charges and refused the demands. At once Tromelin landed an armed party which seized the fort, the customs house, and other government buildings. The king's yacht and a number of merchant vessels were also taken over. After ten days the admiral sailed away, taking Dillon with him.

The British and American consuls protested against this action, and through them appeals were sent to their governments. In addition, a special embassy was sent to France. Dr. Judd was chosen to head the mission. He took with him the two younger princes, Alexander Liholiho, the heir-apparent, and his brother, Lot Kamehameha. Early in 1850 they arrived in Paris and spent several months vainly attempting to right the injustices done by the consul and the admiral, and striving to get a new treaty. On the journey, during which Great Britain and the United States were visited, the young princes—both of whom were to rule Hawaii in future—obtained a valuable idea of the world, and by their attainments and behavior made an excellent impression.

Soon after Dr. Judd's return, a French commissioner, Emile Perrin, arrived on the warship *Serieuse*, and on February 1, 1851, pushed the same ten demands made by Tromelin. Again this cannon diplomacy created high alarm. In self defense, the king signed a secret proclamation putting the islands under the protection of the United States. This document was to be used only if the French attempted to seize the islands. When Perrin learned that the proclamation was in the hands of the American commissioner, he realized he had overstepped himself. He moderated his demands, and signed a temporary agreement with Mr. Wyllie. Perrin then returned to France, and the French shadow never again darkened the Hawaiian skies.

Relations of Hawaii with the United States started inauspiciously. George Brown, the first commissioner, was appointed in 1843; he was the first representative of diplomatic rather than consular rank sent by any foreign nation to Hawaii. His conduct soon occasioned a request for his recall. He was replaced by Anthony Ten Eyck, a man of similar stripe. In his efforts to give American citizens the same special privileges as those of British and French subjects, he became so unreasonable that the king refused to deal with him further. Luther Severance, who arrived in 1851, showed a dignified and respectful attitude that served as a good precedent for his successors.

The occupation of the Oregon Territory and the war with Mexico in 1846, and the admission in 1850 of California, which after the gold rush was to become a populous Pacific Coast state, made it seem that the "manifest destiny" of the United States might embrace the strategically situated Hawaiian Islands. In 1849 the king of Hawaii sent a special ambassador, James J. Jarves, to Washington to negotiate a treaty with the United States, which went into effect in 1850.

In the fall of 1851 the king and his advisers were alarmed at the possibility that filibusters might come from California and overturn the government of Hawaii. The administration of President Franklin Pierce expected that the islands might soon become an American possession. The number of Americans living in Hawaii had greatly increased after the settlement of California, and many of them wanted to see the American flag fly over the islands. Political disturbances in the islands arose, caused by alarm about the decline in the native Hawaiian population, which was hastened by a bad smallpox epidemic in 1853. Animosity among some of the foreign residents of Hawaii was directed against the "missionary influence" centered around Dr. Judd and Richard Armstrong, minister of public instruction, and this faction petitioned the king to dismiss these men, who were charged, among other misdeeds, with having been responsible for the spread of smallpox. The king after due consideration dissolved his ministry and then reappointed all except Dr. Judd, whose place was taken by Elisha H. Allen, former American consul.

During this agitation, the king was requested to take steps that would lead to the annexation of Hawaii by the United States. It was felt that, if the kingdom were overthrown either by filibusters or by internal revolt, immediate annexation by the United States would be the best course to follow. The preparation of a treaty of annexation was in the hands of Wyllie and David L. Gregg, new

American commissioner. Two points of disagreement arose. The king insisted that Hawaii should be admitted to the Union as a full-fledged state and not as a territory. He also asked that the United States pay $300,000 annually to the king and the native chiefs and officials, who would lose their posts after annexation. Mr. Gregg thought that the question of statehood should be left to Congress, and felt that a payment of $100,000 a year would be sufficient. He agreed, however, to include these debatable points. Various causes delayed final signing of the treaty, and the death of Kamehameha III ended this first effort at annexation. It was later learned that the president of the United States would not have approved the treaty as drawn up.

The progress in government achieved during the long reign of the third Kamehameha was stabilized by a new constitution which incorporated the gains made. Three commissioners—Dr. Judd, appointed by the king, Judge Ii, appointed by the House of Nobles, and Judge Lee, appointed by the House of Representatives—submitted the draft of a new constitution, written mainly by Judge Lee, to the legislature. After some amendment, it was passed by the legislature and approved by the king. This Constitution of 1852, which showed the influence of American ideas, was the most liberal yet attained, and gave the people of Hawaii a share in the making and executing of the nation's laws.

CHAPTER NINE

Church, School, and Home, 1824–1854

THE reign of Kamehameha III was the great era of Christian missionary endeavor, and the educational pattern for Hawaii was likewise set in that period. Marked advances in social and cultural life were also achieved during these thirty eventful years.

The first pilgrims sent out by the American Board of Commissioners for Foreign Missions were reinforced by a dozen other parties, consisting of ordained preachers and their helpers, such as teachers, physicians, and artisans. By 1840 such Protestant missionaries were stationed in nearly all parts of the islands. Full admission to the church was not lightly granted to native converts, and during the first seventeen years less than thirteen hundred persons were admitted; but between 1838 and 1840 more than twenty thousand were taken into the church. This harvest resulted from an evangelical drive called the "Great Revival," the work of a small group of energetic preachers such as Titus Coan at Hilo and Lorenzo Lyons at Waimea, Hawaii. By 1840 Hawaii was officially a Christian nation, and although the king never became a member of the church, the constitution he gave the people in that year decreed that "no law shall be enacted which is at variance with the word of the Lord Jehovah."

It has been estimated that in 1840 about 18 per cent of the native population were members of the Protestant Church, and that in 1853 about 30 per cent were members. The number of Protestants who were not church members (including children and believers who had not become active members) swelled the total; in 1853 the census listed a Protestant population of 56,840.

By the end of this period, the native members were making substantial contributions for the support of church activities. In addition, missionaries were sent out by a Hawaiian society to convert the natives of Micronesia and the Marquesas Islands. For some time the missionary policy was directed to training Hawaiians who would become heads of their own congregations. By 1848, nine natives had been licensed to preach; but not until 1849 was a native, James Kekela, ordained and installed as pastor of an independent church.

A further important change in the nature of the mission concerned the status of the American missionaries. During the later 1840's many of them who had been in the field for some years felt that they should return to the United States for the education of their children. Until this time the policy of the American Board had prevented the missionaries from acquiring lands and houses and becoming permanent residents of the islands. The Board had also opposed the naturalization of its workers as Hawaiian citizens. This policy was now reversed to counteract the "homeward current." Missionaries were encouraged to become Hawaiian citizens. The American Board divided up and gave to the individual workers the larger part of the lands, houses, and herds that the mission had acquired in the various islands. Some missionaries bought additional land from the government.

By 1853, the American Board considered that Hawaii had been Christianized, and the old mission organization was dissolved. The status of the new organization, formed at this time as the Hawaiian Evangelical Association, was that of a "home mission" rather than a "foreign mission."

A final result of these various changes was that American missionaries and their families were to become an influential element in the population of the Hawaiian Islands.

The first church for foreigners in Hawaii grew out of the Seamen's Bethel begun in Honolulu in 1833, in charge of a chaplain, the Reverend John Diell. As a result of Diell's interest in foreign residents, he organized in May, 1837, the Oahu Bethel Church. This organization lapsed after the death of its founder in January, 1841; but a new Bethel Church for foreign residents was organized in 1850 by Diell's successor in the seamen's chaplaincy, the Reverend Samuel C. Damon.

The desire for an evangelical church independent of the Bethel was realized on June 2, 1852, with the opening of the Second Foreign Church, later called the Fort Street Church. These two Congregational churches were ultimately combined to form the present Central Union Church of Honolulu.

Until about 1840, the Protestants had a virtual monopoly of religious endeavor in Hawaii. The edict of religious toleration of 1839 opened the way, however, for greater activity by Catholic and other workers. Much of the Catholic story has already been told. It may be remarked that in 1846 a seminary was founded in the Koolau district of Oahu to train Catholic teachers. In 1847 Father Maigret, who had been associated with the mission almost from the beginning, was consecrated Bishop of Arathia; he was to remain as head of the Catholic mission for more than thirty years.

Toward the end of the reign of Kamehameha III another sect entered the field. These were the Mormons.

A group of Mormons headed by Sam Brannan passed through Hawaii in 1846 on their way to California. The first Mormon mission appeared in Honolulu on December 12, 1850, consisting of ten young men from the California gold diggings. Their first thought was to convert the white population, but they soon decided that they should learn the Hawaiian language and work among the natives if they wished any large number of converts. In spite of their youth and inexperience and the necessity of supporting themselves, the first Mormon workers, and others sent out later from Utah, made rapid progress. Almost at the outset they began to appoint native converts to various church offices, and thus gave the Hawaiians responsibility within the framework of the Mormon Church. Against active opposition from Protestant and Catholic missionaries, Mormonism by 1854 had penetrated to all parts of the kingdom.

The most successful and facile preacher among the Mormons was George Q. Cannon, one of the first company. He made the island of Maui a strong center. Early in 1852 Cannon, with the assistance of two educated Hawaiians, began the translation of the Book of Mormon into Hawaiian; the final revision was completed precisely two years later, and was printed in San Francisco.

In 1853 the Mormon leaders were promoting the idea of a "gathering" of all Mormons in Utah, to protect them from the daily temptations of the gentile world. The island of Lanai was judged to be an excellent temporary gathering place for Hawaiians of that faith. A site in the interior of the island was chosen for a town, houses were built and agriculture was begun, and by the end of 1854 the "City of Joseph" was well started as a Mormon community.

Formal education in Hawaii grew out of the work of the Christian missions. Although teaching was not the primary function of the missionaries, it was an essential element of the Christian civilization which they had been instructed to develop in the Hawaiian Islands. Actually, successes in education were achieved readily, and the appeal of the printed page often touched the native heart more quickly than spiritual abstractions. To the Hawaiians, the *pule* (missionary religious instruction) and the *palapala* (missionary education through reading and writing) were inextricably joined.

The desire to learn to read rendered the first missionary schools highly popular. Little could have been accomplished without the assistance of native students who rapidly became teachers. As the better students learned the art, they were sent to other districts to open their own schools. By 1824 there were about two thousand pupils in the schools. Two years later the number had risen to twenty-five thousand, and there were more than four hundred native teachers at work. In 1831 the missionaries reported that there were eleven hundred common schools in the islands, in which about two fifths of the entire population were receiving instruction.

Most of the students learned to read, some of them to write, and a few to do simple arithmetic. The basic textbook was the *Pi-a-pa*, an eight-page pamphlet containing the alphabet, numerals, punctuation marks, lists of words, verses of scripture, and brief poems and other reading matter. As late as 1832, probably half the schools in the islands had nothing to read but this Hawaiian descendant of the hornbook.

Curiously enough, few of the early students were children. So many adults wished to learn the *palapala* that the teachers could give very little time to child pupils. Parents did not want their offspring to go to school until they themselves learned the magical new skill. But after 1829 a strong effort was made to gather the children into schools. A primer was printed especially to interest them.

This first school system in Hawaii, largely unplanned, reached the peak of its value about 1832. By that time the novelty had worn off, and more than half the population had learned to read. This period was also marked by a reaction against the missionaries, and the schools suffered, many of the thatched country schools falling into decay. It was clear that education, and particularly the education of children, would have to be put on a firmer basis. With this in view, the missionaries gave more and more attention to the training of teachers, the preparation of textbooks, and the building of substantial schoolhouses; and they tried to impress on the rulers of the nation the importance of an adequate public school system.

The education of its citizenry was recognized as one function of the government in a law passed on October 15, 1840, which required that common schools should be maintained in every community. Trustees were to be elected by male parents, and provisions were made for the certification and support of teachers. The legislature was to appoint one school agent or inspector for each of the five principal islands. These would be supervised by a school superintendent, and David Malo, a Hawaiian preacher and antiquarian, was the first superintendent appointed in the kingdom. When the word "missionary" in the act was interpreted as discriminating against the organization of Catholic common schools, an amended law of May 21, 1841, was passed to remove this and other objections.

Further progress was made in the latter part of this reign. The Organic Acts passed in 1845 and 1846 established a department of public instruction under a cabinet minister. William Richards, the first minister of public instruction, took office on April 13, 1846, and before his death in November, 1847, made steady advances in getting the educational machinery running.

Richards was succeeded by the Reverend Richard Armstrong, pastor of Kawaiahao Church in Honolulu. Under Armstrong, who served from 1848 until his death in 1860, the trend away from sectarian schools brought more and more responsibilities to the government. The sectarian nature of the schools was a natural result of their historical beginnings. In 1854 Armstrong proposed the consolidation of small schools on a territorial basis, and the avoidance of teaching controversial religious doctrines in the "mixed" schools. This policy was carried out very gradually, and after 1853 the official reports no longer classified the government common schools on sectarian lines.

By the middle of the century, most Hawaiians were literate in their own language. Many of them wished to have their children taught English, which had long ago become the main language of business and government. In 1845 James J. Jarves proposed in a series of editorials that steps should be taken to make English the language of the nation, and advocated that a start be made by teaching English in the mission schools. The missionary view, however, was that in order to preserve the Hawaiian nation, its speech must also be preserved. All instruction in the common schools had been carried on in Hawaiian, and the study of English was not introduced at the Protestant seminary at Lahainaluna until 1846. The closer relations with the United States after the acquisition of Oregon and California, however, caused even the missionaries to recognize the need for a knowledge of English among the natives.

A beginning was made by the legislature of 1853 in promoting the study of English in certain schools, and the next year a law was passed "for the encouragement and support of English schools for Hawaiian youth." By the end of 1854 ten English schools were in operation. They marked the beginning of a movement which, many years later, ended in the abandonment of the Hawaiian language as a medium of instruction in the public schools of Hawaii.

Certain "select" schools which had grown up were gradually taken over by the government. One of these was a family boarding school started by Mr. and Mrs. Amos Starr Cooke in 1839 for the young chiefs. This school was designated by the act of 1846 as the "Royal School" and was put under the Ministry of Public Instruction. The Cookes retired in 1850 after having taught a number of children of the nobility, five of whom afterwards became rulers of Hawaii. English had always been the medium of teaching in this school, and when in 1849 the children of white residents began attending as day pupils, the Royal School became a select English academy; in 1853 it had 121 pupils.

The Oahu Charity School near the mission buildings in Honolulu, started for the education of the children of foreign residents having Hawaiian wives, opened in 1833 as an English-language school. After a number of ups and downs, it was taken over by the government in 1851 and became the Honolulu Free School, supported by a special tax on foreigners.

The high school at Lahainaluna, Maui, was founded by the missionaries in 1831, primarily to train native teachers and pastors. During the reign of Kamehameha III it was the leading school of the kingdom, but the American Board found it difficult to furnish enough money for its support, and in 1849 it was transferred to the government. One of the teachers was Sheldon Dibble, who began the recording of Hawaiian legends and history, particularly from native sources. With the aid of his students, Dibble put out in 1843 through the Lahainaluna press the first published history of the Hawaiian Islands. Dibble was also instrumental in starting an Hawaiian Historical Society, and stimulated such outstanding pupils as David Malo and Samuel M. Kamakau to further research in Hawaiian history.

Other boarding schools were to be found in Hawaii in this period. Among these were the school for boys at Hilo begun in 1836, and a Central Female Boarding Seminary opened at Wailuku, Maui, in 1837. A school for the education of missionary children was opened in 1841 at Punahou, near Honolulu, under the Reverend Daniel Dole. This English school grew steadily, and in 1853 was granted a government charter which expanded its scope under the title of "Punahou School and Oahu College." It was hoped that eventually it would grow up to the latter part of this name.

The number of select schools increased from year to year, and the number of common schools declined, a fact revealing that parents were willing to pay fees to enable their children to attend schools where English was taught and higher teaching standards were held.

The press was early the handmaiden not only of religion and education, but of general culture. On January 7, 1822, the first pages of printing in the Hawaiian language were struck off at the missionary press in Honolulu. Spelling and reading books for schools were rapidly turned out, as well as scripture tracts, a hymn book, and parts of the Bible, which were in demand as fast as they could be translated and set in type. Later, books and periodicals were printed both in Hawaiian and English. In 1832 the New Testament in Hawaiian was completed; in March, 1839, the Old Testament was finished; and by May of that year, the entire Bible was available in Hawaiian.

In 1834 a second mission printshop was set up at the high school at Lahainaluna and on February 14 began issuing the first

Hawaiian newspaper, *Ka Lama Hawaii*. Another small paper, *Ke Kumu Hawaii*, was begun at Honolulu later in 1834. The first quarterly review published in the Pacific was the *Hawaiian Spectator* (1838–1839), printed at the mission press. By 1842, the two printing offices had turned out about a hundred million pages printed in the Hawaiian language.

The first English language newspaper published west of the Rocky Mountains, the *Sandwich Island Gazette*, appeared weekly in Honolulu from July, 1836, to July, 1839, printed by two Americans. This was followed by the *Sandwich Island Mirror*, which was issued monthly for a year. A more pretentious newspaper, the *Polynesian*, began in June, 1840; it was re-established in May, 1844, after having suspended publication for two and a half years, as the official journal of the government, with its editor, James J. Jarves, as "director of government printing." *The Friend*, established in 1843 by the seamen's chaplain, the Reverend S. C. Damon, had occasionally been critical of the government, but in September, 1846, the opposition established its own organ, the *Sandwich Island News*, which ran for about two years. It was followed by two other opposition newspapers: the *Honolulu Times* (1849–1850); and the *Weekly Argus* (1852–1855, the last year under the name *New Era and Weekly Argus*), of which Abraham Fornander was editor.

By the end of the reign of Kamehameha III, Hawaii had already taken on something of the cosmopolitan character which later became so marked. In 1853 foreigners numbered 2,119 out of a total population of 73,134. These foreigners came, as one observer noted, "from nearly every nation under heaven," but the bulk of them were from the United States (692), Great Britain (403), and China (364); and 291 were born in the islands. There were nearly a thousand persons of part-Hawaiian ancestry, but this group, though increasing, was still far from being able to compensate for the decrease of those of full Hawaiian blood. Considerably more than a half of all the foreigners resided in Honolulu, which was the cultural as well as the business and political capital of the kingdom. The total population of Honolulu at this time was 11,455.

A traveler who visited Hawaii in 1845 wrote about the hospitality shown by the foreign residents of Honolulu. "This virtue is not confined to the missionary families, but is a general characteristic of the foreign society. Strangers who come well recommended are immediately introduced into society of a highly intellectual and polished character, consisting of consuls and other resident officers, naval captains and merchants, and American and English ladies, many of whom are highly accomplished." On a smaller scale, this description applied to other towns throughout the kingdom. As the quotation suggests, the foreign population was cosmopolitan not only in racial origin but also in occupation. The civilizing forces at work were not exclusively missionary, as some accounts seem to imply.

Cultural institutions commonly found in European and American communities had begun to make their appearance in Hawaii. Schools, churches, and the press have already been mentioned. In 1850, residents of Honolulu organized an Atheneum Society which conducted a series of public lectures and for a year or two maintained a reading room and library. The Atheneum was succeeded in 1853 by the Honolulu Circulating Library Association. In 1847 the *Polynesian* noted that a thousand dollars' worth of books had been sold in Honolulu in less than two months after their arrival. R. C. Wyllie about this time had in his private library both the sixth and the seventh editions of the *Encyclopedia Britannica*.

The arts of music and the drama were being cultivated. A letter written in 1848 cited as one evidence of civilization the large number of pianos owned by residents of the Hawaiian capital. Mrs. Harriet Fiddes, a singer of considerable ability who resided in Honolulu in 1853 and 1854, gave singing lessons and was frequently heard in concerts either alone or in co-operation with the Honolulu Amateur Music Society. Occasionally, distinguished artists broke the voyage between San Francisco and Australia and gave performances in Honolulu. A notable example was Miss Catherine Hayes, who gave a concert in July, 1854.

Honolulu's first theater, the Thespian, was opened September 11, 1847, and for several months gave more or less regular weekly performances by local amateurs. This was followed by the Hawaiian Theater, which opened in its own building June 24, 1848, with a program including Goldsmith's *She Stoops to Conquer*. The Hawaiian (later called Royal Hawaiian) Theater continued for many years to provide entertainment furnished in part by local actors, amateur and semiprofessional, and in part by professional actors who came to Honolulu for short seasons or stopped there for a little while on the voyage between the United States and Australia. Among the latter was Edwin Booth, who in February and March, 1855, at the beginning of his career on the stage, appeared in several plays, including a command performance of *Richard III* before the king. For about two years, 1853 to 1855, another theater, the Varieties, sought support from the public of Honolulu. Fire removed this competitor of the Hawaiian Theater.

CHAPTER TEN

Prosperity in Paradise, 1824–1854

A STEADY growth in trade, agriculture, industry, and transportation marked the reign of Kamehameha III. During the latter part of this period, prosperity brought by the whaling era was at its height. Such crops as sugar and coffee were established at this time, and the need for field workers led to the importation of foreign labor, a practice that was to be a feature of Hawaiian economy for many decades. Transportation by sea and land was greatly improved.

The fur trade and the sandalwood trade early drew attention to the strategic location of the islands for ocean traffic. Although in the early days some of the natives, such as Governor Boki, engaged in business ventures, commerce was developed more and more by foreign residents. Honolulu soon became the business capital of the "Paradise of the Pacific." Merchant ships brought cargoes from America, Europe, and China. Some of these goods were sold to whalers, some were sold to the people of the islands, and some were transshipped and re-exported to California, Oregon, the Russian settlements to the north, and other islands of the Pacific.

The first representative of a foreign government in Hawaii was John Coffin Jones, a trader who was appointed in 1820 as American commercial agent. As early as 1817 and 1818, James Hunnewell, clerk of a trading house in Boston, ran a store in Honolulu for ten months. Four mercantile firms were doing business there in 1823. In 1826 Hunnewell returned and opened another mercantile house, which was to become C. Brewer & Company, Ltd. After 1830, Americans were driven out of the trade on the northwest coast of America by the activities of the Russians (who prohibited trade with the Indians north of 54° 40′ latitude) and the Hudson's Bay Company. This British concern undertook the exploitation of all the resources of the Columbia River region and established an agency in Honolulu in 1834 which promoted a lively trade between Hawaii and the Oregon country. In 1845 there were, besides the Hudson's Bay Company, two other British firms in Honolulu: Skinner & Company, and Starkey, Janion & Company (which, with a continuous history, is now carried on under the name of Theo. H. Davies & Company, Ltd.).

The Americans in Hawaii concentrated on trade with the American coast from California southward to Valparaiso, and exchanged goods with Chile, Peru, Mexico, and California (where the hide and tallow trade was of first importance until 1849). During the 1840's Valparaiso was a main source of supply for the Hawaiian trade. Imports from Mexico were mainly bullion and coin, which formed the larger part of the money circulating in the Hawaiian Islands. Most of the manufactured goods sold locally or shipped out from the islands were first imported from the United States, China, or Great Britain. The German influence dates from about 1849, when Captain H. Hackfeld arrived from Hamburg and started a firm which eventually became American Factors, Ltd.

The total bulk of trade was of course small and was easily affected by casual events. A writer in 1841 remarked that the visit of the United States exploring squadron under Lieutenant Charles Wilkes was very beneficial to the small trading community, and that the purchase of provisions from the natives put a large amount of money into circulation.

The effect of trade can be seen in the growth of Honolulu during this period. In 1820 it was a village of grass houses with only half a dozen buildings of wood or stone, and three or four small stores. The population numbered between three and four thousand. By 1840 the population had doubled, and included about six hundred foreign residents. Many substantial European-type buildings were found in the town, which had spread out from the waterfront toward Waikiki as far as the Mission, and a system of streets had been laid out. The editor of the *Polynesian* in 1840 gave a long list of stores, public buildings, and shops for tradesmen and artisans, which included four churches, seven schools, a library and reading room, two hospitals for seamen, a government building, consulates of France, England, and the United States, four wholesale and twenty retail stores, two hotels, two taverns, twelve grogshops, two billiard rooms, and seven bowling alleys.

An artist named Emmert in 1853 made a series of pictures (lithographed by Burgess) which show the central part of Honolulu to be well filled with substantial business and government buildings, many of them of two or three stories. Illustrated likewise are many private residences, churches, and schools. In 1850 Honolulu was officially declared to be a city, and Emmert's pictures and other evidence show that it deserved the title.

The whaling industry formed the mainstay of Hawaiian trade for many years. In those days before kerosene lamps and electricity, whale-oil candles and lamps were the main sources of artificial light in the world. Sperm oil was used to lubricate machinery, and many articles were made from the supple whalebone.

A rich sperm-whale fishery was discovered about 1820 off the coast of Japan, and soon many whaling vessels—most of them from the United States—flocked to the Pacific. At that time Japan was closed to foreigners, and Hawaii was the best place for whalers to rest and to get supplies. Between 1840 and 1860, whaling in the Pacific was at its peak. Between 1823 and 1840, an average of about a hundred whaleships stopped at Honolulu and Lahaina in the course of each year. After 1840 there was a sharp increase, and the number remained high up to the Civil War. The years 1846 and 1859 were the highest in the number of arrivals of whaleships in island ports. The increase after 1840 was caused by the discovery of new whaling grounds in the northern Pacific, in the Okhotsk, Bering, and Anadir Seas, and in the Arctic Ocean north of Bering Strait.

The whalers came to the islands in two seasons, the spring and the fall. During these times, the ports were crammed with vessels. At times the ships were moored so close together at Honolulu that a person could walk from one end of the harbor to the other on the decks of ships, without touching shore.

Honolulu had the only good harbor within a radius of two thousand miles at the heart of the whaling grounds, and hence received most of the benefits of the trade, but other parts of the islands also profited by furnishing provisions to the ships. During the forties and fifties Honolulu was the principal forward base of the whaling industry, for six sevenths of the world's whaling fleet was operating in the Pacific. The system of spending one year on a whaling voyage was changed until many ships began to stay out two years or more, spending the summer on the northern grounds and the winter along the equator. Often they would leave their oil and bone in storage at Honolulu, or ship it home in merchant ships, many of which came to this port for the purpose of loading this cargo.

The economic prosperity of the islands during the whaling epoch was almost completely dependent upon the whaling fleets. Government revenue was increased by port charges and duties on imported goods. The business of merchants and warehouse owners and shipyard workers was greatly benefited. Cattle were driven to the ports for slaughtering, or were shipped by sea to Lahaina from the ranches on Hawaii. The demand for firewood began to denude the forest areas. Thousands of dollars a year were spent by the whaling captains for white and sweet potatoes, pumpkins, bananas, molasses, sugar, coffee, coconuts, breadfruit, taro, cabbages, oranges, pineapples, melons, turkeys, hogs, and goats. The sale of agricultural products promoted the growing of provisions needed by the whalers, but the ease with which money could be made selling to the ships probably retarded the development of large plantations, which involved hard work, heavy investments, and high risk of failure.

The whaling era wrought marked changes in the social life of the community. Many sick and disabled seamen were discharged in Hawaiian ports, and the various consuls spent large sums for their care. The presence ashore of thousands of pleasure-bound seamen during several months of each year created grave problems of law enforcement. Disturbances were not infrequent, although they seldom reached the proportions of the celebrated seamen's riot of November, 1852, when a mob of sailors burned down the police station, almost set fire to the fleet in the harbor, and terrorized Honolulu for more than twenty-four hours. Back-country natives came to the ports to sell their wares and remained to swell the number of town dwellers. Many young natives felt the attractions of voyaging about the world; during the three years 1845–47, nearly two thousand of them enlisted as seamen on foreign ships, and Hawaiians, who made excellent sailors, were found in forecastles all over the globe. The laws which provided that a captain should return a recruit to the islands at the end of two years were not strictly obeyed, and the decline in Hawaiian population was undoubtedly affected by the fact that one-fifth of the young men were wandering in foreign parts.

One whaleship seaman, Herman Melville, who was to become famous as the author of *Moby Dick* and other novels about whaling and the Pacific, came ashore and spent four months in the islands in 1843. He signed on as ordinary seaman in the American navy frigate *United States,* which departed on August 17 for New York by way of Cape Horn.

Agriculture on a wider scale began in the Hawaiian Islands in the reign of Kamehameha III. The ancient Hawaiians had intensively cultivated two crops, taro and sweet potatoes, and had even laid out elaborate irrigation systems, but few other vegetable foods were much used by them. Explorers like Vancouver introduced new seeds and plants, as did some early foreign residents. Most prominent of these was the Spaniard Marin, who for his own purposes introduced a wide variety of plants and fruit trees. He also experimented in making nails, tiles, soap, sugar, molasses, castor oil, candles, cigars, wine, brandy, and beer. The missionaries, although somewhat hampered by their many other duties, brought new plants and tools, and gave the natives some instruction in agriculture.

Sugar cane grew luxuriantly on all the islands of the group (Captain Cook wrote of seeing cane plantations), and it had long been thought that raising it could be made profitable. As early as 1802, it is said, sugar was produced by a Chinese on the island of Lanai. Marin made some in 1819, and other small-scale manufacture is reported thereafter. The first attempt to lay out a plantation of any size was made by John Wilkinson, who through the encouragement of Boki had come to the islands with Lord Byron on the Blonde. Manoa Valley, near Honolulu, was chosen as a site, and work began in the fall of 1825. Good tools were lacking, and the natives broke the ground with the o-o, or digging stick. Much capital was consumed by the cost of labor, at twenty-five cents a day. When Wilkinson died in the fall of 1826, more than a hundred acres of cane, as well as many coffee trees, were growing. Some cane was cut at intervals and manufactured into sugar, molasses, and rum; but the enterprise was unprofitable and was abandoned about 1829.

The first extensive agricultural development was not begun until 1835, when the American firm of Ladd & Company obtained a fifty-year lease on a tract of land at Koloa, Kauai. There was much difficulty in getting started, owing to lack of implements and draft animals. The ground was broken by plows drawn by natives. The laborers were paid twelve and a half cents a day and furnished with food. Being paid for their work was a novelty that attracted natives with thrifty ideas, and neighboring chiefs complained that the plantation was leading away their retainers.

The first sugar mill at Koloa was a rude wooden press, but by the end of 1837 an iron mill was set up, and in 1841 an improved mill, run by water power, was installed. The first sugar, turned out in 1837, was poor in quality, and not until 1842 was sugar of even fair quality produced. The Koloa plantation fought along for some years on the verge of success, but not until Dr. R. W.

Wood acquired full possession in 1848 did it get a stable management.

A writer stated in 1840 that missionaries on Kauai, at a distance from Koloa, had set up sugar mills as early as 1838, grinding cane on shares for native growers. In these years many mills were erected in various parts of the kingdom, notably on Maui, Oahu, and Kauai. In 1838 twenty mills run by animal power and two by water power were in operation. These were mere toys compared with later machinery, however, and produced only a small quantity of sugar. The tendency even at this early time was to replace many small mills with larger and more efficient ones, and tiny patches of cane with big plantations under centralized management. In 1836 only eight thousand pounds of sugar were exported; in 1850 the export amounted to three quarters of a million pounds. Sugar was also consumed locally and sold to ships.

The sugar industry, in common with other Hawaiian agriculture, was strongly affected by the rapid settlement of California following the discovery of gold in 1848. The rush of gold seekers into that region caused a critical food shortage. Prices were high and the Hawaiian producers, first in the field, reaped a rich harvest for a little while. But the high prices resulted in the dumping on the California market of produce from other countries. In 1851 the boom in Hawaii collapsed, and in the same year a severe drought occurred in the islands. The sugar planters were hard hit, and a general depression gripped the whole kingdom in 1851 and 1852. But this was a temporary setback, and in the long run the Hawaiian sugar industry was greatly benefited by the settlement of California and Oregon, which provided a convenient and expanding market. Chief drawbacks were the high tariff on sugar imported into the United States and the competition of low-cost sugars from Manila and China. To overcome these difficulties, efforts were made in 1848 and again in 1852 to get a reciprocity agreement with the United States which would permit the importing of Hawaiian goods free of duty; but these efforts did not succeed.

Improvements in field and mill equipment during this period, such as the invention of a deep plow by Samuel Burbank of the Koloa plantation and the introduction (1851) by David M. Weston of a centrifugal machine for separating sugar from molasses, resulted in the production of a better grade of sugar at a reduced cost.

Coffee shared with sugar the promise of being a main staple product of the islands. It has been mentioned that coffee trees were grown by Wilkinson in Manoa. These had been brought from Rio de Janeiro. Other plants were brought from Manila by Richard Charlton. Slips were set out in Kalihi and Niu Valleys near Honolulu. In 1828 or 1829 the growing of coffee was begun by missionaries in Kona, Hawaii, a district which ultimately became famous for its coffee. It was on Kauai, however, that the first large plantations were founded. A large area was planted at Hanalei in 1842, and another was started there a few years later. In 1847 there was a plantation at Hilo, Hawaii, and several small ones on Oahu. The first record of coffee exportation was 248 pounds in 1845. Drought, floods, and labor difficulties caused the production to vary greatly from year to year. In 1850 the amount exported was 208,428 pounds; in 1851, 27,190 pounds; in 1854, 91,090 pounds.

Attempts were made in this period to develop some other staple crops. Principal among these were silk and cotton.

Silk raising was an interesting and at first a promising experiment carried on for about ten years (1836–45) at Koloa and Hanalei, Kauai. Mulberry trees were planted, silkworm eggs were imported from China and America, and some good silk cocoons were produced. Several small shipments of raw silk were made; but droughts, violent winds, and insect pests caused heavy losses, and the enterprise was abandoned about 1845.

Experiments with raising and weaving cotton have a longer history. It was reported as early as 1825 that the natives were raising a cotton plant of excellent quality. The missionaries became interested in the possibility of starting a weaving industry, and in

1835 Miss Lydia Brown, sent out by the American missionary board, began teaching the art of spinning and weaving at Wailuku, Maui. The young native women finally became quite proficient in spinning and in working the loom, and after a year and a half a class was graduated "clothed in garments of their own manufacture." The governor of Hawaii lent his aid and in 1837 had a stone building put up at Kailua to be used as a cotton factory. Before the spring of 1839 about six hundred yards of cloth had been made at Wailuku and four hundred yards at Kailua. Fields of cotton were planted at several places, and for a few years it seemed that a profitable industry would be founded. But for various reasons the first interest slackened, and although there was a revival of cotton growing during the Civil War, when some good cotton was exported, the attempt was thereafter abandoned.

The main vegetable produce at this time was potatoes, which were sold in large quantities to the whale ships. Cultivation of the Irish potato began about 1840, especially in the Kula district of Maui. This region was very productive and a boom developed in 1849-50, when the needs of the California market were at their height. A story was often repeated about a man who, after having visited the mines of California, came back to Maui quite satisfied, saying, "California is yonder in Kula. There is the gold without the fatigue and sickness of the mining country." The wealth of "Nu Kalifonia" vanished, however, when the boom collapsed in 1851. Thereafter the people of the American West began raising their own potatoes, and the export market declined.

After the collapse of the potato boom, attention was turned to the expansion of wheat raising, particularly on the island of Maui. A flour mill was built in Honolulu in connection with D. M. Weston's machine shop (which developed into the Honolulu Iron Works). The mill was completed in May, 1854, and began turning out corn meal and wheat flour. Thereafter flour appeared on the list of exports from the islands for about a dozen years. The raising of wheat was extended to Kau on the Big Island, and at one time there were three flour mills in the kingdom, one in

Honolulu and two small ones on Maui. But the industry was not a permanent one.

The grazing industry had its start in the reign of Kamehameha III. The cattle and goats left in the islands by early voyagers had run wild and multiplied to such an extent that hides and goat skins were notable export products. The demand for beef led to the establishment of ranches. At the end of the reign, it was estimated that there were about forty thousand cattle in the group, including at least twelve thousand wild ones. From 1835 to 1840 about five thousand hides were exported annually. In 1840 a *kapu* was placed upon the killing of wild bullocks, but during the last decade of the reign an average of more than two thousand hides were exported each year, as well as some quantities of salted beef. The cattle industry is associated with the entrance of a picturesque group of foreigners, Spanish or Mexican cowboys—the Hawaiians called them *paniolos*—who not later than 1830 were to be seen at Waimea galloping after wild cattle and lassoing them in dashing style. The word *paniolo* (as meaning "cowboy") stuck in the Hawaiian language, but a writer of 1859 reported that "the imported vaqueros of Hawaii have disappeared before the march of time. . . . In their place has sprung up a class of Hawaiian mountaineers, equally as skillful horsemen as their foreign predecessors, but leading a vagabond sort of life."

A significant proof of the general interest in agriculture at the middle of the century was the organization of the Royal Hawaiian Agricultural Society, which included not only farmers, planters, and graziers but also businessmen and government officials, all of whom were eager to see the natural resources of the country wisely developed. The Society was active for several years and by its meetings, publications, exhibits, and experimental garden did much to promote the objects in which it was interested.

One of the problems to which it first gave attention was that of labor. During the reign of Kamehameha III the native population diminished by fifty per cent, and there were not enough laborers to supply fully the needs of the plantations and other enterprises that were being started. Under the auspices of the Agricultural Society, some three hundred Chinese laborers were brought into the country in 1851 and 1852 to serve under contracts for a term of five years. An act passed by the legislature on June 21, 1850, provided the legal basis for the contract labor system which existed in Hawaii throughout the latter half of the century.

In addition to uncertain markets and shortages of labor, early agricultural enterprise suffered from a scarcity of capital. Interest rates were high, and few firms were able to sustain themselves during the development period before profits began to come in. One means suggested to overcome this lack was the establishment of a bank, but no bank was started during the reign of Kamehameha III.

The growth of transportation and communication furnishes an interesting measure of a nation's civilization. For the people of Hawaii, travel by sea has always been of first importance. The ancient Hawaiians spent much of their time on the sea in their canoes. Foreigners and foreign ideas came to the islands in ships. Kamehameha the Great built up a fleet of foreign-style sailing vessels for use both as war vessels and troop transports. Some of these were later used for trading ventures, and the government continued in the shipping business until about 1846. Several of the chiefs also had sailing vessels which they used for trading. At the beginning of the reign of Kamehameha III, many small vessels owned by natives were in service among the islands.

In the early days, foreign ships often carried passengers and freight between the various islands of the group, but a law passed in 1846 limited inter-island service to vessels registered under the Hawaiian flag. By the end of 1851, 67 vessels, with an average tonnage of 60 tons, were so registered; most of these were in the coasting trade.

Shipbuilding had been carried on in the islands from the time the *Britannia* had been built under Kamehameha I, and many excellent vessels were turned out. In the early fifties, the custom began of having the larger ships built in American yards from specifications suited to the needs of the Hawaiian inter-island trade. One of the first of these was *Ka Moi* (or *Sovereign*), a large schooner built in 1853 at New London, Connecticut. Even in the fifties and sixties, however, travel between the islands was a slow, dangerous, and uncomfortable experience. Since the ships were small, even the cabins of first-class passengers were crowded and hot. Other passengers camped on deck among their heaps of baggage, dogs, pigs, chickens, and food for the voyage. Despite misery, seasickness, and frequent shipwrecks, there was a surprising amount of travel among the islands at this time, especially by the native Hawaiians.

Steam navigation came to the islands as a result of the settlement of California and the branching out of the United States shipping companies into the Pacific. In the summer of 1851 Captain William A. Howard of San Francisco obtained for his associates a seven-year franchise for inter-island steamer service, and in January of the following year returned with the steamer *Constitution.* This 600-ton propeller proved too large for the work, and after making one round trip between Honolulu and Lahaina returned to San Francisco.

Howard's franchise lapsed, and the privy council offered these rights to any company that would first put into inter-island service a steamer of the proper size. The winners in this contest were a group of San Francisco business men brought together by Richard H. Bowlin, a Honolulu attorney. In the fall of 1853, this company put into operation a small side-wheel steamer, the *S. B. Wheeler,* which began regular service toward the end of the year under the name of the *Akamai.* At the same time the operating group, the Hawaiian Steam Navigation Company, was granted a ten-year franchise on inter-island steam navigation and towage under the Hawaiian flag. Two other steamers were put on the run, but all three were either wrecked or withdrawn from service within a few years, and in 1856 the franchise was declared void. Not until 1860, when the *Kilauea,* a 414-ton screw steamer, began a long and varied career of inter-island service, did steam navigation on this run begin operating on something like a permanent basis.

Oceanic transportation of both cargoes and passengers from the earliest days of the kingdom was carried on in fur traders, sandalwood ships, and, after 1820, whaling vessels. In the era of the clipper ships, especially the fifties and sixties, many famous sailing vessels touched at Hawaii. The establishment of mercantile firms in the islands brought fairly frequent ocean service between Hawaii and the United States, Great Britain and her colonies, and Germany. In 1850 James Hunnewell, Henry A. Peirce, and Charles Brewer formed a partnership to carry on a freighting business between Boston and the important ports of the Pacific; in later years the business was conducted by Brewer and his sons, and the firm of C. Brewer & Company was the Honolulu agent for this line. The development of shipping to California and Oregon made it easier to travel to eastern United States by way of San Francisco and Panama than by the old route around Cape Horn, but for many years large quantities of merchandise still went around the Horn.

In the fifties, certain ships came to be regarded as packets between San Francisco and Honolulu, and in 1855 a line of clipper barks was established under the name of the Regular Dispatch Line, operating the *Frances Palmer* and the *Yankee*. Projects for scheduled steamer service between California and Hawaii were talked about as early as 1850, but although the *Polynesian* made a trial voyage in 1854, nothing was accomplished before the reign of Kamehameha V.

The needs of ocean-going vessels for safe harborage, wharves, and rigging docks were responsible for the growth of such ports as Honolulu, Lahaina, and Hilo. A shipyard was set up in Honolulu Harbor as early as 1827. This harbor, although safe, was hard to enter. Ships were towed in through the channel by small boats, or by gangs of natives pulling on the ship's hawser as they marched along the reef on the eastern border of the channel. This method lasted down to the middle of the century, although toward the end of that period oxen were sometimes used. After about 1850, the need for extensive improvements along the Honolulu waterfront became evident, and the government began a series of dredging and filling operations that would enable harbor facilities to keep up with the needs of ocean commerce.

Land travel of a comfortable sort was very slow to develop in the islands. It was easier for the old Hawaiians to go from one coastal settlement to another in canoes than to tackle the interior on foot. Still, there were a few trails on all the islands. The missionaries were the first foreigners to travel much by land, and their pedestrian journeys are graphically described in missionary annals. The introduction of horses early in the nineteenth century made riding horseback a common means of travel as well as a popular recreation. The Hawaiians became avid equestrians, and riding and racing became sports that vied in popularity with swimming and surfing. Use of the horse as a draft animal developed more slowly.

The employment of wagons and carriages which followed in due course required the building of roads. At first these were short and were confined to towns. The need for a road on Oahu through Nuuanu Valley and down the *Pali* to the Koolau district was early made clear. In 1837 work was done on the *Pali* trail to make it a safe footpath. By 1845, a "horse-road" was built and was soon in constant use by riders of horses and mules. In 1861 the road was first driven over in a one-horse wagon, as a stunt, but it was some time before there were many practicable carriage roads even on Oahu. An amusing foreshadowing of events is found in the remarks of a writer in the *Polynesian* in 1852, who said that the residents of Oahu would "never be satisfied till a tunnel is dug through the *pali,* suitable for the passage of carts and wagons."

Mail service in the earlier years of the kingdom was a slow and casual affair. Even in the thirties a letter might take two or three years to arrive by sailing ship from Europe or the United States, and the latest European news might reach Hawaii by way of China. Until 1846 the Hawaiian government assumed no responsibility for the mails. Ships carried mail free, and it was received and forwarded by merchants or other private persons. The Organic Act of 1846 provided for setting up a postal system, but more than four years elapsed before anything was done to carry out this measure. Meanwhile, the need for a stable postal service had been emphasized by the settlement of California, and the United States by 1849 had provided mail steamship lines between the Atlantic coast and Panama and between Panama and west-coast ports.

The Hawaiian mail service was finally put on an official basis at the end of 1850, when the treaty of that year with the United States provided for the exchange of mails. A royal decree at the same time established a post office in Honolulu and set up postal rates. Henry M. Whitney, who was named postmaster, began operating the system at once. In 1851 a revised law lowered the rates on letters and authorized the issuance of the first Hawaiian stamps, in denominations of two, five, and thirteen cents. These stamps, printed from type, were the earliest of the "numerals" long prized by collectors. The law provided for the selling of stamps for domestic use, but until 1859 this service was in actuality free. It was feared that charging for inter-island mail would discourage the frequent exchange of letters among the natives, but when in 1859 the two-cent rate was put in force, the system seemed to work very well and the sale of stamps brought in a good revenue. The Civil Code of 1858–1859 firmly established the service under a postmaster-general, and Hawaii had a mail system well suited to the needs of the kingdom.

Book 3

The Middle Period of Change
(1854–1874)

CHAPTER ELEVEN

The Last Two Kamehamehas

THE reigns of the royal brothers, Kamehameha IV (1854–1863) and Kamehameha V (1863–1872), comprise the middle period of the Hawaiian kingdom, in which there were changes and developments of great significance and interest. There was a marked swing away from American missionary influence toward a closer relationship with England, symbolized by the introduction of the Anglican church. In government, there was a swing away from American democratic political ideals as expressed in the Constitution of 1852 to a new constitution in which popular rights were subordinated to the power of the king. In foreign affairs, there was a continuous effort to stabilize and improve relations with other countries and to make secure the independence of Hawaii—in part at least for the purpose of counteracting the tendency toward political union with the United States. In the realm of business and industry, Hawaii shifted to a new, more solid economic foundation.

These developments will be described in this chapter and the two following. But first, something must be said about the kings themselves.

Kamehameha III of happy memory died on December 15, 1854. His nephew and heir, Prince Alexander Liholiho, was immediately proclaimed king under the title of Kamehameha IV. He was formally inaugurated on January 11 at Kawaiahao Church and took his oath to maintain the Constitution of 1852.

The new king, a month less than twenty-one years of age at the time of his inauguration, was one of the sons of Kinau and Governor Kekuanaoa and was a grandson of Kamehameha I. His high mental ability had been supplemented by a good education in English; he was very fluent in that language as well as in Hawaiian. His visit to England with his elder brother Lot had perhaps strengthened his aristocratic leanings, as it had aroused an admiration for the British form of government and the English church. His attitude toward Americans may have been prejudiced by the unkind treatment he and his brother had received while traveling in some parts of the United States and by his feelings about the institution of slavery in that country. At all events, although some of his most trusted advisers were Americans, he did not want his country to be swallowed by the American giant and he shaped his policy accordingly.

Kamehameha IV was tall, slender, and handsome. He was frequently troubled by attacks of asthma which caused him suffering and interfered with his work. At one time, to strengthen his body, he took some lessons in boxing. He was passionate and quick tempered. He had a youthful tendency to dissipation, and some observers thought he acted occasionally in an arbitrary manner. Yet he had, with real ability, served in the government for three years as a member of the privy council, and he took seriously his position as head of the state and leader of his people.

An early and joyous event of the new reign, offering hope that the dynasty would be perpetuated, was the marriage of the king, which occurred on June 19, 1856, at Kawaiahao Church. In this wedding the ritual of the Church of England was followed. The bride was Miss Emma Rooke, to whom Alexander had long been betrothed. The young queen was a woman of kind and lovable nature who brought to the palace a high degree of refinement and culture. She came of prominent families of both English and Hawaiian blood. She was the granddaughter of John Young, adviser to Kamehameha I, and was the great-granddaughter of Keliimaikai, younger brother of that king. In infancy she had been adopted by her uncle, Dr. T. C. B. Rooke, an English physician of Honolulu. She had been educated in the Chiefs' Children's School by the Cookes, and afterward by an English governess. Her sympathies were strongly in favor of England and English institutions and, as will be seen, the inception of the Episcopal Church in Hawaii was in part due to these strong sympathies.

The birth of a son to the royal pair on May 20, 1858, was greeted with joy by their subjects. The boy was christened Albert Edward Kauikeaouli Leiopapa A Kamehameha. With the approval of the privy council he was granted the title of "His Royal Highness the Prince of Hawaii" (*Ka Haku o Hawaii*). In 1859 he was officially designated and proclaimed as heir and successor of Kamehameha IV. The child was bright and attractive and was tenderly loved by the king and queen. Mr. Wyllie wrote of them, while they were visiting him on the island of Kauai: "We were all quite charmed with the private life of the royal pair, always addressing each other familiarly as 'Aleck' and 'Emma' and uniting in a just pride of and affection for their interesting and precocious son."

Four years this happy family lived together. Then the child was stricken with a most serious illness. In anguish the parents watched by the bedside, hoping for the early arrival of the English bishop who was expected to christen the royal child. But death would not wait, and another clergyman was called in to perform the sacrament of baptism. The little prince died four days later on the morning of August 27, 1862.

The death of his son was a severe blow to Kamehameha IV. The king's health, undermined by asthma, was further weakened by grief at the loss of his heir. He died on November 30, 1863, after a brief illness, at the age of twenty-nine years.

Following the death of the Prince of Hawaii, no formal arrangement had been made regarding the succession, but after the death of Kamehameha IV the cabinet, the privy council, and the *kuhina nui* acted promptly in proclaiming the late king's elder brother, Prince Lot, as king of the Hawaiian Islands under the title Kamehameha V.

The new king, like his brother, was well educated and had traveled widely. In 1860 he had journeyed to the Pacific Coast and visited California and British Columbia. Kamehameha V did not have the brilliant mental attainments of his predecessor, but he had a better grasp of practical matters. He had served as minister of the interior during the last six years of his brother's reign, and for more than a year had headed the department of finance. During his reign he entered personally into all the discussions of important issues; he selected ministers who shared his opinions, and gave them full support. Some of his policies aroused fierce opposition, but it is clear that he sincerely believed that his acts were directed to the good of the nation.

Kamehameha V, "the last great chief of the olden type," believed that the mantle of his grandfather, the conquering Kamehameha I, gave to the king the right to lead the people firmly into the proper paths. His ways of thinking and acting were despotic, but his was a benevolent despotism. He wished his subjects to be hardworking and thrifty, and felt that they must be protected from thoughtless waste and idle temptation. When it was proposed that the law against selling liquor to the natives be repealed, he said, "I will never sign the death warrant of my people," and the proposal was defeated.

Like his brother, Kamehameha V reigned for nine years. He was a bachelor. By the Constitution of 1864 which he promulgated, his sister, the Princess Victoria Kamamalu, was designated as his successor. She died in 1866, and at that time and later there were many suggestions that the king ought to marry in order to provide an heir to the throne. But the king declined to marry. And he likewise declined, even on his deathbed, to state in the constitutional manner who his successor should be. He died, rather unexpectedly, on his forty-third birthday, December 11, 1872. On the next day he lay in state, while in the shadow of somber *kahilis* (royal standards) his ministers and his subjects marched past to give a farewell glance at the last monarch of the line of Kamehameha.

The policies of these royal brothers during their reigns were quite similar. When Kamehameha IV came to the throne, the problems demanding first attention were those arising from the foreign relations of the country and, foremost of all, from relations with the United States. The danger of annexation had been barely averted in the closing days of the reign of Kamehameha III. Some substitute policy still had to be found to prevent annexation. Many sugar planters who were Americans by birth felt that if Hawaii were annexed to the United States the industry would be more prosperous, since heavy import duties into the markets of California and Oregon would not then have to be paid. The government sought another way to meet the problem—a reciprocity treaty which would permit American and Hawaiian products to be exchanged free of duty.

The idea was not new; some attempts of that sort had been made, unsuccessfully, a few years before. But now it was decided to send the best available representative to Washington to make a new and strong effort to secure such a treaty. This mission was entrusted to Judge William L. Lee, to whom was also committed another important diplomatic mission—to see if it was possible to get the great powers, the United States, Great Britain, France, and Russia, to unite in a treaty guaranteeing the independence of the Hawaiian kingdom. Hence Lee was named envoy extraordinary and minister plenipotentiary to all those governments.

David L. Gregg, the American commissioner to Hawaii, strongly supported the idea of a reciprocity treaty. In Washington, President Franklin Pierce and Secretary of State William L. Marcy were likewise favorably inclined, and a treaty was drawn up and signed by Marcy and Lee on July 20, 1855. The treaty was enthusiastically approved in Hawaii, but it was never ratified by the United States Senate, owing mainly to the opposition of the sugar planters of Louisiana. Some relief was given to Hawaiian sugar producers when the United States tariff on sugar was lowered by the act of March 3, 1857, from 30 to 24 per cent. Efforts to get a reciprocity treaty were renewed a few years later.

Working on the other part of his mission, Lee conferred with the representatives of the great powers in Washington and learned that it would be quite impossible to get those powers to agree on a treaty guaranteeing Hawaiian independence. He was assured, however, that all of them favored strongly the maintenance of Hawaii as an independent nation. The veteran minister of foreign relations, R. C. Wyllie, clung tenaciously to the hope of getting a joint guarantee of Hawaiian independence. In 1861 he persuaded Sir John Bowring, one-time British governor of Hong Kong, to see if something could not be accomplished in Europe. Bowring tried hard but without any success. It was an impracticable project, and after Wyllie's death in 1865 the effort to gain such a treaty of guarantee was abandoned.

An issue in foreign relations that Kamehameha IV inherited from his predecessor was the attempt to obtain a new treaty with France similar to those obtained from Great Britain and the United States. Negotiations were carried on for several years, with Allen and Wyllie representing the kingdom of Hawaii and Commissioner Emile Perrin representing France. The most troublesome clauses were those in which the French insisted on a reduction in import duties on French liquors, and on the use of the French language on a parity with English. A treaty embodying a compromise was signed by the plenipotentiaries on October 29, 1857. Article 10 provided that the importation and sale of French wines should not be prohibited in Hawaii, the duty on common wines should not be more than 5 per cent, the duty on wines of higher quality might be 15 per cent, and the duty on French brandy should not be more than three dollars a gallon. The treaty was ratified by the French emperor on March 20, 1858, and after some discussion, by Kamehameha IV on September 8, 1858. The French treaty as finally ratified included a provision that after the lapse of ten years certain articles, including the objectionable tariff article, might be terminated by either country through an official declaration giving twelve months' notice to the other. Accordingly, on April 15, 1873, those articles came to an end as a result of the appropriate action by the Hawaiian government.

Overtures toward diplomatic relations with the Japanese Em-

THE LAST TWO KAMEHAMEHAS

pire were made in 1860. Japanese sailors rescued from drifting derelicts had arrived at the islands from time to time, and in the 1840's three Japanese became naturalized Hawaiian citizens. The opening of Japan by Commodore Perry in 1854 was noted with interest in Hawaii, and in March, 1860, Honolulu was visited for a fortnight by the first Japanese embassy sent to the United States. This group was making a passage across the Pacific in the U.S.S. *Powhatan,* flagship of Commodore Josiah Tatnall. While the ambassadors were guests of the Hawaiian government, Minister Wyllie addressed a letter to them asking that a treaty be nego-tiated similar to that between Japan and the United States. Wyllie learned, however, that the Japanese were not willing to enter into treaty relations with any more countries, and he could not even obtain permission to appoint Hawaiian consuls in the open ports of Japan. Nevertheless, efforts were continued and in 1871 a treaty was concluded between the two countries.

Meanwhile, political developments within the kingdom pointed to a radical change in the constitution. Though Kamehameha IV at the time of his inauguration readily promised to maintain the liberal Constitution of 1852, he and his advisers soon became greatly dissatisfied with some features of it which seemed to them to be too democratic, limiting too much the powers of the king. A few changes were made in the constitution during this reign, but the popularly elected House of Representatives refused to permit the radical changes desired by the king and his ministers. Kame-hameha IV is reported to have expressed regret at having taken the oath to maintain the Constitution of 1852. The attitude of his successor Kamehameha V was revealed when, upon his accession, he refused to take this oath.

The new king felt that the Constitution of 1852 was far in ad-vance of the needs of the people at their current stage of develop-ment. He believed that the privilege of voting should be granted only to those subjects who had some education and owned prop-erty, and who thereby showed that they were well informed and industrious. He feared that universal suffrage would end in the establishment of a republic in Hawaii, and that such a republic would inevitably be annexed by the United States. "Hawaii has scarcely emerged from a feudal state," he said, "and already the American influence pushes us toward a republic." He therefore felt that the first major act of his administration should be directed toward revising the Constitution of 1852 or replacing it with a new one.

During the period when the constitution was being changed, the cabinet consisted of the following men: Wyllie for foreign affairs; Charles de Varigny, a Frenchman, for finance; C. G. Hopkins for the interior; and C. C. Harris, an American lawyer who had long resided in the kingdom, as attorney general. Elisha H. Allen, an American, was chancellor and chief justice, and his associates on the supreme court were G. M. Robertson (British) and Robert G. Davis (American-Hawaiian). All these officials had taken the oath to support the constitution.

Giving some hint of his intentions, the king refrained from calling the legislature to meet at the proper time in April, 1864. Instead, on May 5 he issued a proclamation calling a convention in which delegates elected by the people would meet with the nobles and the king on July 7 "for the purpose of consulting on the revision of the Constitution." This was not the constitutional method of amending the existing document and the announcement aroused violent protests in the newspapers, in public meetings, and in private discussions. In May and June the king made a speaking tour around the islands, explaining his purpose. He was politely received, but the speeches of Wyllie, who went with him and bitterly attacked the Constitution of 1852, did more harm than good. When the returns from the election of June 13 came in, it was clear that a majority of the delegates were against the king's plan.

The convention met on July 7, The king presided except when illness kept him away. From the first, debate was long and acrimonious, and not until July 19 was the proposed draft of the new constitution read. This draft had been prepared by the cabinet. As the discussion went on, article by article, it became clear that the opposition was concentrated on only a few provisions. Article 62, which came up on August 8, was the rock on which the convention was wrecked. This article defined the qualifications of voters, and included a literacy test and a property qualification. Neither side would yield. On August 13 the king, who believed that universal suffrage would destroy the monarchy, dissolved the convention. He said, in part: "As we do not agree it is useless to prolong the session, and ... on the part of the Sovereignty of the Hawaiian Islands I make known today that the Constitution of 1852 is abrogated. I will give you a Constitution."

During the following week the nation was without a written constitution. The new one promised by Kamehameha V was signed by him on August 20, 1864, and on the same day he took the oath to maintain it.

The Constitution of 1864, as might be expected, strengthened the hand of the king and freed him from the control of the privy council and the *kuhina nui*, an office which was abolished. The cabinet was given more responsibility for the policies and conduct of the government, but was subject to the king's control. The qualifications for voting limited the privilege to male subjects of the kingdom who (if born since 1840) must be able to read and write, and who must be possessed of real estate valued at $150, or of leasehold property renting at $25 a year, or of an income not less than $75 a year.

In spite of the high-handed way in which the new constitution was put through, it remained in force for twenty-three years—longer than any other Hawaiian constitution before annexation. It was now possible for the king to make the influence of the crown pervade every function of government. Angrily it was pointed out by the opposition that if the king could give and take away the fundamental law of the land at his own pleasure, no safeguard was left for the rights of the people. For years the argument went on between the faction which favored the new constitution and a strong throne and the one which favored more liberal government and demanded the restoration of the Constitution of 1852. The constitutional issue was to be given prominence in the manifestoes of the two men who sought to succeed Kamehameha V at his death; but while he lived no efforts to change the Constitution in any important respect met with success, and actually only one minor amendment was made during his reign.

The outbreak of the Civil War in the United States caused a flurry in foreign relations. The Hawaiian government had worked out a policy of neutrality during the Crimean War in 1853. Minister Wyllie believed that belligerent rights should be accorded to the Confederacy, but the king did not wish to take a step that might displease the government at Washington. News that Great Britain and France had proclaimed their neutrality in the American war strengthened the arguments of Wyllie, and on August 26, 1861, the king signed a proclamation asserting Hawaii's neutrality in the event of armed conflict in the Pacific. Circumstances at the moment made this declaration acceptable to the United States.

The terrific strain which the Civil War put upon the people of the United States made them very sensitive to any appearance of anti-American sentiment in foreign countries. For this reason, the British leanings of the king of Hawaii, the introduction of the Anglican church into the island kingdom by Kamehameha IV, and the abrogation of the liberal Constitution of 1852 by Kamehameha V caused a distinct coolness in relations between the United States and Hawaii. Some small but irritating causes of controversy arose during the war years.

Both the government in Washington and the one in Honolulu, however, felt the importance of keeping relations on as cordial a basis as possible. On its part, the United States government made a friendly gesture when in 1863 the status of its representative in Hawaii was raised to that of minister resident. This was the first time any foreign power had been represented in Honolulu by an officer of such diplomatic rank. The action was recognized as a compliment to the Hawaiian kingdom and was greatly appreciated.

The idea of a reciprocity treaty came forward again at this time. The Civil War had brought great prosperity to the sugar industry of the islands, but toward the close of the war a corresponding drop in prices was seen to be imminent. Toward the end of 1863 the American minister resident in Honolulu, James McBride, submitted to his government various reasons why a treaty of reciprocity should be made with the island kingdom. The question was briefly raised in the United States Senate. In the spring of 1864 the Hawaiian government, alive to the value of such a treaty, sent Chief Justice Elisha H. Allen to Washington on a mission of which the main purpose was to negotiate a treaty of reciprocity. Allen discussed the subject with the president, the secretary of state, and other officials, all of whom were friendly; but at the end Secretary of State Seward was obliged to inform him that because of the war the negotiation of a treaty at that time was "inconvenient and inexpedient." Though Allen failed to accomplish the main end of his mission, he did succeed in creating a better feeling in Washington toward the island government.

The next American minister to Hawaii, General E. M. McCook, became greatly interested in strengthening the American position in the islands by means of a reciprocity treaty. While in Washington in the early part of 1867 he obtained from Secretary Seward authority to negotiate such a treaty. At this very time the Hawaiian sugar industry was in the midst of an acute post-war depression and the government, at the urgent request of the planters, appointed Minister of Finance C. C. Harris to proceed to Washington in a new attempt to get the desired treaty. McCook and Harris met in San Francisco and drafted a treaty which was signed by them on May 21, 1867.

The news of this event which reached Hawaii on McCook's return was greeted with joy, and the treaty was ratified by the king's government without unnecessary delay. In Washington, on the other hand, although the president quickly submitted the document to the Senate, many obstacles speedily arose. Congress was busy with problems of southern reconstruction and was carrying on a bitter struggle with President Johnson. Opponents of the treaty argued that the United States would get little benefit and would lose a source of income needed to meet the enormous debt incurred during the war. They said that the measure would profit only the sugar growers of Hawaii and the importers of the Pacific-coast states. This time the southern sugar planters were not able to lead the opposition, for their industry had been ruined by the war and few of the southern congressmen were truly representative of their sections. A strong fight for the treaty was led by Senator Charles Sumner of Massachusetts, and both Harris and Allen were energetic in promoting the scheme. But apathy and delay caused postponement, and when ratification finally came to a vote on June 1, 1870, the measure was defeated.

The successive hopes and fears aroused on the reciprocity issue caused great unrest in Hawaii. The belief was widely held that revolution might overturn the throne or that annexation of Hawaii might take place as a measure of American defense. The king himself seemed to fear the intimidation that might result through American interference. During June and July, 1867, the American naval vessel *Lackawanna* was visiting the islands, under the command of Captain William Reynolds. This officer had formerly been a resident of the islands, and appeared to side with a party opposing the government. His manner created fears that some threatening gesture would be made that would influence the negotiations going on in Washington; and the king refused to act on the treaty until the *Lackawanna* had withdrawn from the harbor.

CHAPTER TWELVE

A New Economic Foundation

MOMENTOUS economic changes began to take place in the middle period of the kingdom. The most marked were first, the decline of whaling, and second, the establishment of the sugar industry as the foundation of Hawaii's economic structure. Early in 1862 the minister of finance wrote, "We are in a sort of transition state,—turning from nearly a total dependence on the whale fisheries of the northern seas to the internal resources of the country." The internal resources were almost exclusively agricultural, and the most promising agricultural product was sugar.

The decline of whaling as a factor in Hawaiian life is graphically shown by figures on arrivals of whaling ships in the ports of the islands. During the first three years of the reign of Kamehameha IV (1855–1857) the annual average number of such arrivals was 400; during the last three years of the reign of Kamehameha V (1870–1872) the annual average was 71; in the last two years it was 47. The North Pacific whale fishery had reached its turning point in the year 1852; thereafter an ebb tide set in. But the fact that whaling was dying out was not generally recognized until a few years after the opening of the reign of Kamehameha IV. By 1860 the trend was too obvious to be overlooked.

During this period a vigorous attempt was made to develop whaling as a local Hawaiian industry. As far back as 1831 a ship had been sent out on a whaling voyage by one of the foreign residents of Honolulu, but the business did not really take hold until about 1854. In that year six whaleships claimed Honolulu as home port. The island fleet grew until 1858—the banner year—when it included nineteen vessels. One writer says that "Honolulu was by this time imbued with the 'oil fever' and realized the advantages of her position and facilities to prosecute the industry." The results of that year's effort were not very encouraging, but did not destroy the local interest in whaling. From 1856 to 1870 a dozen whaleships, on the average, were sent out from Honolulu each year. For the next decade the average was four, and the business came to an end as a local industry in 1880.

Reasons commonly assigned for the decline of whaling were the increasing scarcity and shyness of whales; the rising cost of outfitting ships; the necessity of longer voyages, involving heavy expenses for refitting at points far distant from the home ports; and the deadly competition arising from the introduction of illuminating gas and of illuminating oils and lubricants refined from coal and petroleum. The competition of petroleum became more important during the huge development of that industry following the drilling of the first successful oil well in Pennsylvania in 1859. Added to these natural causes of decline were others that were more or less accidental. The Civil War in the United States brought the withdrawal of a large part of the whaling fleet from the Pacific. Of the ships that continued in operation, many were destroyed by a Confederate cruiser, the *Shenandoah*. After the war, the business revived to some extent, but in 1871 more than thirty whaleships were locked in north of Bering Strait, and destroyed in the ice packs. There was a similar but less serious disaster in 1876. After that, whaling ceased to be of much economic importance to Hawaii.

By the time the whaleships finally disappeared from its ports, Hawaii's economy was rather solidly based on agriculture. Conversion from the whaling era to the planting era—in which Hawaiian economy still lies in the main—was not easy and was not accomplished without considerable stress and strain, but it was gradually effected in the middle period. Among the products of the soil which were the major source of Hawaii's income from this time onward, sugar was by far the most valuable. The history of Hawaii cannot be told without putting the spotlight on sugar.

Again figures tell the story. In the first three years of the reign of Kamehameha IV (1855–1857) the amount of sugar exported from the Hawaiian Islands averaged 255 tons a year; in the last three years of the reign of Kamehameha V (1870–1872) the average was 9,586 tons a year—nearly thirty-eight times as much. These figures are small by present-day standards, but so also were the Hawaiian community of that day and its financial resources. The significant point is that the upward trend which started in this period went right on through succeeding decades. Despite numerous difficulties and a few times of crisis, the Hawaiian sugar industry, like Old Man River, kept rolling along.

Most writers on the subject mention that in 1857 the number of sugar plantations was reduced to five, and state this fact in a way to imply that there had been a serious falling off in production. This, however, was not true. There had been a sharp drop in production in 1855, but in 1856 production was better, and in 1857 was not very far from the highest point that had been reached up to that time. Furthermore, the price of sugar was good in the years 1856–1858, and hence sugar planters were well off, although mercantile business was in a depressed state.

The Civil War in the United States raised prices still higher and gave a great stimulus to sugar planting in Hawaii. Many new plantations were established, and in 1865 the export was ten times what it had been in 1860. The expansion in these years was too rapid, and based too much on borrowed capital. After the war prices dropped. Business failures in San Francisco and Honolulu forced a number of plantations into bankruptcy in 1867 and there were heavy losses. One effect was to bring the capitalization of these plantations more nearly into line with their actual value. The year of misfortune, 1867, was marked by a drop in production. The decline was more than recovered in 1868, and in 1871 for the first time the sugar export exceeded ten thousand tons.

The advance of the sugar industry was due in part to improvements in mills, machinery, and production methods. The first irrigation ditch for sugar cane was dug in 1856 on Kauai, and another was dug about ten years later on Maui; these demonstrated the feasibility and value of such projects. The vacuum pan (in which sugar syrup could be boiled down without scorching) was introduced in the early 1860's. Steam power came into extensive use in sugar mills. The sugar produced was of high quality, much of it being of what were known in the American market as "grocery grades," so good that they went directly into consumption without having to be refined.

This was the period in which the sugar-refining industry was being developed in San Francisco. One of the leaders there was Claus Spreckels, who at a later time became prominently associated with the sugar industry in Hawaii. There was some competition between the better grades of Hawaiian sugar and that put out by the San Francisco refineries. An attempt was made in the later 1860's to reconcile these interests, and for two years an arrangement was in effect under which the Hawaiian planters turned about half or two thirds of their crop into "refinery grades" which were sold to one of the San Francisco refineries. It was supposed that the lower price received would be more than offset by the lower cost of production. But the planters were not quite satisfied with the results, and the arrangement was not continued.

With the growth of the sugar industry, the plantations came to be closely tied up with the larger business houses in Honolulu. The plantation agency system, under which these business houses furnished much of the capital and served as agents for plantations, became a prominent feature of the Hawaiian economy. The system was not new, but it expanded greatly during this transition period. The earliest such agent was the firm of Ladd & Company, which in 1835 had established the Koloa Plantation on Kauai and began handling its business; the agency for that plantation afterwards passed to H. Hackfeld & Company. Four of Hawaii's later "Big Five," or their predecessors, became agents for sugar plantations in this middle period. The business house having the most extensive interest of this kind was Walker, Allen & Company, agent for about a dozen plantations, among them some of the largest in the kingdom. The failure of this company in 1867 carried with it all these plantations. Nearly all were reorganized and their agencies passed to other companies.

The growing of sugar did not absorb all the energy of the agriculturists of Hawaii. Some attention was given to other products, of which one was rice. Early attempts at rice culture were not encouraging, and the success finally achieved was a tribute to the persistent efforts of H. Holstein, manager of the garden of the Royal Hawaiian Agricultural Society, who began experimenting with rice in 1858. For two years, using China rice, he met only failure, but in 1860, with seed rice from South Carolina, he got such promising results that in 1861 a craze for rice planting swept over Oahu and parts of the other islands. In some places, taro already growing was pulled up to make room for rice. After the first excitement came a recession, followed in turn by a substantial advance. In the last four years of the reign of Kamehameha V the exports of rice and unmilled "paddy" averaged more than a million and a quarter pounds each year. Probably as much more was consumed locally. Among products of the soil, rice became second in importance to sugar in the Hawaiian economy and held that position for many years.

Coffee raising, which had been so very promising at the close of the reign of Kamehameha III, was seriously set back by an insect pest. The blighting effect was so great that the large coffee estates in the Hanalei district of Kauai were converted into sugar plantations. The coffee industry came to be more and more localized on the island of Hawaii, especially in the Kona district, and fell into the pattern of small patches farmed by individual owners or lessees. The production and consequently the amount exported continued to vary greatly from year to year.

The livestock industry, in cash value of its product, held a high place and did very well during the third quarter of the century. It was especially important on Hawaii and Oahu and was for many years the dominant agricultural enterprise on those islands. The grazing interests claimed in 1856 that their contribution to national wealth was greater than that of the sugar planters. This was probably true for that year, although the spectacular march of the sugar industry in the 1860's placed it well ahead of livestock. Production did expand greatly in hides, tallow, beef, and goatskins. Wool growing became important in the fifties and sixties. The royal family had valuable herds of cattle and flocks of sheep on Oahu and on Molokai (where the king established a sheep station in 1859). Prince Lot was the first president of a Graziers' Association organized on Oahu in 1856 by those engaged in the livestock industry.

Another natural product which figured largely in the foreign commerce of Hawaii in this period was *pulu*, a silky or woolly fiber which grows at the base of the fronds of the tree fern and which was discovered to be useful as a filling for mattresses and pillows. After the settlement of California, a market for *pulu* was found in San Francisco, and this article was exported for about thirty years (1851–1884). The trade was at its height in the sixties and seventies, and was handled by a small group of exporters. It recalled the bad old days of the sandalwood trade, since it made severe demands on the health of the poor people who gathered the stuff in the damp fern forests.

Sugar, rice, coffee, *pulu*, and products of the livestock industry —these were the commodities that made up the bulk of Hawaii's domestic exports in the reigns of the last two Kamehamehas. The value of domestic exports increased in twenty years from less than $275,000 to more than $1,500,000. Many times it was pointed out that the best and surest base for national prosperity was the natural resources of the country, which had produced these exports. Hawaii was therefore passing from the erratic economy of the whaling era toward a sounder economic foundation that was rooted in the soil.

All these important changes in Hawaiian economy increased the need for better means of transportation among the islands and between the islands and foreign markets.

As has been told, most of the early attempts by foreign private interests to provide inter-island steamer service ended in failure in 1856. Partly in response to government initiative, the Honolulu firm of C. A. Williams & Company undertook to provide a steamer and run it in inter-island service. Williams and his associates received from the legislature various privileges and a charter of incorporation as the Hawaiian Steam Navigation Company. The 414-ton screw steamer *Kilauea* was built to their order in Boston in 1859 and arrived at Honolulu on June 28, 1860. After several months' trial, the steamer was sold to a new company with the same name, in which the government held a substantial amount of stock.

For seventeen years, with numerous interruptions—one of two years' duration—the *Kilauea* shuttled back and forth between Honolulu and other ports in the kingdom. For three years (1862–1865) a little steam schooner, *Annie Laurie,* supplemented and at times substituted for the *Kilauea.* The latter was rather too large for the business then available, what with competition by sailing schooners and heavy costs for alterations, frequent repairs, accidents, and running expenses. In 1865 the government sold its interest in the ship, but two years later had to provide a subsidy to keep the steamer going, and in 1869 and 1870 had to buy and repair the vessel at heavy expense in order to insure a continuation of her service. During the last half dozen years before 1877, the *Kilauea* was owned and run by the government, and toward the end began to show a profit.

In the reign of Kamehameha V steamer transportation between Honolulu and San Francisco and between Honolulu and Australasia became a reality. This came about mainly as a consequence of American interest in the Pacific and the Far East, but the desire of the British colonies in the South Pacific for faster mail and passenger service to England contributed something to the final result.

There had been for many years desultory talk and abortive plans for transpacific steamship lines. The close of the Civil War enabled the United States to give greater attention to the subject, to which the building of a railroad across the country to the Pacific coast gave impetus. In February, 1865, Congress passed an act authorizing the payment of half a million dollars annually for a monthly mail steamship service between the United States and China, with calls at the Hawaiian Islands and Japan. The contract for this service was awarded to the Pacific Mail Steamship Company. Before the line was fully in operation the company was freed from the requirement of calling at the Hawaiian Islands, because it was shorter and therefore cheaper to follow the northern great-circle route across the Pacific and because harbor facilities at Honolulu were inadequate.

At about the same time (on March 2, 1867) Congress authorized a monthly mail steamship service between San Francisco and Honolulu for a maximum of $75,000 a year. A contract was awarded to the California, Oregon, & Mexico Steamship Company and this service, which proved to be permanent although not always given by the same company, was inaugurated with the steamer *Idaho,* which arrived at Honolulu on September 17, 1867. Previously, in the early part of 1866, the steamer *Ajax* of the California Steam Navigation Company had made two round trips between San Francisco and Honolulu.

Completion of the Pacific railroad across the United States in 1869 aroused interest, both in that country and in the British colonies of Australia and New Zealand, in founding a steamship line between those colonies and San Francisco, touching at Honolulu. The S.S. *Wonga Wonga,* pioneer vessel of the new line of steamers from Sydney, arrived in Honolulu on April 19, 1870, connecting with the *Idaho.* After several such trials, the Pacific Mail Steamship Company in the fall of 1875 instituted a monthly mail-steamer service, which was permanent under that and other companies, connecting the ports of San Francisco, Honolulu, and the British colonies.

With steamers bringing travelers to the islands in greater numbers, the people of Honolulu became aware of the need for more and better hotel accommodations for tourists. Because private interests seemed unequal to the task of providing a suitable hostelry, the government assumed the burden and in 1871 and 1872 the Hawaiian (later called Royal Hawaiian) Hotel was built in Honolulu at the corner of Richards and Hotel Streets, at a cost of more than $110,000. The hotel was an ornament to the city and added greatly to the comfort and pleasure of a visit to the Hawaiian capital. But it nearly doubled the national debt and is said to have been the main cause of the temporary political downfall of the two cabinet ministers, Dr. John Mott Smith and C. C. Harris, who were the chief promoters of the project.

The Hawaiian Hotel was not the only item of public works undertaken in these years. For the accommodation of steamers, new wharves and warehouses were built and dredging operations were carried on to improve the harbor. The lighthouse at the entrance to that harbor was permanently lighted on August 2, 1869. Planning was carried on toward a new royal palace, and preliminary work was undertaken. Construction was begun in 1872 on a large and ornate government legislative and office building (*Aliiolani Hale*), which was completed in 1874. And there were numerous lesser projects.

Many of these public works were admitted by all to be necessary, but some of them, especially the government building and the hotel, were characterized by critics of the government as luxuries which the little kingdom could ill afford at such a time. As it happened, the rapid expansion of the sugar industry slowed down after 1869, and the years 1872 and 1873 were a time of depression, during which there was much gloomy talk about what would happen if some relief, preferably a reciprocity treaty with the United States, were not obtained for the country's principal industry.

CHAPTER THIRTEEN

The Changing Community, 1854–1872

KAMEHAMEHA IV and Kamehameha V, like earlier kings of that dynasty, were vitally interested in the conditions and prospects of their native subjects and sought to find some way of saving the Hawaiian race from the extinction with which it seemed to be threatened. Closely related was the problem of a labor supply for the expanding industries of the country. These were important topics to which public attention was directed during these reigns. At the same time, changes in community life came in religion and education, recreation and entertainment.

The native population dropped from seventy to fifty-seven thousand between 1853 and 1866, and by 1872 it fell to less than fifty thousand. In July, 1863, Wyllie wrote, "Unless we get more population, we are a doomed nation." The possibility that the native race of the islands could be given a fresh start by the importation of workers from other Polynesian stocks was seriously considered. Kamehameha IV, addressing the legislature in 1855, said, after commenting on the apparent failure of bringing in a number of coolies from China: "It becomes a question of some moment whether a class of persons more nearly assimilated with the Hawaiian race could not be induced to settle on our shores. . . . Such immigrants, besides supplying the present demand for labor, would pave the way for a future population of native-born Hawaiians, between whom, and those of aboriginal parents, no distinguishable differences would exist." No funds were then available for the experiment which he proposed. In 1859, ten South Sea islanders were brought in to work on the Koloa Plantation. The idea of strengthening the Hawaiian stock by immigration of others of Polynesian blood continued to have strong advocates and it was tried from time to time, without much success.

The rescue of the native population from extinction was likewise attempted through the establishment of medical services for the Hawaiian people. The birth rate was low and the death rate was high. The deaths of thousands of Hawaiians were caused by epidemics such as measles in 1848 and smallpox in 1853 (when 2,485 deaths were reported from 6,405 smallpox cases). Kamehameha IV, in his first message to the legislature in 1855, said: "Our first and great duty is that of self-preservation. Our acts are in vain unless we can stay the wasting hand that is destroying our people. . . . I would commend to your special consideration the subject of establishing hospitals."

Some hospitalization for foreigners was available in Honolulu at this time, but none existed for the native population, among whom the need was greatest. Government funds were for some time unavailable for the purpose, but in 1859 the legislature passed a law permitting the formation of an association for the establishment in Honolulu of a hospital for sick and destitute Hawaiians. When the corporation had acquired funds to the amount of $5,000, the minister of the interior might convey to it government lands of an equal value. The law permitted the establishment of hospitals on Maui, Hawaii, and Kauai under similar conditions. The king signed this law on April 20, 1859, and then he went out personally to solicit funds. He obtained pledges to the amount of $14,000, and an organization was incorporated under the name of Queen's Hospital.

By the end of 1860 a two-story stone building had been raised and occupied at the present site in Honolulu. Funds for maintenance came mainly through government appropriations. The hospital, although its facilities were available for foreigners and for a few paying patients, was run primarily for the benefit of poor Hawaiians. At first somewhat hesitant, the natives soon came to use and appreciate its services. Dr. William Hillebrand, who was head physician, in 1863 reported of the Hawaiian patients: "Their faith in the old *kahunas* has not been demolished yet, but faith in the foreign *kahunas* seems to have sensibly increased. . . . I have not seen a native yet who, once having been an inmate of the Hospital, was not anxious to avail himself of its benefits again." Queen's Hospital will stand as the finest monument to the memory of Kamehameha IV and Queen Emma.

Leprosy was a disease that required drastic handling. This affliction, it is said, was brought into Hawaii in the reign of Kamehameha III, presumably from China (the native name for leprosy was *mai pake*—the Chinese disease). Unchecked, it had spread over the islands. Kamehameha V warned of the danger when he said to the legislature in 1864: "The increase of leprosy has caused me much anxiety, and is such as to make decisive steps imperative upon us." A law was then passed which set up a receiving station at Kalihi, near Honolulu, and the small, isolated peninsula of Kalaupapa on the north side of Molokai was chosen as the site for a leper settlement for cases considered incurable. By the end of this reign, about eight hundred lepers had been segregated from the rest of the population and removed to the Molokai settlement. Nearly all these cases were native Hawaiians.

The decline in the native population was an important element in the labor problem, which was becoming acute by the time Kamehameha V mounted the throne, owing to the increased demand for labor in the expanding sugar industry. Dissatisfaction with Chinese coolie workers led to discussion of other sources of supply. Steps were taken at once to collect information to guide the government in its decision, and in April, 1864, a Planters' Society was organized, mainly to work out answers to the labor question. Wyllie, as owner of the large Princeville Plantation on Kauai, was one of the leading spirits. The government's interest resulted on December 30, 1864, in the creation of a Bureau of Immigration to superintend the importation of foreign laborers and to promote and encourage the introduction of free immigrants from abroad.

The Bureau appointed Dr. William Hillebrand to proceed to China and send back enough Chinese laborers to meet immediate needs, and to investigate sources of labor supply for the future, such as India and Malaya. Before the end of 1865, 522 Chinese (including 52 women) had been sent by Hillebrand to Honolulu. His report made it clear that China was the most available source of labor, and during the remainder of this reign a sufficient number of Chinese came in to fulfill the most urgent needs of the planters. But there was much objection in Hawaii to the extensive introduction of Chinese laborers.

The Bureau as well as private groups made further attempts to introduce other Pacific Islanders, but only a few were brought in.

Through the negotiations of Eugene M. Van Reed, consul general for Hawaii in Japan, 148 Japanese laborers came to the islands in 1868. It took some time for these workers to become acclimated, and various misunderstandings arose in interpreting contract agreements. When their three-year contract expired in 1871, thirteen of the Japanese chose to return to their native land; the remainder obtained passports permitting them to remain in Hawaii. The treaty between Hawaii and Japan which was signed in 1871 included provisions permitting Japanese laborers to go to Hawaii, but no more importations of such laborers were made for many years.

During the reign of Kamehameha V, about two thousand laborers, men, women, and children, were brought into the islands. Of these about 10 per cent were South Sea islanders, and 85 per cent were Chinese. The problem of labor supply was to become more pressing as time went on.

Laborers brought into the kingdom worked under contracts authorized by the "Act for the Government of Masters and Servants" which had been passed in 1850. Under the provisions of this law a laborer who refused to serve according to the terms of his contract could be arrested, brought into court, and imprisoned at hard labor until he consented to serve; if he absented himself from his work without leave he could be compelled to serve double the time of his absence. Some other parts of the law were designed to protect the interests of the laborer.

Opposition to this law gradually arose because it was felt that the system was in theory akin to serfdom and slavery, because of various abuses of the law which in practice favored the employer, and because many persons in Great Britain and America frowned upon the spread of the "coolie trade," as they called it.

This criticism came to a head in 1869. At this time the reciprocity treaty was pending in the United States Senate, and if ratified would cause an expansion of the sugar industry and a need for a large force of laborers. In October, a meeting attended mainly by the planter contingent, after an energetic debate, adopted resolutions that more laborers were needed; that Chinese laborers had, on the whole, been satisfactory and that more should be brought in; and that the contract labor system had been necessary and advantageous. Meetings of working men, business and professional men, and government officials were immediately held to discuss these resolutions. These "citizens' meetings" adopted resolutions opposing further introduction of Chinese coolies and calling for repeal of the contract labor law, especially the penal portion of it. Similar resolutions were passed by meetings of native Hawaiians. The leading Chinese merchants of Honolulu expressed their opposition to the indiscriminate importation of Chinese coolies.

The campaign against the obnoxious features of the labor system was carried into the legislative session of 1870, when a vigorous effort was made to repeal the Masters and Servants Law. It failed, and an attempt, equally unsuccessful, was then made to amend the law. The persistent attacks on the system bore fruit in the 1872 session, when three acts were passed which ameliorated some of the harsh features of the law, although the penal sections were not removed. Charles Nordhoff, who visited all the islands in 1873, believed that much of the criticism of the Hawaiian labor system was not justified.

One of the important developments—perhaps the most impor-

tant—in the reign of Kamehameha IV was the establishment of the
Episcopal Church in the kingdom, an event that had political as
well as religious significance. Many English and American residents of Honolulu had in their homelands been members of the
Church of England or of the Protestant Episcopal Church of
the United States. The organization of a church of that faith in
the islands had often been considered, but had never been carried out. King Kamehameha IV became actively interested in the
plan about 1859, as the result of an emotional crisis in his life.
Queen Emma was ardently interested, and hoped to have the
Prince of Hawaii brought up under the direction of a tutor
belonging to the Episcopal Church.

Minister Wyllie, who was personally sympathetic to the plan,
had written several times to Bishop William I. Kip of California,
asking him to send an Episcopal clergyman to Hawaii, but the
bishop had no helpers to spare from his own field. On December
5, 1859, by command of the king, Wyllie wrote to Manley Hopkins, Hawaiian consul general in London, informing him of the
earnest desire of the king and queen "to promote the establishment of an Episcopal Chapel or Church" in Honolulu. The king
offered to donate a site for the church, and engaged to pay a
clergyman $1,000 a year and to provide a parsonage. A few days
later, a meeting was held in Honolulu, and when it was known
that the king and queen were supporting the idea, a committee
was appointed to raise a building fund for the proposed church.

The project publicized by Hopkins was reinforced by a letter
from Kamehameha IV to Queen Victoria. On December 15, 1861,
the Reverend Thomas N. Staley of Queen's College, Cambridge,
by virtue of a license granted by Queen Victoria to the Archbishop
of Canterbury, was consecrated as bishop of the new missionary
diocese in Hawaii.

It was intended that the English and American branches of the
Episcopal Church should co-operate in the new enterprise; but the
Civil War in the United States interfered, with the result that the
final establishment was distinctly English in tone. When reports

from England began to speak of setting up an episcopate in Hawaii, the American missionary group who had been established there since 1820 became alarmed, fearing that the erection of a Church of England mission might be followed by attempts at political domination. Apparently there was no justification for their fears of aggression. The Hawaiian king and his advisers, however, did believe that the Anglican Church would strengthen the Hawaiian monarchy.

Kamehameha IV and Queen Emma eagerly awaited the arrival of Bishop Staley and his party in Honolulu. They intended that the first important act of the bishop would be the baptism of the Prince of Hawaii. Queen Victoria had consented to be the godmother of the royal child, and great preparations had been made. But when the bishop reached Honolulu on October 11, 1862, the prince was dead. In his last hours he had been baptized by the pastor of Kawaiahao Church, using the ritual of the Church of England.

A charter of incorporation was granted to the new church shortly after the bishop's arrival, under the name of the Hawaiian Reformed Catholic Church; it was commonly called the English Church. The king and queen were the first communicants, confirmed on November 28. Minister Wyllie, Justice G. M. Robertson, Attorney General Harris, and the high chief David Kalakaua were also soon confirmed. The king further demonstrated his piety by translating into the Hawaiian language the English Book of Common Prayer. On March 5, 1867, the cornerstone was laid for the Anglican Cathedral erected in the heart of Honolulu.

Under royal patronage, the Episcopal Church gained a position of consequence in the islands. Unfortunately, it became involved in a bitter controversy on church doctrines with the old established American Mission.

The founding of the Episcopal Church in Hawaii occurred at about the same time that an important change was made in the organization of the pioneer Protestant mission, which up to this time had been controlled, and in part financed, by the American

Board of Commissioners for Foreign Missions. For some years the Board had felt that Hawaii was a Christian nation and that religious work should be placed fully in the hands of a self-governing local organization of the Hawaiian churches. In 1863, as the results of a survey by Dr. Rufus Anderson, Foreign Secretary of the American Board, this Board virtually withdrew from the field, leaving the work under the jurisdiction of the Hawaiian Evangelical Association, which was now enlarged to include the native pastors and the lay delegates elected from the different islands. The Hawaiian Evangelical Association elects an executive body, usually called the "Hawaiian Board," which handles the business of the association.

The fiftieth anniversary of the landing of the first missionary group sent out by the American Board was celebrated in June, 1870, with a jubilee.

The Mormon Church in the islands experienced during this period a kind of second birth under rather trying circumstances. By the close of the reign of Kamehameha III, as has been told, this religious group had made very satisfactory progress, with an experimental settlement under way on the island of Lanai. In 1858, however, all the *haole* missionaries were recalled to Utah because of the Mormon War, and the native church members were left to fend for themselves.

Walter Murray Gibson, the villain of the Mormon drama in Hawaii, arrived from Utah in 1861 and assumed leadership of the group. This "scheming, dreaming genius," as a Mormon pamphlet calls him, seized power, transferred the title to church lands to his own name, and in general used the church to further his own selfish ends. He was later to become a stormy figure in Hawaiian politics. He was expelled from the church in 1864 and other men were sent from Utah to take charge of the field. But through Gibson's acts, the Mormons had lost their property on Lanai, and it was decided to erect a new headquarters at Laie, on the northern shore of Oahu. In 1865 a large party of Mormons arrived from the United States to settle at Laie. Here a number of agricultural efforts were at last successful, and after hardships and despair, a profitable sugar cane plantation brought revenues to support the work of the Mormon Church in Hawaii and elsewhere in the Pacific.

A religious episode of some interest to the foreign residents of Honolulu was the organization of a Methodist Episcopal Church in 1855, with the Reverend W. S. Turner of the California Conference as its first pastor. A church building and parsonage were built at the corner of Kukui Street and Nuuanu Avenue. The organization never gained much strength and seems to have had some internal dissension. It was finally given up in 1861. The religious needs of those in the community who had evangelical Protestant leanings could well be taken care of by the two Congregational churches already existing in Honolulu. The former Methodist premises were the buildings first used by the Episcopal Church when it was established in 1862.

Public education during this transitional period of the kingdom drew closer to the pattern of American school systems. The Ministry of Education was abolished in 1855 and was replaced by a three-man Board of Education (Richard Armstrong, president, with Prince Lot Kamehameha and Elisha H. Allen). When Dr. Armstrong died in 1860, the king named as president of the Board his father, the venerable Mataio Kekuanaoa. The latter appointment did not work out to the benefit of public education, for Kekuanaoa, although an able man, knew little English and was handicapped in dealing with such problems. The lack of trained professional leadership in teaching, which was thus glaringly revealed, was corrected in the reorganization act of 1865. This act set up a Bureau of Public Instruction of five members, and made other improvements in the interests of good management. Most important, it created the position of inspector general of schools. Abraham Fornander, the first inspector general, was a journalist who lacked proper knowledge of teaching practice, and his administration has been characterized as one of "vacillation and lack of progress." He had previously been extremely critical of the American missionaries, and when he began to make many changes in the local schools they accused him of trying to destroy the work they had done. Nevertheless, the system set up in 1865 did eventually make a place for professional leadership. Under H. Rexford Hitchcock, who became inspector general in 1870, and Charles Reed Bishop, who in 1874 became president of the Board, the way was smoothed for a more efficient public school program on the American plan.

Steamship service, which had become permanent by the end of this period, made travel to and among the islands quicker and less difficult. Tourists began to be a feature of community life. Travel by land—on horseback over trails and rudimentary roads —was still not easy, although the life of the visitor could be pleasant, if one can judge by the experiences of such visitors as Miss Isabella Bird and Charles Nordhoff. Each toured the islands the year after Kamehameha V died and each wrote a book narrating experiences and giving pictures of island life. Even at that time there was only one really good hotel in the entire kingdom, the Hawaiian Hotel in Honolulu, which had opened for business in 1872. Elsewhere, travelers were accommodated in the homes of residents, either *haole* or Hawaiian. Miss Bird was an Englishwoman, Nordhoff an American, but they separately agreed that there were many persons of culture and refinement not only in Honolulu but also in the smaller towns and on the plantations. Both praised the friendliness and hospitality of the Hawaiians, and both give amusing descriptions of some Hawaiian customs, such as *lomi-lomi* (a massage to remove soreness and fatigue) and surf-riding (Nordhoff said that Hilo was one of the few places where this sport could be seen).

Another visitor who did much to advertise the islands was Mark Twain, who appeared in Hawaii in January, 1866, on the steamer *Ajax*, as a correspondent of the Sacramento *Union*. His writings about Hawaiian conditions and personalities were widely copied in American newspapers. One thrilling story on which he was able to scoop his journalistic competitors was the arrival of fifteen

crew members of the clipper ship *Hornet,* which had burned near
the equator. The survivors had managed to reach the island of
Hawaii after a voyage of forty-three days in an open boat.

From these and from other writers, and from newspaper accounts, one gets a picture of a community in which attention was
given to the amenities of life as well as to the business of money-
making. There were in Honolulu a number of clubs and fraternal
and social organizations, as well as literary and musical societies
for mutual improvement of their members. For entertainment the
populace from time to time had its choice of circuses, minstrel
shows, Swiss bell ringers, fireworks displays, balls, concerts, lectures, debates, and amateur dramatics. Visitors were sometimes
entertained with a *luau* or native feast, which was likely to be
accompanied by an exhibition of the hula. The hula had long
been frowned upon by the missionary element on the ground that
it was a pagan practice if not indecent, but it still was offered even
before such distinguished visitors as H.R.H. the Duke of Edin-
burgh.

The annals of the Royal Hawaiian Theatre under the enter-
prising management of Charles Derby furnish a list of surpris-
ingly varied entertainments. This small playhouse, described by
the author Charles Warren Stoddard as a "quaint, old-fashioned
building in the midst of a beautiful garden," was sometimes the
scene of performances by traveling British actors on their way to
the United States, and hence the Hawaiians saw such repertories
in advance of American audiences. Not only dramas and skits, but
singers, minstrels, cyclorama and diorama displays, "dissolving
views," and even grand opera appeared on the boards at the Royal
Hawaiian. A visiting actor, Walter Montgomery, in 1870 gave
several Shakespearean programs at Buffum's Temperance Hall,
one of which consisted in the recital of the entire play *Macbeth*
from memory.

The Royal Hawaiian Band was organized in 1870 as a government institution, under the leadership of W. Northcott. Two
years later Captain Henry Berger, its conductor for many years

and composer of the music of the Hawaiian national anthem, *"Hawaii Ponoi,"* arrived from Germany and took charge of the band.

Gala events were horse races upon the plain and regattas along the shore, where hotly contested races would be arranged for schooners, whaleboats, gigs, and native canoes. Speaking of a regatta in 1859, the *Advertiser* commented: "The sport is one for which our Hawaiian boat boys are admirably adapted, and in which they show great ambition and skill. There never was a better place for regattas than our harbor."

The beginnings of the Waikiki colony as a fashionable seaside resort came in this era. In 1865 one of the local newspapers reported: "Quite a little community of foreign families are now residing at the beach at Waikiki. The distance from town is so short that a person may be in town at his business all day, and go out at evening, when the change of atmosphere is truly refreshing, while the surf bathing cannot help but be invigorating."

CHAPTER FOURTEEN

Lunalilo, the People's King

KAMEHAMEHA V died without an heir to succeed him on the throne. He had failed to exercise the right which the constitution gave him to name his successor. His death therefore left the throne vacant, and it was the duty of the legislature to elect a king from among the native nobility. This was a unique circumstance. Never before had the common people of the kingdom been given a chance to express their opinions on who should rule over them.

For several weeks Hawaii had no king. Who should be chosen? The members of the cabinet, on the day after the death of Kamehameha V, ordered the legislature to meet on January 8, 1873, for the purpose of electing a new ruler of Hawaii.

Two active candidates for the throne were William Charles Lunalilo and David Kalakaua. Lunalilo was considered the highest ranking chief, and was popular among all classes of natives. He was liberal in his opinions—a fact which had kept him out of any office under Kamehameha V—and it was known that he did not favor the Constitution of 1864. Kalakaua also belonged to a noble family, and he had been in public office under the late king. Popular favor seemed to fall upon Lunalilo, and on the day after the death of Kamehameha V, a mass meeting of natives voted unanimously that Lunalilo was their choice.

Lunalilo published an address to the people a few days later, stating that he believed the people should express their views on the choice of a king, and submitting his claims for their decision. He recommended that a vote should be taken on January 1 to make the people's wishes known. "The only pledge that I deem it necessary to offer to the people," he declared, "is that I will restore the constitution of Kamehameha III of happy memory, with only such changes as may be required to adapt it to present laws, and that I will govern the nation according to the principles of that constitution and a liberal constitutional monarchy."

A large mass meeting was held the day after Christmas, at which the candidacy of Lunalilo was endorsed, and a committee was appointed to arrange for the plebiscite he had proposed. A resolution was unanimously adopted "that we the people of Honolulu do hereby instruct our four representatives in the Legislative Assembly to vote for Prince W. C. Lunalilo for king, and for no one else."

Kalakaua responded on December 28 with his own address to the people, couched in figurative ancient style. It began with the words, "O my people! My countrymen from old! Arise! This is the voice!" Kalakaua made the charge that foreigners were backing Lunalilo, and urged the people not to vote on January 1. His platform promised "to preserve and increase the people, so that they shall multiply and fill the land with chiefs and common people;" "to repeal all the personal taxes;" and "to put native Hawaiians into government offices, so as to pay off the national debt." He also promised to amend the Constitution of 1864, but warned: "Beware of the Constitution of 1852 and the false teachings of the foreigners who are now grasping to obtain the control of the government if W. C. Lunalilo ascends the throne."

The people did not fear these dark warnings. On New Year's Day, they went to the polls to cast their ballots, as Lunalilo had suggested. The votes, when counted, were almost unanimously in favor of Lunalilo.

A week later, the Legislative Assembly met for the purpose of electing a new king under the constitution. A throng of people surrounded the building. One by one the votes were cast. The first was for Lunalilo—and so were all of them to the end. Lunalilo, the people's choice, was king.

The new sovereign was inaugurated amid a magnificent ceremony on the following day at Kawaiahao Church. At once King
Lunalilo fulfilled his election promise by submitting several proposed amendments to the constitution, the most important being
one to do away with the property qualification for voters. Thirty
amendments altogether were passed by the special legislative session of 1873, and referred for final action to the regular session
of 1874.

The cabinet members announced by the king on January 10,
1873, were with one exception of American origin, and two of
them came from missionary families. Charles R. Bishop was minister of foreign affairs; Edwin O. Hall was minister of the interior; Robert Stirling, a Scotsman, was minister of finance; and
A. Francis Judd was attorney general. Although it was believed
that Lunalilo favored American ideas, at the time of his election
he had a remarkable popularity among all classes of his subjects.
Unfortunately, by the end of his brief reign he had lost much of
this support.

Lunalilo, who was born on January 31, 1835, was descended
from a brother of Kamehameha I. His mother was Kekauluohi,
who had been *kuhina nui* of the kingdom. She died when Lunalilo
was ten years old. The child was brought up as a spoiled prince,
living in idleness, but he did obtain a good education at the Royal
School under Mr. and Mrs. Cooke. He was intelligent and witty,
and had a remarkable memory and gift for mimicry. By disposition he was gentle, fair-minded, and truthful, but his indecisive
nature might well have resulted in harm to the nation. Weakness
in health soon developed into a serious case of tuberculosis, and
although he was sanguine about his recovery, wiser observers were
soon worrying about who would succeed to the throne if the disease should prove fatal.

Lunalilo, like his three predecessors, sought to conclude a reciprocity treaty with the United States. The need for such a treaty
was greater than ever, for 1872 had been a year of serious financial

depression. It was felt that a reciprocity treaty would bring economic prosperity.

The Honolulu Chamber of Commerce in February, 1873, adopted a resolution asking the king to make another attempt to secure a reciprocity treaty. In view of the previous history of this question, it was clear to most observers that the United States would do nothing unless some special inducement could be offered to make such a treaty seem attractive to the American people. The idea that the Pearl River lagoon might be given to the United States for use as a naval station was suggested, and in June the king, upon the advice of his cabinet, agreed that this proposal should be made. The "Pearl River scheme," however, aroused much opposition, especially from the native Hawaiians, and when it was clear that the legislature would not approve such a cession of territory to a foreign nation, the king became lukewarm about the plan, and in November the offer was withdrawn. It turned out that the United States was not seriously interested in the proposed treaty, even with the cession of Pearl Harbor. The attempt to gain reciprocity in the reign of Lunalilo was therefore dropped.

The sugar planters of Hawaii, faced with high American tariffs, had begun to cultivate the export market in Australia and New Zealand, and there was talk that a reciprocity treaty with these South Pacific countries might be made.

An awkward incident of Lunalilo's reign which revealed somewhat the anti-foreign temper of the natives was the mutiny of the Household Troops. These troops were the military body of the kingdom, although their duties included little more than guarding some government buildings and providing an escort of honor for the king. Their chief officers were a drillmaster—an Austrian named Joseph Jajczay—and an adjutant general. Captain Jajczay was a martinet whose discipline was resented by the soldiers. They also had some grievance against the adjutant general, who had charge of supplies and equipment.

When Captain Jajczay attempted one day early in September

to punish some of the men for a serious breach of duty, they attacked him, but were stopped before they could injure him seriously. The mutiny which thus broke out was to last for five days. The mutineers, in possession of the barracks on Palace Walk (now Hotel Street), brought over several cannon from the palace grounds during the first night, and prepared to hold their ground. They refused to return to their duties until the drillmaster and the adjutant general were dismissed. They had the sympathy of many native Hawaiians, and it was feared that any attempt to dislodge them from the barracks would lead to bloodshed and possibly civil war.

The king, who was commander-in-chief of the troops, was ill in his cottage at Waikiki. When other efforts had failed, his aid was invoked to settle the mutiny. He interviewed some of the rebels on the fourth day, and next morning sent a letter asking the men to leave the barracks and return to their homes, promising that he would forgive their disobedience. The soldiers complied, and the next day the king issued an order disbanding the Household Troops. "The soldier's mutiny," concluded Attorney General Judd in a private letter, "had one good result, the disbanding of a useless and expensive army."

Leprosy, in spite of the steps carried out during the previous reign, was still a serious menace. The segregation program had not been fully completed, and many lepers were still at large in the community. The natives did not understand the seriousness of the disease or the need for preventing infection. Lepers were hidden by families or friends, for they feared that being sent to Molokai was a sentence of death. The Board of Health during the reign of Lunalilo made an active campaign to enforce the law. Almost five hundred patients were taken to the Molokai station during 1873, a much larger number than had ever been sent there in one year. This unpleasant step was necessary if the rest of the people were to be protected from the ravages of disease, but this health measure was resented by many and resulted in much popular dissatisfaction with Lunalilo's government.

The illness of the king, who was unmarried and thus without an heir, made it an urgent matter of policy that he name his successor to avoid leaving the throne vacant for a second time. He did not seem to favor strongly any of the eligible candidates for the succession, and was strongly opposed to David Kalakaua, whose cause was already being promoted by certain newspapers. A majority of the seven *alii* who comprised the total membership in the House of Nobles were known to favor Kalakaua, but one way in which Lunalilo might control the vote there would be to create a number of new nobles who shared his views. Henry A. Peirce, minister resident of the United States in Hawaii, wrote in September: "It is expected that Lunalilo will create a sufficient number of new nobles to ensure the confirmation of the person selected by him for the future sovereign of these islands. No one believes he will choose Kalakaua as his successor."

The king was taken to Kailua, Hawaii, in November in the hope that the Kona climate would improve his failing health. His condition became rapidly worse. It became clear to everyone but himself that he could not live much longer, and when he was brought back to Honolulu two months later, he was urged again to name his successor. "The public mind seems to be settled upon Kalakaua as the coming man," wrote Minister Bishop on January 21, 1874, "and as it is very doubtful if a majority of the nobles would approve of any other, we have tried our best to have the king appoint him." But no appointment was made.

Lunalilo died on February 3, a year and twenty-five days after he mounted the throne. His body was wrapped in the feather cloak of his mother and taken to the Royal Mausoleum. When his tomb in Kawaiahao churchyard was finished, the body was removed there in the midst of a thunderstorm. Just as the coffin entered the gate, a sharp crash of thunder was heard. The natives told each other that this was a heavenly sign of recognition of the high rank of their beloved Lunalilo.

Lunalilo was the first Hawaiian to leave his property to a benevolent institution. He is best remembered for the Lunalilo Home, erected under the terms of his will "for the use and accommodation of poor, destitute, and infirm people of Hawaiian blood or extraction, giving preference to old people."

The election of a king was again the most vital issue in the kingdom. The cabinet selected February 12, 1874, as the date on which the Legislative Assembly would meet for this purpose.

Kalakaua, the day after Lunalilo's death, formally announced that he was a candidate. On the next day a similar announcement was made by Queen Dowager Emma, the widow of Kamehameha IV. Since her return in 1866 from a trip abroad, where she had become a friend of Queen Victoria, she had lived quietly, devoting herself to charitable works. She was loved and respected by natives and foreigners alike, but many of them did not like the idea of having her as a sovereign. "The Hawaiian people," said one newspaper, "will love her as a benefactress and hate her as a politician."

Queen Emma, in the brief campaign that followed, won the support of many natives, especially on Oahu. The British element in the islands was, naturally, strongly on her side. Most of the other foreigners, including almost all the Americans, were enthusiastically for Kalakaua. He also had a strong following among the natives, especially on the other islands. When the legislature met, thirty-nine of the members voted for Kalakaua and six for Queen Emma.

Kalakaua was at once declared king, and a committee was appointed to notify him of his election. The courthouse in which the election was held had been surrounded by a throng of people, mainly supporters of Queen Emma. The success of the populace in demonstrating their will at the Lunalilo plebiscite had filled them with a fiery determination. The results of the vote passed from mouth to mouth, and when the notification committee attempted to leave the building they were attacked by members of the angry crowd.

Some representatives were wounded before they could get back inside. The mob then forced its way into the courthouse, sacked the various offices, and destroyed furniture, books, and papers. Other native members of the assembly were assaulted, and it seemed that an open rebellion would break out.

The newly elected king, together with Minister Bishop and the governor of Oahu, in order to prevent further riot and possible loss of life, asked the American minister and the British commissioner to land marines from three warships in the harbor. These were the American vessels *Portsmouth* and *Tuscarora*, which were cruising in these waters with an eye out for protection of American interests, and the British ship *Tenedos*. The armed forces were landed at once, and by evening had restored order. The marines remained on shore for about a week, by which time the new regime was firmly established.

Kalakaua took the oath of office on February 13. On the same day, Queen Emma acknowledged him as king, and advised her supporters to do the same. To settle at once the troubling question of the succession, King Kalakaua immediately proclaimed his younger brother, William Pitt Leleiohoku, as his heir. But Kalakaua was destined to be the last male ruler of the Hawaiian kingdom.

Book 4

Later Years of the Kingdom
(1874–1893)

CHAPTER FIFTEEN

Reciprocity, the Wonder-Worker

THE great event of the early years of the reign of Kalakaua was the conclusion of a reciprocity treaty with the United States. Even though much had been expected of such an agreement, the actual effects far exceeded the most extravagant predictions of what it would do. Reciprocity, it is sometimes said, made sugar king in Hawaii. It certainly caused an enormous expansion of the sugar industry, whose influence was felt in many directions, political and social as well as economic. The prosperity of the kingdom came to be dependent on maintenance of the reciprocity arrangement. Thus Hawaii was bound by powerful economic ties to the United States, and the American government was able, after a while, to obtain from the island kingdom the concession of a right to use Pearl Harbor as a naval coaling and repair station.

When the reign began, there seemed to be very little prospect of obtaining a reciprocity treaty, but within a few months the subject came up, almost as a matter of routine. The sugar factors and businessmen of Honolulu presented an urgent petition to the king, predicting economic disaster to the country unless relief to the plantation interests was speedily obtained. Kalakaua passed this petition on to the legislature with his approval, and they put through an act to facilitate negotiations. With the advice of the cabinet and privy council, the king appointed Chief Justice E. H. Allen as envoy to the United States to conduct the negotiations, and associated with him as special commissioner H. A. P. Carter, head of the firm of C. Brewer & Company. They sailed on October 18, 1874, for San Francisco on their way to Washington.

Kalakaua decided to go to the United States himself. He had already been thinking of making such a journey, and it was strongly suggested that his going at this time might improve the chances of getting the treaty. Accordingly, on November 17, he left his island realm on the United States warship *Benicia*, as a guest of the American government. His party included Governor John O. Dominis of Oahu, Governor John M. Kapena of Maui, and Henry A. Peirce, United States minister to Hawaii. Never before had the king of any country visited the United States, and Kalakaua's good-will tour was a great triumph. Wherever he journeyed, he was given the honors due a visiting monarch of a friendly and independent nation. In Washington he was received in state by President U. S. Grant, and was presented to the members of both houses of Congress. Afterwards he went to New York and to various places in New England—among them Boston, where the first missionary party had set out, and New Bedford, home port of many of the whaleships that had once thronged Hawaiian waters. The king returned to Honolulu on the United States warship *Pensacola* on February 15, 1875. He had been wholly successful in promoting a friendly feeling toward Hawaii among the people of the United States.

Allen and Carter arrived in Washington in the middle of November and set resolutely to work. Their task was not easy. The administration of President Grant was at first decidedly lukewarm. Since Secretary of State Hamilton Fish would not proceed until he had a reasonable expectation of favorable action by Congress, the Hawaiian envoys had to become lobbyists as well as diplomats. By the middle of January they had won their case and on January 30, 1875, the treaty of reciprocity was signed.

The treaty was approved a month and a half later by the United States Senate, after an additional article had been inserted. It was ratified by King Kalakaua on April 17. Enabling acts which permitted the treaty to go into effect were passed by Congress and the Hawaiian legislature in 1876. The treaty finally went into operation on September 9, 1876. That was a red-letter day in the history of Hawaii. The dream of reciprocity was an accomplished fact.

This epochal treaty was not lengthy. It provided that unrefined sugar, rice, and virtually all other Hawaiian products should be admitted to the United States free of customs duties. In turn, a large list of American products and manufactured goods were admitted free into Hawaii. The clause inserted by the United States Senate—without which the treaty probably would have been rejected—provided that, as long as the agreement remained in effect, the king of Hawaii would not offer the same kind of treaty to any other nation, and that he would not "lease or otherwise dispose of . . . any port, harbor, or other territory in his dominions, or grant any special privilege or rights of use therein, to any other power, state, or government." The treaty was to continue for a term of seven years; at any time after that, it could be terminated by either the United States or Hawaii by giving one year's notice of intention to do so.

Why was the United States ready at this time to sign a treaty embodying terms which had been refused to Kalakaua's predecessors? Undoubtedly the king's visit had been very helpful, although he took no direct part in the negotiations. It appears certain that the arguments of Minister Peirce sent to his own government had a favorable effect. Yet there were stronger influences at work. At this time, America had almost a monopoly of Hawaiian trade. American capital and brains had built up much of Hawaii's industry, particularly sugar. But English business interests were still strong, and when the sugar planters, hampered by high United States tariffs, looked about for better markets, they found a welcome in the British colonies. More than a third of the sugar exported in 1873 was sent to Australia, New Zealand, and British Columbia. The American government was told that the entire crop of 1875–76 would be sent to those places. If trade were to swing that way, Hawaii might soon drift into the British sphere.

To forestall such a turn of events off its Pacific shores, the United States was willing to try reciprocity.

The effects of the treaty soon began to exceed the most sanguine expectations. Now that a profitable market was assured, capital began to flow in larger volume into agricultural enterprises. Production leaped ahead. Transportation, construction, merchandising, and other businesses associated with the production of sugar and rice also boomed. The demand for a greatly increased labor force had to be met, and was met—with a marked effect upon the complexion of Hawaii's future population. The income of the government was greatly increased, permitting a corresponding increase of expenditures for public works and other purposes.

The most spectacular effect of reciprocity was the increase in output of sugar and rice. In four years the production of sugar more than doubled, and the proportional increase of the rice crop was nearly as great. In 1875 Hawaii exported twenty-five million pounds of sugar; fifteen years later, the amount was more than two hundred and fifty million pounds. The increase in production was so great that sugar growers in the United States protested that it could not be true; they insisted that the Hawaiians must be nefariously importing sugar from other countries and transshipping it under the treaty terms. This charge was investigated and found to be false. Not only was Hawaii really turning out the amount it claimed—the industry pushed ahead, and thereafter doubled its tonnage of sugar shipments every ten years!

This result was achieved by the expansion of old plantations and the founding of many new ones; by building bigger mills and equipping them with better and more efficient machinery; by the application of fertilizers to the cane fields; and by the development of huge irrigation projects. In other words, output was increased by using all the methods of large-scale agriculture, for the production of sugar in the Hawaiian Islands, it must be emphasized, is a large-scale enterprise all the way along the line.

One of the most truly noteworthy features of the growth of the sugar industry in this period was the development of irrigation.

The production of a crop of sugar requires enormous quantities of water, equal to ten feet of rainfall a year. Few of the plantations can get along without irrigation. The beginnings of this practice in modern times go back at least to 1856, when the first ditch of any size was dug to supply the Lihue Plantation on Kauai. From that beginning, irrigation had, by the time the reciprocity treaty went into effect, become standard practice on many plantations, even though on a small scale.

The first great venture was the Hamakua Ditch on the island of Maui. S. T. Alexander and H. P. Baldwin formed the plan of bringing water from the dripping northern slopes of Mount Haleakala to the dry central plain where they owned a small plantation at Paia. Borrowing money from a few other men, the two obtained a lease from the government and began the work. The cost was about $80,000—an immense project for that time.

The district was rugged and gashed with deep ravines. To get the water across these, it was necessary to lay large and heavy pipes down each side and across the bottom, making an inverted siphon. When the construction men came to the final obstacle, the deep gorge of Maliko, it was necessary for them to lower themselves down the cliffs by holding on ropes. They refused to endanger themselves in this way, and work stopped. Then Manager Baldwin, who had lost one of his arms in a mill accident, showed his leadership. He slid down the rope using his legs and his one good arm, with which he successively gripped and released the rope to grab a new hold lower down. This exhibition of courage so shamed the workmen that they followed Baldwin down the rope. To keep them heartened and to inspect the progress of the work, Baldwin day after day went through this risky performance.

When the Hamakua Ditch was finished, it ran for seventeen miles and had a daily capacity of forty million gallons. Soon Claus Spreckels, another sugar operator, ran a second ditch in the same district, below the Hamakua Ditch; it was thirty miles long and had a capacity of fifty million gallons. A few years later a third ditch was dug, on the other side of the plain. The once barren acres of central Maui have ever since been a flourishing region of tall cane. Under Baldwin's guidance in the last year of Kalakaua's reign, a large ditch was dug to deliver thirty-five million gallons daily to the Makaweli Plantation on Kauai. These pioneer ditches, big as they seemed at the time, have been surpassed by huge projects in later years. The first artesian well was bored in July, 1879, at Ewa Plantation, and thereafter, with the aid of giant pumps, the underground water supply of Oahu was made available for use.

The construction of new mills required the importation of expensive milling and harvesting machinery. Much of this came from the United States, but many mill outfits were imported from Great Britain. The Honolulu Iron Works was called upon to increase its labors by turning out plantation equipment. New methods of operation were put into use. The first diffusion-process plant for sugar manufacture was introduced by Col. Z. S. Spalding for the Makee Sugar Company, Kauai, in 1888.

All this development required great sums of money. It had been said, in the old days before 1876, that the three needs of the sugar industry were a good market, available capital, and a supply of cheap labor. The reciprocity treaty provided the market and, when that was assured, capital became available. A large amount of money was brought into the islands, principally from the United States. A great proportion of this was in the form of loans to plantation companies and agencies. But some men brought money and invested it on their own account. The most prominent of these invaders was Claus Spreckels, who had already made a fortune as a sugar refiner in California. He had fought the reciprocity treaty, but when it became a reality he went to Hawaii and invested heavily in sugar land, sugar mills, and irrigation systems. His son, J. D. Spreckels, founded the Oceanic Steamship Company, which served the islands for many years. Claus Spreckels also became an important figure in the political history of Hawaii.

With the exception of Spreckels, the leaders in the development of the sugar industry were, by and large, men who had been born in the islands or had lived there for a long time and had grown up with the business. S. T. Alexander and H. P. Baldwin were sons of missionaries. James Campbell was an Irish sailor and carpenter who settled ashore and founded the Pioneer Mill Company in 1861. Valdemar Knudsen, who was the son of a president of Norway, after a career as a forty-niner lost his California gold and made a new fortune in Hawaiian sugar. Captain James Makee, a Massachusetts whaling captain put ashore near death after being attacked by a ship's cook, lived to become King Kalakaua's partner in sugar planting. Paul Isenberg, son of a German pastor, rose from overseer on a Kauai estate to become a great sugar proprietor. An ex-seaman named Benjamin F. Dillingham discovered that one could drill to the subsoil pools on Oahu and flood the fields with life-giving water.

To this roster must be added the businessmen who diverted part or all of their attention from merchandising to sugar raising, and who composed the companies in Honolulu that served as agents for the plantations. The agency system, already well established before 1876, became steadily more important after that date. Most powerful among this group in the 1880's was the firm of Wm. G. Irwin & Company, which represented the Spreckels interests and controlled about one third of the total production. Other important agents were H. Hackfeld & Company, C. Brewer & Company, Theo. H. Davies & Company, Castle & Cooke, G. W. Macfarlane & Company, and F. A. Schaefer & Company. The agency system filled the obvious need for a centralized handling of the business of a number of plantations. These agents or "factors" took care of the sale and shipping of sugar crops, the purchasing of all materials needed by the plantations, the insurance of plant and equipment, the financing of new or expanding ventures, and a hundred and one other functions that could more efficiently be performed by a central management. Agencies were an obvious business growth to meet the needs of the times.

The third need of the sugar industry—an adequate supply of

laborers—was made more pressing by the tremendous increase in production. This need could not be met by drawing upon the native population. The population of Hawaii in 1875 was at its lowest point in history. Since that time it has increased steadily and rather rapidly; but this rise was not caused by increase of the Hawaiian stock. The natives continued to decline in numbers. In 1878 they comprised 82 per cent of the whole population; in 1890 they were less than one half. Even though Kalakaua's government spent money on printing a handbook of "Sanitary Instructions for Hawaiians" to spread medical knowledge, even though more money was spent in the fight against leprosy, the Hawaiian race dwindled. Another epidemic of smallpox in 1881 made the situation worse.

The increase in population was due to the importation of laborers from several parts of the world. During the years between 1877 and 1890, more than 55,000 immigrant laborers were brought into the Hawaiian Islands. Half were Chinese, about 8,000 of whom came from California. The Chinese were competent field laborers, but many of them preferred independence, and sought to set up stores or small vegetable farms. Many of them liked town life and flocked to swell the population of Honolulu. It was feared that the influx of oriental people might change drastically the type of community that had grown up in Hawaii. The government set up restrictions against the immigration of Chinese, and began seeking immigrants from other lands who might be more suitable. One purpose of the trip that King Kalakaua made around the world in 1881 was to study places from which a supply of immigrant laborers might be brought to Hawaii.

The Bureau of Immigration in 1876 set in motion the plan of bringing families from the Portuguese islands in the Atlantic. The value of such an immigration had long been recognized. To assist in this project, the Bureau was able to get the assistance of Dr. William Hillebrand, who had rendered similar service in the Orient some years before. He had returned to Europe and his research in botany had taken him to the Madeira Islands. He arranged that a group of Madeirans should emigrate to Hawaii in 1878. Thereafter a number of others from the Portuguese islands came, for it was found that they took cheerfully to plantation life and proved to be good citizens. Unfortunately the cost of bringing them was very high.

The resistance of the Japanese government to the idea of allowing their people to emigrate was broken down in 1885, and in 1886 a treaty was made under which numbers of Japanese laborers came to Hawaii. Several thousand Japanese came in each year thereafter. When the movement ended in 1908, some 180,000 Japanese had come to the islands and about 126,000 had left them, some to go to the mainland, most to return to Japan.

During the reign of Kalakaua, a substantial number of workers were brought in from several other countries, such as Germany, Scandinavia, and the South Sea islands. Hawaii was fast becoming the melting pot of races. By 1890, the census showed a total of 90,000 inhabitants. Of these 41,000 were Hawaiians, 15,000 were Chinese, 12,000 Japanese, 9,000 Portuguese, 2,000 Americans, 1,300 British, and 1,000 Germans.

The lack of co-operation in the Hawaiian sugar industry was unfavorably commented upon by Charles Nordhoff, who visited the islands in 1873. The old Royal Hawaiian Agricultural Society, into which the Planters' Society of 1864 had merged, had been disbanded in 1869. By 1882, questions relating to the labor supply and other matters of interest to the planters and their agents as a group finally brought them to see the need of joint effort, and in that year the Planters' Labor and Supply Company was organized. The group began in the same year to share its knowledge through the publication of the *Planters' Monthly*, edited at first, oddly enough, by three lawyers, S. B. Dole, W. R. Castle, and W. O. Smith. The company did not at the beginning engage in scientific research and experimentation.

Transportation and communication facilities were expanded to take care of the new industrial needs. The shipping of thousands of tons of sugar alone required a small fleet of vessels. Sugar was only part of the freight that had to be carried, and there was an ever-growing volume of passenger traffic. Steamships acquired the bulk of this business, but they did not have a complete monopoly, and square-rigged sailing ships and schooners were found in the ports of the islands throughout the century.

The government in 1877 had the 382-ton wooden steamer *Likelike* built in San Francisco for inter-island service. This vessel and the old *Kilauea* were purchased by Samuel G. Wilder, who shortly thereafter organized the Wilder Steamship Company, which operated a growing fleet of ships. Competition soon arose and in 1882 the Inter-Island Steam Navigation Company was organized; in 1905 the latter absorbed the Wilder company and continued in business until 1950. By that time airplanes had become the principal carriers of passengers, mail, and fast freight between the islands.

ship Company for many years maintained the line which it had established in 1875 between San Francisco and the British colonies "down under," with Honolulu as an intermediate stop. The Oceanic Steamship Company, a Spreckels enterprise, in 1882 inaugurated a monthly service, soon expanded to semi-monthly, between San Francisco and Honolulu. Ultimately this company extended its operations to Australia and New Zealand. Thus Hawaii was brought closer to other lands, and tourists from many parts of the world began to visit the colorful island kingdom in search of sunshine, health, and recreation.

The need for roads, bridges, and railroads on the islands became more urgent. The government began building better roads. Men with engineering vision started the construction of small-gage rail lines. The franchise of the Oahu Steam Railway (under the Oahu Railway and Land Company) was granted to B. F. Dillingham and associates in September, 1888, and this roadbed had reached Ewa within a year. By the end of the reign of Kala-

kaua there were railroads in operation on the islands of Maui,
Hawaii, and Oahu.

The ground was broken for a mule-drawn street railway in
Honolulu in 1888. In that year the streets of the city were first
lighted by electricity. The first telephone lines were erected on
Maui and in Honolulu in 1878. Soon thereafter the king had a
line installed between the palace and his boathouse. Within a
few years an extensive telephone system was in operation, not
only within the city, but to the other side of the island. The first
steam fire engine was imported by the city in 1879. A parcel post
system in co-operation with the United States was inaugurated in
1889. In the same year, the first section of an inter-island submarine cable system, running between Maui and Molokai, was
laid.

It should be clear, from the foregoing recital, that the reciprocity treaty very quickly became of supreme importance to the
Hawaiian economy. With the exception of anti-American foreigners in Hawaii and some natives who feared that too close relations with the United States might lead to the loss of Hawaii's
independence, most people in the islands were anxious to have
the treaty continued.

In the United States, however, the case was different. There,
the opposition became stronger and more outspoken as the effects
of the treaty began to develop. It was charged that Spreckels, with
the aid of the treaty and his investments in Hawaiian plantations,
was erecting a sugar monopoly on the Pacific coast. The people
of Oregon complained that the treaty favored San Francisco at
the expense of other west-coast communities. The San Francisco
Chronicle, extremely hostile to Spreckels, was vigorous in as-
saulting the treaty and bitter in denunciation of what it called
the "slave labor system" of Hawaii. Eastern sugar refiners feared
the new competition, and joined with the cane planters of re-
constructed Louisiana in introducing resolutions in Congress to
end the agreement. Complaints were made that free trade with
Hawaii caused a loss to the United States treasury. The organized

opposition to the treaty reached a peak about 1883, in which year it could be terminated by action of either country.

The Hawaiian government in 1877 appointed a minister resident to represent it in Washington. This minister (E. H. Allen until 1883 and then H. A. P. Carter) gave most of his time and effort to defending the treaty and preparing the ground for its renewal. Successive administrations in Washington were generally friendly to the treaty, recognizing it as an important instrument of American policy in this part of the world. It was this political consideration that saved the treaty for Hawaii.

Minister Carter was able to negotiate with Secretary of State Frelinghuysen a simple convention providing for extension of reciprocity for another term of seven years. This was signed on December 6, 1884, but final approval of it was delayed for almost three years.

The election of Grover Cleveland, who took office in 1885, did not change the American policy toward Hawaii. Thomas F. Bayard, the incoming secretary of state, was a friend to the reciprocity idea, and pushed it along. He was disagreeably surprised, however, when on April 14, 1886, the Committee on Foreign Relations of the Senate, in reporting favorably on the Frelinghuysen agreement, included an amendment which would give the United States the "exclusive right to enter the harbor of Pearl River, in the Island of Oahu, and to establish and to maintain there a coaling and repair station for the use of vessels of the United States." There was another long delay, but on January 20, 1887, the Senate, by a narrow vote, adopted the Pearl Harbor amendment and gave its consent to the ratification of the treaty as thus amended.

The amendment threatened to upset the whole scheme. Secretary Bayard was at first strongly opposed to it, but finally became convinced, by threatening international complications in the Pacific, that the treaty should be ratified even with the Pearl Harbor amendment, which he considered of little value to the United States.

In Hawaii the government then in power, dominated by Walter Murray Gibson, declared that it was unalterably opposed to the Pearl Harbor amendment. But Gibson was overthrown by a revolution in the summer of 1887 and the Reform ministry which came into office, taking into consideration the importance of the treaty to Hawaii and the same international complications that alarmed Bayard, consented to ratify the treaty as amended, on the condition that "Hawaiian sovereignty and jurisdiction are not impaired."

Assurances were given by the American government that no threat to Hawaiian independence would result from the treaty. Accordingly, the renewal treaty was ratified by Kalakaua on October 20, 1887, and was proclaimed by President Cleveland on November 9. Reciprocity was fated thereafter to remain in effect until the United States annexed Hawaii more than a decade later. During that time the American government never took advantage of its treaty rights to use the Pearl River Harbor.

CHAPTER SIXTEEN

Kalakaua Rex

A N UNRELENTING struggle for political power went on during
most of the reign of Kalakaua, and culminated in a series
of revolutions that foretold the downfall of the monarchy in the
following reign.

Personally, Kalakaua was a man of very pleasing, even impressive manner, who could converse agreeably in English or Hawaiian with the court that he built up around him, or take his place
in the highest circles of society at home and abroad. He was de-
lighted with ceremonials and military display. He was a lover
of music and encouraged that art. Literary men such as Robert
Louis Stevenson, who passed the first half of 1889 visiting in the
islands, found his companionship worth seeking. Henry Adams,
who had an audience with the king in 1890, reported that he
"talked of Hawaiian archaeology and arts as well as though he
had been a professor." Kalakaua had worked hard to improve and
advance himself. He had practiced public speaking and writing
and had acquired considerable skill in the art of persuasion. He
thoroughly understood the Hawaiian character, including the
deference still paid to the *alii*. With these qualities added to the
prestige of his high office he was well equipped to be an effective
leader of his own people and to win their support for whatever
course he might choose to follow.

Politically, Kalakaua believed that the king should be, liter-
ally, the ruler of the country, and he lost no opportunity to make
his personal influence felt at every turn. He had gained considerable experience in the practical details of government, both in

administrative positions and in the legislature. He was a champion of the ideas of Kamehameha V, who had given the country the Constitution of 1864. The powers that this constitution gave to the king were used by Kalakaua to the limit, nor did he hesitate to appeal directly to the people and to bring pressure upon them to influence their votes.

Universal suffrage, abolished by the Constitution of 1864, was restored by one of the amendments proposed by Lunalilo and finally adopted in the legislative session of 1874, although almost all the thirty other amendments proposed under Lunalilo were rejected. Kalakaua made skillful use of this universal suffrage and for a long time was able to control affairs by appealing with catchwords or personal prestige to the mass of voters.

Kalakaua started out rather well. He appointed good ministers, including one of the native chiefs. Soon after his accession, he made a tour of the kingdom and produced an excellent impression on everyone. In his speeches he promised to do many things that would promote the best interests of the people. He actively and effectively supported the movement for a reciprocity treaty.

In the summer of 1878 Kalakaua began a practice that was one of the great evils of his reign. He dismissed his ministers and appointed an entirely new cabinet. Under the constitution he could do this, but preceding kings had not abused the power. The new ministers appointed at this time were able men, better, perhaps, than the ones they replaced, but the practice was a bad one. Its evils became apparent two years later.

Claus Spreckels, who had acquired land on Maui for a sugar plantation, applied for an extensive water privilege on the northeast side of the island. The cabinet rejected the application. Spreckels then, with the aid of a personal loan to the king, induced him to dismiss the ministers and appoint others, who promptly granted the requested water right for thirty years at $500 a year. This was the beginning of Spreckels' baleful meddling in Hawaiian governmental affairs.

After another lapse of two years, Kalakaua in 1880 dismissed the members of his cabinet and turned the ministry over to a foreign adventurer. Celso Caesar Moreno was an Italian soldier of fortune who arrived in Honolulu in 1879 with a scheme for starting a steamship line between that port and China. By flattery and by encouraging the king's ideas of a huge foreign loan for military expansion, Moreno obtained the support of Kalakaua. Abetted by Gibson in the legislature of 1880, the king and his henchmen put through a subsidy bill for Moreno's steamship line, and tried to pass a ten-million-dollar foreign loan, a bill to permit liquor to be freely sold to Hawaiians, and a bill to license the sale of opium in the kingdom. Fortunately, these latter schemes were defeated in the legislature. The king then, on August 14, prorogued the legislature at noon, and about an hour later dismissed his cabinet and appointed Moreno as prime minister.

A hurricane of protest against the interloper at once arose from all sides. Five days later, Moreno's resignation was announced. He left for Europe at the end of the month with a secret commission as plenipotentiary to the great powers; the commission was soon revoked but later caused trouble. With him Moreno took to Europe three youthful Hawaiians who were to be educated abroad at the expense of the government. One of these young men was Robert W. Wilcox, who was to become the most prominent revolutionary figure in the latter part of the reign.

The boom that followed the signing of the reciprocity treaty brought prosperity to the Hawaiian Islands. Never before had the government enjoyed such prospects of a rich income, and it now seemed possible for it to do many things that it had previously been unable to afford. Kalakaua decided that the time had come for his kingdom to take a more prominent place in world affairs, and he began by considering the idea of making a tour around the globe.

Preparations were soon made for the journey. Princess Liliuokalani, the king's sister, who had been proclaimed heiress to the throne after the death of Prince Leleiohoku in 1877, was named as regent during the king's absence. The king departed in Janu-

ary, 1881, accompanied by his chamberlain, Col. C. H. Judd,
and his attorney general, W. N. Armstrong, who was to study
the question of obtaining emigrants from the various countries
visited. The royal party went first to San Francisco, and from
there took a steamer for Japan.

A royal salute greeted the vessel as it entered the Bay of Yeddo,
and the king was invited to be the guest of the Japanese emperor.
The celebration in Kalakaua's honor was magnificent. He was the
first king of a western, Christian nation that had ever set foot
in Japan, and too much honor could not be paid him by the enthusiastic Japanese.

The king continued his tour through China, Siam, India,
Egypt, and the great European capitals; and everywhere he received the respect and courtesy due a visiting monarch. By way
of the United States, Kalakaua returned to Honolulu at the end
of October, to be greeted by a triumphal celebration of homecom-
ing. He was the first king in history ever to make a trip around
the world.

The coronation of King Kalakaua and his consort Queen Kapiolani, which was held soon after his return, was likewise an international occasion. This ceremony had been authorized by the
legislature in 1880, but had been delayed. The date of February
12, 1883, the ninth anniversary of Kalakaua's election, was set
for the coronation. Its purpose was to confirm the royal family as
the ruling dynasty of the kingdom, and to bring the Hawaiian
nation to the attention of the world.

The crowning of king and queen was performed in the sight
of some eight thousand people who gathered in front of the recently completed Iolani Palace, the cornerstone of which had been
laid at the end of 1879. A pavilion and amphitheater, decorated
with the coats-of-arms of the nations of the earth, provided a vivid
setting. The ceremony was witnessed by a gathering of officials
representing the United States, Great Britain, France, Germany,
Sweden and Norway, Japan, Portugal, the Netherlands, Belgium,
Denmark, Mexico, and Russia. Officers of American, British, and

French warships sent to honor the event stood at attention in their bright uniforms.

The ritual was a combination of the customs Kalakaua had seen used in Europe with the sacred observances of the ancient Hawaiian chiefs. The regalia included a costly jeweled crown, a scepter, and a sword of state, all made in Europe. Upon the king was bestowed the robe of Kamehameha I, made of 450,000 feathers of the *o-o* bird, while he stood beside the *puloulou* or tabu stick (a seven-foot tusk of narwhal) and the *kahili*, symbolic of Hawaiian chieftainship. With his own hands the man who had become king by ballot placed upon his head and that of his consort Kapiolani the royal crowns, which thereafter were never worn again.

Two days later a statue of Kamehameha the Great, erected in front of *Aliiolani Hale*, (now the state judiciary building) was unveiled by the king. The money for this statue was appropriated by the legislature of 1878 to commemorate the discovery of the islands by Captain Cook a hundred years before. T. R. Gould, an American sculptor residing in Italy, designed a statue which showed the robed founder of the kingdom gazing into the future with his hand clasped about the barbed *pololu*, a spear signifying peace. On its way from Italy, this statue had been lost in the sea at the Falkland Islands. A replica was then made, and it was this replica which was unveiled; it still stands in Honolulu. The original statue was later salvaged, and was set up in Kamehameha's homeland of Kohala, Hawaii.

The ideal of statesmanship personified in Kamehameha's statue had little influence upon the monarch who now, in his palace across the street, was pursuing a course which in the end brought ruin to the monarchy. In this course he was aided and abetted by Walter Murray Gibson. It is difficult to decide whether Kalakaua or Gibson was the more responsible for the unwise political and financial policies, and for the more than unwise practices, that prevailed during the years from 1880 to 1887.

Gibson, who became head of the cabinet in 1882, cleverly seconded Kalakaua's political aspirations. During the next five years Gibson held each of the cabinet posts, sometimes several of them at the same time. Other ministers came and went, but he stayed on. Gibson was well educated and at times shone with a perverted brilliance. Some of his ideas were good, but all were designed to promote his own interests; and he was completely unscrupulous in method. The result was a regime of political corruption such as might have been found in some of the larger cities of the United States at about the same time.

The legislative session of 1882 had been one of the most corrupt that had ever met in Honolulu. One of the first acts was to convey to Claus Spreckels, the sugar baron, some 24,000 acres of crown lands at Wailuku, Maui, to settle a claim which he had purchased for $10,000. The prohibition against furnishing intoxicating liquor to natives was repealed, with evil consequences. The appropriation bill was swelled to double the estimated government income. As a result of another bill, silver coins bearing the head of Kalakaua were minted in San Francisco and put into circulation; Spreckels made a profit of $150,000 on this coinage transaction.

Under the Gibson regime further scandals arose. In 1884, some Reform members were elected in spite of heavy government patronage to their opponents, and several noxious bills—such as one to charter a dubious "state bank," a bill to set up a lottery, and an opium licensing bill—were barely defeated. This opium bill was, however, passed by the legislature of 1886, and gave the government the right to sell an opium monopoly license for $30,000. Among the lesser scandals of the administration were the sale of public offices, defrauding of the customs revenue by abuse of royal privilege, illegal leasing of lands to the king, neglect of the public roads, and sale of exemptions to lepers, who might thereby escape being sent to Kalaupapa. The leper segregation and treatment program was allowed to break down, and the effect on the people can be studied in the labors of Father Damien, who died in 1889 in the leper settlement on Molokai, having himself fallen victim to the disease.

One of the most alarming political weapons in the armory of Gibson was the deliberate stirring up of racial antagonisms. His cry of "Hawaii for the Hawaiians" was designed to win the votes of the natives. To promote his secret slogan of "Hawaii for Gibson," he tried in every way to arouse hatred of non-Hawaiians—in particular those who had long resided in the islands and were prominent in business and social life.

Kalakaua's grandiose dream of heading a Pacific empire of native peoples was fostered by Gibson. Renewal of the reciprocity treaty in 1887 was clouded by international complications which arose when the colonial policies of Great Britain and Germany in the Pacific clashed with Kalakaua's vision of a Polynesian League which, under his leadership, would arise in that ocean.

Kalakaua, encouraged by Gibson, had attempted to form an alliance with Samoa as the first step in this scheme of empire. On December 23, 1886, he commissioned John E. Bush as envoy extraordinary and minister plenipotentiary to the king of Samoa. Bush and several companions arrived at Apia in January, 1887, and were welcomed by King Malietoa, who was thereupon presented with the Grand Cross of the Order of Oceania. A convention was concluded on February 17 between Samoa and Hawaii to form a political confederation, and Minister Carter in Washington was asked to represent Samoan as well as Hawaiian interests there.

The king of Hawaii formally ratified this agreement on March 20, and in order to make a show of his naval might, he hastily fitted out an old steamship to represent him in the South Pacific. This vessel, renamed the *Kaimiloa*, carried a crew composed mainly of boys released from the Honolulu house of correction. Before the ship sailed a disturbance broke out on board which resulted in the dismissal of three officers. When the *Kaimiloa* reached Samoan waters, trouble again erupted. R. L. Stevenson, who knew Samoa and knew mutineers, wrote of Kalakaua's disorderly navy: "The *Kaimiloa* was from the first a scene of disaster and dilapidation; the stores were sold; the crew revolted; for a great part of a night she was in the hands of mutineers, and the Secretary lay bound upon the deck."

The German government's annoyance was great. Since 1884, Prince Bismarck had played with the idea of building up a place in the sun among the islands of the South Pacific. The possibility that Kalakaua might support Malietoa in a conflict with rising German influence in Samoa could easily give Germany an excuse to intervene in Hawaii, where revolution was brewing. After Gibson's downfall in the summer of 1887, however, the Samoan "alliance" was quickly brought to an end and Kalakaua's South Sea bubble collapsed.

Many of the opponents of the Gibson regime belonged to a younger generation of citizens, some of them of foreign ancestry and others of native Hawaiian stock. Allied with them were many foreigners who had long resided in the country or who had identified themselves with it in a business or professional way. These men were concerned to see that the government was run honestly and efficiently. The spendthrift policy of Kalakaua was glaringly obvious; between 1880 and 1890, for example, the public debt rose from $388,900 (with a treasury balance almost enough to cover this sum) to $2,600,000. Financial extravagance and mismanagement, added to the outrageous political and other scandals since 1880, alienated nearly all the foreigners as well as many of the natives.

A secret political organization called the Hawaiian League was formed about the beginning of 1887. This league, which aimed to reform the government by means of a more liberal constitution, soon recruited hundreds of members in all parts of the kingdom. It comprised foreigners, Hawaiian citizens (both naturalized and those born in Hawaii of foreign parents), but no native Hawaiians belonged to it. Two factions developed within the league. One, the radicals, advocated the overthrow of the monarchy, the setting up of a republic, and annexation by the United

States. The other faction, the conservatives, were in the majority. They felt that Hawaii should remain independent but that the king should have his powers limited by a constitution that would permit the people to rule through their elected legislature, which would control the cabinet. Should the king refuse to accept such a constitution, the conservatives were ready to join with the radicals in an effort to overthrow the monarchy. The members of the league obtained arms, and were ready to fight if necessary to make their views prevail.

The immediate occasion for the outbreak of the Revolution of 1887 was a bribery affair connected with government licensing of the sale of opium. The king was shamefully involved. Revelation of the details of this affair aroused the anger of the citizenry against the king and against the system of government which permitted such iniquities.

The leaders of the Hawaiian League decided that the time for action had come. One man advocated a march on the palace by the league's riflemen, but this advice was overruled, and instead, a public mass meeting of protest was held on June 30, 1887, in the armory on Beretania Street. At this meeting, attended by people of all classes, creeds, and nationalities, unanimous resolutions were passed denouncing the government and demanding that the king dismiss his cabinet and the registrar of conveyances (who had acted as go-between in the opium bribery scandal), and that he make a pledge that he would never again interfere in politics.

Bloody revolution was avoided by this display of popular strength. The king, most of whose troops had deserted him, granted all the requests of the people with little delay. Before doing this, however, he called in the representatives of the United States, Great Britain, France, and Portugal, and offered to transfer to them his powers as king; but they refused and advised him to lose no time in signing a new constitution. A new cabinet was appointed and drew up a new constitution, which was signed by Kalakaua on July 6 and went into effect the next day. Gibson had been arrested on July 1, but the charge against him was nol-prossed and on July 12 he left Honolulu for San Francisco, where he died six months later.

The "Bayonet Constitution" of 1887 was a revision of the Constitution of 1864 promulgated by Kamehameha V, but it contained important changes. Cabinet ministers could not be dismissed by the king except in accordance with a vote of the legislature. No official act of the king would be valid unless approved by the cabinet. The king's veto of a bill could be over-ridden by a two-thirds vote of the legislature. Nobles, instead of being appointed by the king, were to be elected by voters who had a fairly large income or amount of property (in practice, this article placed the election of nobles in the hands of voters of foreign birth or ancestry). No member of the legislature, while in that position, could hold any other public office. Finally, the right to vote was extended to resident foreigners of American or European birth or descent if they took an oath to support the constitution.

The Reform ministry which came into office at this time included W. L. Green, premier and minister of finance; Godfrey Brown, minister of foreign affairs; Lorrin A. Thurston, minister of the interior; and Clarence W. Ashford, attorney general. These ministers gave the country an efficient administration, but some parts of their program antagonized the native Hawaiians. Thurston and Ashford were the most aggressive members of the cabinet, and their treatment of the king was rather brusque and unconcilia-tory, and further alienated him instead of winning him over to their policies.

Kalakaua naturally resented his loss of authority and prestige. He soon discovered that he still had some shreds of power—most valuable was the veto of legislative acts—and he used these skill-fully to annoy and sometimes to embarrass the ministers. The majority of the native Hawaiians greatly disliked the subordinate position in which the Constitution of 1887 placed them and were aggrieved that their highest *alii*, the king, had been stripped of so much of his power. On the other side, a widening rift showed itself in the ranks of the Reform Party and serious dissension arose within the cabinet.

For these and other reasons there developed, especially among the Hawaiians, a strong opposition to the Reform administration and the Constitution of 1887. The opposition came to a head in the insurrection of 1889 led by Robert W. Wilcox.

Wilcox was one of the students who had gone abroad with Moreno in 1880 at government expense. He studied engineering and military science in Italy, but was recalled in 1887 by the Reform cabinet, who did not think his education would be of great value to the nation. He immediately began plotting against the Reform administration and in 1889 formed a revolutionary organization which armed itself and prepared to take over the government. At dawn on the morning of July 30, with about one hundred and fifty followers, Wilcox surrounded the palace and government buildings and set up field pieces.

The king was not in the palace at the time. Lieutenant Robert Parker Waipa, head of the palace guards, refused to surrender. The cabinet acted quickly to suppress the revolt. The revolutionists took refuge in a large royal bungalow on the palace grounds, and were soon fired upon by a band of sharpshooters consisting mainly of *haole* residents. After a day of sniping by both sides, a white tablecloth was flown from one of the bungalow windows. Wilcox surrendered and the uprising was over, with the loss of seven revolutionaries dead and a dozen wounded.

Later, when Wilcox was tried for treason, he stated that he planned to take possession of the palace and have the king sign a new constitution which would restore the old prerogatives of the king and the people. He claimed to have the sanction of the king for his deeds; and he was acquitted by a native jury under the ancient doctrine that "the king could do no wrong."

The revolutionary movement had failed to dislodge the Reform cabinet. Political maneuvering was more successful. In the election that took place in the fall of 1887, the Reform Party was victorious. But the king soon rallied his forces and drew upon the large number of people who might still support him. He was aided by the formation of a society called the *Hui Kalaiaina* (Political Economy Party) among the native Hawaiians, whose purpose was to restore the Constitution of 1864. By working through this society and by other methods, the king's party grew stronger. The Reform Party, weakened by dissension, did not have a majority in the legislature of 1890. A serious quarrel among its own members and lack of support in the legislature caused the Reform cabinet to retire on June 13, and a compromise cabinet was appointed.

After the close of this legislative session in November, King Kalakaua, a sick man, left for California on the United States cruiser *Charleston*, hoping that his health would improve in a different climate. His condition grew worse instead of better. He died on January 20, 1891, in San Francisco. His body was brought back to his homeland on the *Charleston*, and amid a stately ceremony that would have pleased this ceremonious king, Kalakaua was buried on February 15. His sister, Liliuokalani, who had been regent in his absence, was proclaimed queen on January 29, and took the usual oath to support the constitution of the land.

CHAPTER SEVENTEEN

Liliuokalani and the Provisional Government

LILIUOKALANI came to the throne at a difficult moment in the history of Hawaii and her whole reign was one of trouble. It was a time of great economic distress. The political controversies which had characterized so much of the reign of Kalakaua quieted down in the latter part of 1890, but they were not settled and broke out with greater fury a year or two later. These causes of turbulence and the queen's determined hostility to the Constitution of 1887 brought on the crisis of January, 1893, and the downfall of the monarchy.

The new sovereign was in the full vigor of mature womanhood when she ascended the throne. A newspaper reporter who talked with her in 1893 described her face as "strong and resolute." "Her voice was musical and well modulated . . . and she spoke remarkably pure and graceful English. Her manner was dignified, and she had the ease and the authoritative air of one accustomed to rule." She had been educated in the Chiefs' Children's School and had long been a prominent member of the social group around the throne. She had taken an active part in benevolent work for her own race. Like other members of her family, Liliuokalani had a taste for music and a marked musical talent; her best memorial is her beautiful song *Aloha Oe*. Twice she had served as regent during her brother's absence from the kingdom, and she was well fitted to take firm hold of the reins of government. Her political ideas were similar to those of her brother, but she had a stronger will than Kalakaua and a resolute purpose to regain for the throne some of the power and prestige that it had lost during his reign.

The economic depression which gripped the country during the whole reign of Queen Liliuokalani stemmed from the McKinley Tariff Bill enacted by the American Congress in the summer of 1890. This law removed the tariff on all raw sugars imported into the United States from foreign countries and gave a bounty of two cents a pound to sugar producers in the United States. Thus at one stroke was wiped out the differential advantage that Hawaiian sugar had enjoyed in the American market over sugar produced in other foreign countries. The effect was disastrous. Property values dropped. The production of sugar fell off sharply. Employment was curtailed and wages cut. To alleviate as much as possible the evil effects of the McKinley Bill, a strong effort was made to negotiate a treaty providing for complete freedom of trade between the two countries, but it was impossible to agree on terms that were acceptable to both governments.

The depression caused by the McKinley tariff, coupled with the growing political strife, created an atmosphere or condition of the public mind that was very favorable for the growth of revolutionary ideas, and one in which the thought of annexation to the United States made a strong appeal to certain elements in the community. The situation posed a dilemma for the sugar planters and their agents. Annexation would result in political stability and it might, though this was by no means certain, give the sugar industry the benefit of the two-cent bounty on sugar; but it would almost certainly interfere seriously with the Hawaiian labor system.

Revolution and annexation were much talked about during these years, and a small Annexation Club, a secret organization, was formed in Honolulu in the spring of 1892, composed of *haoles* who had come to the conclusion that annexation offered the only hope for stable government in Hawaii.

The prelude to revolution was the long legislative session of 1892. In that session the fighting issues were control of the cabinet and the attempt to change the constitution. Two issues of lesser importance were an opium licensing bill and a lottery bill.

The members of the legislature were divided among three parties: the Reform Party; the National Reform Party, which supported the queen and her views; and the Liberal Party headed by R. W. Wilcox, J. E. Bush, and others, who at the outset opposed the queen and apparently favored any change that would give them a place in the government. In the spring of 1892 some of the Liberal group talked loudly about a republic and got themselves arrested for treason, but the charge was soon dropped.

The cabinet which had been appointed by Queen Liliuokalani soon after she ascended the throne belonged to the National Reform Party. After the legislature convened in 1892, the Reform and Liberal Party members formed a coalition—it was a strange combination—and on August 30 succeeded in voting the ministry out. Then they tried to bring into practice the principle, recognized in Great Britain, that the cabinet must be selected from the group in power in the legislature. The queen resisted this attempt and appointed successively two sets of ministers from among her own followers, each of which was quickly voted out by the legislature. She then, on November 8, named a cabinet composed entirely of members of the Reform Party. This looked like a concession and was so considered, but it may have been a shrewd move designed to divide the enemy. The Liberal Party leaders were displeased because they had not been given a place in the cabinet. Some of them turned against the Reform Party, aided in the passage of the opium and lottery bills, and on January 12 combined with the National Reform Party in voting out of office the recently appointed cabinet.

The legislature was to close two days later. The queen signed the opium and the lottery bills and appointed a cabinet from her own party. These acts were severely criticized, but if the queen had been content with her victory thus far, it is entirely probable that there would have been no serious trouble. But she had decided to do away with the hateful Constitution of 1887 (even though she had sworn to maintain it) and her attempt to do so led swiftly to the overthrow of the monarchy.

The queen's decision was the culmination of a movement running through nearly the whole period since 1887, aimed at securing important changes in the constitution or a new one modeled more or less on that of 1864. One method proposed was the holding of a convention. This plan had been given the strong support of both Kalakaua and Liliuokalani, but it was defeated in the legislative sessions of 1890 and 1892.

The queen's new constitution, much like that of 1864, had been prepared. All arrangements had been made for its promulgation immediately after the prorogation of the legislature, which occurred at noon on Saturday, January 14. The queen thought it was necessary for the members of the cabinet to sign the constitution. The ministers, knowing the temper of the community, refused to sign and warned her of the fatal consequences of her proposed action. There was a long and heated argument, but the ministers persisted in their refusal, and late in the afternoon the queen announced to the expectant crowd outside the palace that the grant of a new constitution would be postponed for a while.

Reports of the queen's proposed action aroused a storm in the community comparable to those of 1880 and 1887. On Saturday afternoon a Committee of Safety was organized to study the situation and plan whatever actions might be considered necessary. The committee, dominated by members of the Annexation Club, decided that the time had come to abrogate the monarchy, set up a provisional government, and apply for annexation to the United States. This decision, of course, was not announced publicly. To test the sentiments of the people, a mass meeting was held on Monday afternoon, at which resolutions were adopted denouncing the action of the queen and authorizing the Committee of Safety to do whatever was necessary "to secure the protection of life, liberty and property in Hawaii."

The queen and her advisers became alarmed and on Monday morning they issued a notice saying that no change would be made in the constitution except in the way presented by the constitution itself. But this promise came too late.

The Committee of Safety proceeded with its plans and preparations. On Tuesday afternoon, January 17, they took possession of the government office building, *Aliiolani Hale,* and read from the steps a proclamation abrogating the monarchy and setting up a Provisional Government headed by Judge Sanford B. Dole, "to exist until terms of union with the United States of America have been negotiated and agreed upon." A volunteer military force was quickly organized, and before nightfall the situation was well under control. Upon the demand of the Provisional Government, the queen surrendered her authority in a document in which she protested against the acts of the revolutionists and stated that she "yielded to the superior force of the United States . . . until such time as the Government of the United States shall upon the facts being presented to it undo the action of its representative and reinstate me in the authority which I claim as the Constitutional Sovereign of the Hawaiian Islands."

The wording of this document was based upon the fact that on Monday afternoon, United States Minister John L. Stevens had caused troops to be landed in Honolulu from the cruiser *Boston.* He stated that this was done for the protection of American lives and property. It was well known, however, that Stevens favored annexation and was very friendly with the group to which the revolutionists belonged. By the queen and her advisers, his action was taken to mean that he would recognize and protect the Provisional Government. He did in fact very quickly recognize that government.

Without delay, the Provisional Government appointed five commissioners to proceed to Washington and negotiate for the annexation of Hawaii to the United States. The commissioners had a very friendly reception in the American capital, and a treaty of annexation was quickly drawn up. It was signed on February 14, 1893, and immediately submitted to the Senate by President Harrison, but the Senate failed to act upon it in the few days remaining before the change of administration.

President Cleveland, upon the advice of his secretary of state,

Walter Q. Gresham, withdrew the treaty from the Senate and sent to Hawaii a special commissioner, James H. Blount, to make an investigation of the circumstances relating to the overthrow of the Hawaiian monarchy. Blount flatly charged that the revolution was the result of a conspiracy between Minister Stevens and the revolutionary leaders. On the basis of Blount's report, President Cleveland came to the conclusion that the United States ought to undo the revolution and put Liliuokalani back in power. For that purpose he sent a new minister, Albert S. Willis, to Honolulu. Willis made an honest effort to carry out his mission, but it was an impossible task. The Provisional Government refused to give up. Furthermore, it emphatically denied the truth of Blount's charges and said that the United States government had no right to meddle in this way in the internal affairs of Hawaii. Congress thought that the United States should follow a hands-off policy, and therefore President Cleveland could take no further action.

These developments extended into the spring of 1894. Relations with the United States necessarily absorbed much of the time of the Provisional Government, but its leaders gave needed attention to internal administration and local affairs. As few changes as possible were made in the civil service. The former royal palace was made the executive building of the government and *Aliiolani Hale* became the judiciary building. Amendments were made in existing laws to conform to the new style of government. Among legislative acts of the Provisional Government were the repeal of the opium and lottery laws recently enacted, an act to create the fire department of Honolulu, one to establish and regulate the National Guard of Hawaii, and one to provide for a constitutional convention. This last act foreshadowed the establishment of the Republic of Hawaii.

Book 5

Hawaii in Transition

(1894–1900)

CHAPTER EIGHTEEN

The Republic of Hawaii

THE Republic of Hawaii was a kind of interim government. Its purposes, all of which were successfully carried out, were to give a greater appearance of regularity and permanence than did the Provisional Government, to keep the way clear for annexation whenever the United States government became ready to take up that question again, and in the mean time to maintain in authority the group that had carried through the Revolution of 1893. The constitution of the Republic contained a number of novel features, and the government thus set up, during its short life of six years, had several rather difficult problems to deal with in domestic affairs and in foreign relations.

The Provisional Government by its origin, its name, and its form was recognized as being a temporary affair. When it became clear that annexation was not possible during the term of President Cleveland, attention was directed to setting up a permanent government for the Hawaiian Islands. An act was passed on March 15, 1894, providing for the holding of a constitutional convention, to consist of the president and the eighteen members of the executive and advisory councils of the Provisional Government and also eighteen delegates chosen by voters whose qualifications were defined in such a way as to make certain that they were supporters of the regime. Of the delegates elected, fifteen were Hawaiian born and five were native Hawaiians.

The convention met on May 30, 1894. A draft of a proposed constitution, largely the work of President Dole and Lorrin A. Thurston, was submitted to the convention by the executive council as a basis for discussion. This was thoroughly debated and many amendments in detail were made by the convention. The completed constitution was adopted by the convention on July 3. By its own terms, and also by authority of an act of the Provisional Government approved on July 3, the new constitution was promulgated and became effective on the Fourth of July, 1894, as the constitution of the Republic of Hawaii.

The government created by this document was in many respects similar to that of the United States. There was an executive body consisting of the president, elected by the legislature for a term of six years and not eligible for re-election, and the four cabinet members appointed by him; a legislature of two houses, Senate and House of Representatives, each having fifteen members; and a judiciary similar to that already existing. There was also a council of state—this was a unique feature—of fifteen members, which had power to appropriate money in times of national emergency when the legislature was not in session. Members of the legislature and voters had to be able to speak, read, and write either English or Hawaiian, and they also had to take an oath to support the Republic of Hawaii and promise not to "encourage or assist in the restoration or establishment of a monarchical form of Government in the Hawaiian Islands." Property qualifications were prescribed for members of the legislature and for voters eligible to elect senators. The constitution contained some material not usually found in such documents, as for example provisions relating to naturalization, registration, and voting. Some of the requirements for naturalization were designed to exclude orientals from citizenship unless they were born in Hawaii, just as the language qualification of voters was intended to debar orientals from voting. The constitution named Sanford B. Dole as president of the Republic until the end of the year 1900.

This was a republic more in name than in origin or in actual fact. The men who devised the constitution did not believe that a democracy in a full sense, with universal suffrage, was a workable form of government for Hawaii under the conditions existing in 1894, but they believed that in time such a government could be made to work satisfactorily. They recognized, although they did not say so publicly, that the Republic of Hawaii was a combination of minority rule with a representative form of government. What they were trying to provide for was an efficient government and honest administration.

Liliuokalani protested to Great Britain and the United States against the establishment of the Republic, but the protest was unavailing. The new government was soon recognized by all the foreign powers with which Hawaii had diplomatic relations.

During the summer and fall of 1894, partisans of the former queen, including some foreigners, made secret plans and collected weapons and ammunition to be used in an armed attempt to restore the monarchy. The time set for the uprising was early on the morning of January 7, 1895, but rumors had put the government on guard, and an advance unit of the insurrectionists was intercepted at Waikiki on the night of January 6. In a brief exchange of shots, a prominent supporter of the government, Charles L. Carter, was mortally wounded. Martial law was proclaimed. During the next few days, two or three skirmishes occurred and several of the rebels were killed and some wounded. Within two weeks the revolutionary uprising was completely suppressed and its leaders, including Robert W. Wilcox, were captured.

About two hundred persons in all were arrested for active or passive complicity in the rebellion. Among them were Liliuokalani and her two nephews, the young princes David Kawananakoa and Jonah Kuhio Kalanianaole. While confined under mild imprisonment in the former royal palace, Liliuokalani signed and sent to President Dole a document in which she formally abdicated and renounced all claims to the throne; she also signed the oath of allegiance to the Republic of Hawaii, and announced her intention to live quietly as a private citizen.

The prisoners were tried for treason and lesser offenses by a military commission created for the purpose, and nearly all were found guilty. Heavy sentences—death in a few cases—were imposed by the military court. But on the insistence of President Dole and a substantial body of public opinion, a policy of clemency was adopted. The death sentences were commuted to imprisonment, and the pardoning power was used so generously that all offenders were free within a few months.

Victory of the government over the insurrectionists put the Republic of Hawaii in a strong position and enabled it to give needed attention to problems of local administration and foreign relations.

One of the most troublesome of these was the perennial question of labor supply and population. The Wilson-Gorman Act passed by Congress in 1894 discontinued the bonus to sugar producers in the United States and restored the tariff on sugar imported into that country, so that the Hawaiian sugar industry once more enjoyed the benefits conferred by the reciprocity treaty. Consequently the labor question again became urgent. In the 1880's the government had, with some difficulty, begun the introduction of contract laborers from Japan in order to counterbalance the Chinese, and restrictions had been placed upon the immigration of Chinese. In the 1890's the situation was reversed. The Hawaiian authorities found, as one writer notes, that " the antidote had been over-applied." By 1896, the Japanese comprised nearly a fourth of the whole population. There were real fears that Hawaii might become a Japanese colony. Various measures were therefore adopted to reduce the volume of Japanese immigration and to encourage the immigration of Chinese. Yet during three years (1895-1897) that this policy was followed, the number of Japanese immigrants still exceeded the Chinese by more than two thousand. In the same period, 723 Portuguese and 227 German immigrants were brought in under government auspices.

After 1894 the immigration of Japanese was a voluntary movement, that is, it was not dependent upon the labor convention of 1886, and was conducted by several emigration companies in Japan chartered by the Japanese government. In 1896 the Hawaiian officials became convinced that frauds were being practiced by these companies in order to evade the restrictions imposed by the Hawaiian government, and in the spring of 1897 the immigration authorities in Honolulu refused admission to about twelve hundred Japanese immigrants on the ground of such frauds. The Japanese government came to the defense of the rejected immigrants and a sharp controversy developed between the two governments. Besides the immigration question, there were a few other points in dispute. While the diplomatic contest was in progress between Hawaii and Japan, the question of annexation of Hawaii to the United States became active again.

The victory of the Republican Party in the election of 1896 awakened strong hopes among the annexationists both in Hawaii and in the United States. It is true that president-elect McKinley had not, during the campaign, shown any interest in the Hawaiian question, but the party platform was favorable to annexation and there was a strong expansionist faction among the Republicans.

Efforts to gain the support of the new president in the cause of annexation were successful, but for several months the attention of the administration and Congress (in special session) was absorbed by the work of tariff revision. Powerful interests in the United States, including the sugar trust and the rapidly growing beet sugar industry, with both of which Claus Spreckels was now associated, were again demanding abrogation of the Hawaiian reciprocity treaty. Under these circumstances, a new annexation treaty was negotiated. It was signed at Washington on June 16, 1897, and was transmitted to the Senate on the same day by President McKinley. The treaty was not approved by the Senate during the special session of Congress, but came up for action in the regular session which began in December. In Hawaii the treaty was approved by the Hawaiian Senate and was signed by President Dole on September 10, 1897.

In the United States, the same interests which opposed the reciprocity treaty opposed also the treaty of annexation and were able to prevent favorable action upon it. Though it was clear that a majority of the senators would vote for the treaty, the majority was a little short of the two thirds necessary for ratification. Hence it was decided to try a different method of annexation, by a joint resolution which would require only a simple majority of each house of Congress. This method had been followed in the annexation of Texas in 1845. Two such resolutions were introduced, one in the Senate on March 16, 1898, and one in the House of Representatives on May 4.

Between these two dates the Spanish-American War began and the American squadron under Commodore Dewey won its sensational victory over the Spanish naval force in the Philippines. The Hawaiian government threw aside its neutrality and did all it could to aid the Americans. Pearl Harbor had not been developed under the lease of 1887, and Honolulu became a mid-ocean stopover for the United States troops that were sent across the Pacific to follow up Dewey's victory. The American soldiers were enthusiastically welcomed and given a taste of Hawaiian hospitality. The first Hawaiian Red Cross group was formed at this time to render service to the "boys in blue."

The war gave decisive support to the cause of annexation. The joint resolution that had been introduced in the House of Representatives was passed by that body on June 15; it was then passed by the Senate on July 6, and signed by President McKinley the following day. News of the Senate's action was received in Honolulu on July 13 amid great excitement.

The idea of annexation was not palatable to the Japanese nation, which had just won a war against China and was now the leading Asiatic power. In June, 1897, within a few days after the signing of the annexation treaty, the Japanese government formally protested to the United States against the proposed annexation, on the grounds that it would disturb the status quo in the Pacific and that it would endanger the rights of Japanese subjects in Hawaii and might postpone the settlement of the pending claims of Japan against the Hawaiian government.

The United States government denied that any Japanese interests would be jeopardized by the contemplated union and gave assurances that all vested rights of Japan and Japanese subjects would be respected. Ultimately Japan withdrew the protest against annexation, but she continued to press her claims against the Hawaiian government. The latter suggested arbitration. Japan agreed, but only on conditions that were wholly unacceptable to Hawaii. After the annexation resolution was approved, the American government urged very strongly that the differences between Japan and Hawaii be settled before Hawaii's problems were turned over to the United States along with its sovereignty. Finally the Hawaiian government, without admitting that its position was wrong, agreed to pay an indemnity of $75,000 and Japan accepted that sum as a full satisfaction of her claims.

Transfer of the sovereignty of the Republic of Hawaii to the United States took place in a short but impressive ceremony on August 12, 1898. On that day, to the sound of twenty-one gun salutes from shore batteries and the U.S.S. *Philadelphia*, the Hawaiian Islands became a part of the great American republic. In form, however, the government of the islands continued to be that of the Republic of Hawaii for nearly two years longer. The annexation resolution said in substance that the existing government should continue, subject to the direction of the President of the United States, until Congress made some other provision for the government of the islands. It was expected that Congress would do this very soon, but a long delay occurred because of the great questions of national policy resulting from the war with Spain. For two years, therefore, President Dole and his associates carried on the government virtually under the constitutions and laws of two countries at once, but subject always to the higher authority of the president of the United States.

A speculative boom in sugar began immediately after annexation had been effected. The numerous projects for expansion of sugar production created a large demand for more laborers. The annexation resolution put a stop to Chinese immigration but left the way open for immigrants of other races. Some plans were made for bringing laborers from Europe, and a small number arrived from that region, but the broad stream of immigration flowed from Japan. During the two years 1898 and 1899, 24,524 men and 5,152 women arrived from that country. Although many of the earlier immigrants returned to Japan, the census of 1900 showed that Japanese (to the number of 61,111) comprised about two-fifths of the whole population.

Probably the worst problem that troubled the government and the people of Hawaii in this short period was an epidemic of bubonic plague which broke out just at the end of 1899. Five cases resulting in five deaths were reported on December 12. There had been an epidemic of cholera in 1895, but this was potentially more dangerous, and drastic measures were taken to control it. Reports of Board of Health officials and volunteer inspectors who went into the infected district revealed almost unbelievable over-crowding and fearfully insanitary conditions existing in the slum area of Honolulu, within which most of the cases occurred. The connection between rats and the plague was suspected even if not clearly understood, and rat-control was practiced. Quarantine, in-spection, and disinfection were the methods first used in fighting the epidemic. These proved inadequate, and the officials then resorted to the burning of buildings known to be infected. On January 20 one of the official fires got out of control and before nightfall nearly thirty-eight acres of "Chinatown" slums had been reduced to ashes and more than four thousand persons rendered homeless. This purge by fire did not destroy the disease, and it was not until April 30 that the epidemic was officially declared to be over and the port quarantine removed. There had been eighty cases of plague and seventy deaths, most of them in Honolulu; and there had been huge losses by fire and disruption of business.

By a curious coincidence, April 30, 1900, was also the day on which President McKinley approved the "act to provide a govern-ment for the Territory of Hawaii," the Organic Act which was to be Hawaii's constitution for more than half a century.

Book 6

Hawaii, from Territory to State

(1900 — 1959)

CHAPTER NINETEEN

Territorial Rule

HAWAII became, about two years after annexation, an incorporated territory of the United States, and in that status it was
destined to continue for nearly sixty years. Under the American system of government, the territorial status is one of preparation for statehood. It has been shown in earlier chapters that
American influence had for decades been very powerful in this
group of islands and had been decisive in shaping most of its
institutions. President Lincoln, in a letter to Elisha Allen in 1864,
had written of Hawaii: "Its people are free, and its laws, language,
and religion are largely the fruit of our own teaching and example." Nevertheless, becoming an actual American territory necessi-
tated many little changes and adjustment in the details of government, in politics, and in social and economic relationships. These
developments will be sketched in the following pages. Attention
will be given first to those which relate to government and
politics.

The annexation resolution ("Newlands Resolution") directed
the president of the United States to appoint five commissioners
to recommend to Congress "such legislation concerning the
Hawaiian Islands as they shall deem necessary or proper." The
commissioners appointed by President McKinley were three members of Congress—Senators S. M. Cullom and J. T. Morgan and
Representative R. R. Hitt—and two citizens of Hawaii, S. B.
Dole and W. F. Frear. The commissioners held a series of meetings and conducted hearings in Honolulu and other places in the

islands in the fall of 1898, and their report was presented to Congress in December of that year.

The most important work of the commission was the drafting of a bill to provide a government for the Territory of Hawaii. The bill as drafted gave the outline of a government following in general the familiar American pattern and similar in many respects to that of the Republic of Hawaii. It contained a few features, some of them copied from the constitution of the Republic of Hawaii, which were unorthodox from the American standpoint and not to be found in state constitutions or in the organic acts of territories on the mainland. Most important of these were sections prescribing property qualifications for members of both houses of the legislature and for voters for senators; the section on citizenship was so drawn as to exclude all orientals, even those who were citizens of the Republic of Hawaii; another section placed the appointment of the territorial judges in the hands of the governor, a power usually reserved to the president; one section made the supreme court of the territory the judge in cases of contested elections of legislators instead of leaving that function to the two houses respectively; still another section permitted a voter to concentrate all his votes for representatives on one candidate; and there were a few other minor novelties in the bill.

The bill prepared by the commission was introduced in both houses of Congress in December, 1898, but congressional action was long delayed and it was not until April 30, 1900, that the bill, as amended by House and Senate, received the approval of President McKinley and became a law. The Organic Act went into effect on June 14, 1900, and on that day Hawaii became an organized territory of the United States. Sanford B. Dole was appointed by the President as first governor of the territory. There had been vigorous opposition in Congress to the exceptional and novel features in the original bill for the territorial government, and most of them were removed. Congress wanted Hawaii to be a truly American territory, with the greatest possible measure of self-government and with no property qualifications limiting the right to vote.

There were numerous amendments to the Organic Act, but none of these affected the general structure of the territorial government, which as set up was similar to that of most of the states of the Union. The differences arose from the controlling authority possessed by the national government. The Congress, having erected the territorial government, could also abolish it and substitute some other, such as a commission government or even military or naval administration. The principal executive officers of the territory, the governor and the secretary, were appointed by the President; the secretary became acting governor in event of the absence or disability of the governor. Heads of the various departpartments of the territorial government were appointed by the governor. Judges of all courts of record in the territory (territorial supreme court and circuit courts, and a federal district court) were appointed by the President; district magistrates, corresponding to justices of the peace in some states, were appointed by the chief justice of the territorial supreme court. The legislature consisted of two houses (Senate, fifteen members, and House of Representatives, thirty members); it could pass laws on substantially the same range of subjects as do state legislatures, but Congress had the right to amend or invalidate any territorial law. Actually, Congress never exercised this right.

By virtue of the Organic Act all persons who had been citizens of Hawaii at the time of annexation became citizens of the United States. Under this Act the people of the island territory—the common people—had more political power than they had ever possessed under their native kings. For more than twenty years after 1900 the Hawaiians (including part-Hawaiians) comprised an absolute majority of the electorate, and for another decade they outnumbered any other racial group in the voting population. For many years, therefore, the native Hawaiians had the power to say who should sit in the territorial legislature.

At first they showed a tendency to follow unwise and irresponsible leaders. The results of the first election were not encouraging to the cause of good government. Preliminary to this election, Republican and Democratic party organizations were formed. In addition, there was organized a Home Rule Party, one of whose slogans was "Hawaii for the Hawaiians." Robert W. Wilcox was the Home Rule candidate for delegate to Congress. He was elected, and the Home Rulers also won a substantial majority in each house of the legislature. The first legislative session was one long wrangle, with many days wasted in debate on trivial matters. It came to be called the "Lady Dog Legislature," because it spent so much time on a bill to reduce the tax on female dogs, a bill which finally became a law over the governor's veto.

The people soon gained political experience and learned the folly of irresponsible leadership. Wilcox, when he sought re-election in 1902, was defeated by his Republican opponent, Prince Jonah Kuhio Kalanianaole. The latter continued to serve as Hawaii's delegate to Congress until his death in 1922. The racially slanted Home Rule Party was not a really serious factor after the first two elections and it disappeared following the 1912 campaign. Improvement in the behavior of the body politic is reflected in comments contained in the annual reports of the governor to the Secretary of the Interior. Governor Dole (1900–1903) was very critical of the conduct and accomplishments of the first two legislatures. Not many years later, Governor Frear (1907–1913) wrote in complimentary terms of the businesslike attitude of the three legislatures which met during his administration and the excellent work done by them. Since that period, not all Hawaii's legislatures have deserved unstinted praise, but the general average has been high enough to compare favorably with legislatures of the states on the mainland. Their deliberations have resulted in placing much progressive legislation on the statute books.

In one respect, however, the legislature signally failed to perform its duty, by persistently refusing to reapportion its own membership. The original apportionment of members in the legislature was based approximately on the population as distributed among the islands in 1900. This basis gave Oahu six of the fifteen senators and twelve of the thirty representatives. The Organic Act directed the legislature to reapportion its membership after each decennial census. Since 1900 the population has increased much more rapidly on Oahu than it has in the rest of the territory. By 1930 Oahu had more than half, by 1940 more than three-fifths of the total population, and it was therefore entitled to more than half the seats in the legislature. But all attempts at reapportionment were defeated by the adverse votes of members from the other islands.

Decentralization of the government by the creation of counties was a very live issue during the early years of the territory. There was a strong local demand for such action, especially by residents of the islands other than Oahu. A badly drawn and defective act was passed by the first legislature (1901) but was killed by a pocket veto. A committee of the United States Senate which conducted an investigation into Hawaiian affairs in 1902 commented at great length and in a sharply critical tone about the absence of local governments and recommended that Congress pass a county government act for the territory if the legislature failed to do so during its next session. The legislature of 1903 passed such an act, but it was declared unconstitutional. A new act was passed in 1905. This survived the constitutional test, and the county governments came into existence in July of that year. In 1907 a law was enacted creating a municipal government for the "City and County of Honolulu," including the whole island of Oahu, and this superseded the Oahu County government at the beginning of January, 1909.

The major problems in setting up these local governments centered about the division of the functions of government between the territorial and county organizations and the adjustment of their financial requirements. The arrangements first made were not entirely satisfactory and these problems became a continuing source of controversy. Nearly every legislature has dealt with them in some way, and the subject was considered in the convention of 1950 which drafted the constitution for the state of Hawaii. Article 7 of the state constitution gives to the legislature, authority to create local governments in the state possessing such powers as are conferred by general laws. It removes one source of frequent irritation in the relations between the local and the territorial governments found in the practice of giving legislative mandates to the counties, laws requiring the latter to make certain payments or to perform certain acts, many of them being things that the local governments would not do of their own free will or would not do in the way the legislature commanded.

Financial problems were especially difficult in the early years because, upon the establishment of the territorial government, the customs revenues were diverted to the federal government, but the latter did not assume all the obligations to which those revenues formerly had been applied. For this reason and because of the added expense of the county governments, the territory had to find some new sources of revenue. The first important innovation was the enactment of an income tax (1901). Such a tax had been tried, not very successfully, in some of the states. Hawaii was a pioneer in putting into effect a workable tax of this type. As the territory grew in population and in economic stature, attaining industrial and civic maturity, government finances became big business. In 1901 receipts of the territorial government were $2,140,297; expenditures were $2,818,382. For the fiscal year 1958 the corresponding figures (for territorial and local governments) were about $200,000,000 and $195,000,000. In 1957 the legislature enacted (over the governor's veto) a tax law making important changes in the tax system which had, as one result, a large increase in the revenue from taxes. Most students of the subject will be likely to agree that, on the whole, Hawaii's governmental financial problems have been well handled.

For over fifty years Hawaii's political complexion predominantly Republican, though many Democrats, some appointed and some elected, have held public offices in the territory and its sub-

Hawaii Visitors Bureau

1. The power of erosion: Waimea Canyon on the island of Kauai, carved out of ancient lava by the waters running from Mount Waialeale, "wettest spot on earth."

2. A crater in the sky: part of the world's largest dormant volcano—Haleakala, "the House of the Sun," on the island of Maui. The Hawaiian Islands are composed of volcanic peaks.

Hawaii Visitors Bureau

3. Kamehameha I
(the Great)

4. Kamehameha II
(Liholiho)

The First Kings of Hawaii
(photos from Public Archives of Hawaii)

5. Kamehameha III
(Kauikeaouli)

6. Kamehameha IV
(Alexander Liholiho)

7. Kamehameha V
(Lot Kamehameha)

8. William C. Lunalilo

The Later Rulers of Hawaii
(photos from Public Archives of Hawaii)

9. David Kalakaua

10. Liliuokalani

11. Today the famed Nuuanu Pali is a peaceful beauty spot; but in 1795 the invading army of Kamehameha the Great forced many of the defenders of Oahu to plunge over the vertical cliffs of this windward escarpment.

12. Early view of Lahainaluna Seminary, Protestant mission high school for boys founded in 1831 on the island of Maui. Reproduced from an engraving made on copper by a student at the school.

13. Early view of the Honolulu waterfront from the sea, from a drawing made soon after the middle of the nineteenth century.

14. The southeastern part of the town of Hanarura at Oahu, 1826.

15. Looking along Queen Street toward Diamond Head, with old fort of Honolulu at lower right; Court House beyond corner of fort; Kawaiahao Church in background. Lithograph, G. H. Burgess, 1857.

16. First street tramway in Honolulu opened January 1, 1889.

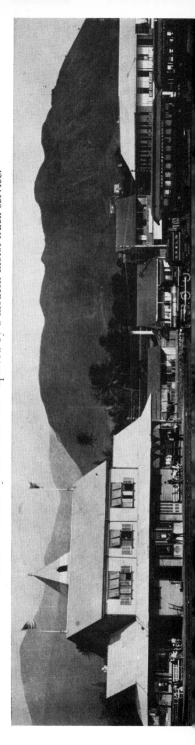

17. The days of the windjammers: sugar clippers and inter-island schooners moored in Honolulu Harbor, 1882.

18. Early railroading days: Oahu Railway and Land Company Depot in Honolulu about 1890. Recently the operations of this rail system have been replaced by a modern motor-truck service.

19. The king's cottage in Waikiki in the 1860's. It occupied the present site of the Royal Hawaiian Hotel.

20. Hawaii becomes a part of the United States. Transfer of sovereignty, August 12, 1898; at Iolani Palace, Sanford B. Dole, president of the Republic of Hawaii and later its first governor, paves the way for annexation and fifty years of territorial government.

divisions. In fifty-nine years the territory had twelve governors, seven of them being Republicans (total length of service, thirty-three years) and five Democrats (twenty-six years). Because the governor was appointed by the president, the governorship was not a barometer of local politics. Election results give the best indication of political trends. Until 1954 the Republicans were particularly successful in electing their legislative candidates, obtaining strong majorities in both houses of the legislature in every election except those of 1900 (when the Home Rulers were victorious) and 1946. In the latter election the Republicans gained a majority of one in each house, but a special election to fill a vacancy converted the majority in the House of Representatives to a tie, and the result was an unseemly squabble between Republicans and Democrats in the legislative session of 1947. In the elections for delegate to Congress, the Democrats were successful five times out of thirty-one, the Home Rulers once, the Republicans twenty-five times.

However, in the election of local officials, especially of the City and County of Honolulu, the Democrats have shown greater strength. As a result of these elections, Democrats have occupied the mayor's office for a greater number of years than have Republicans. Other elective local offices have been divided between the parties. During much of the time, the mayor and the majority of the Board of Supervisors have been of opposite political faiths, and this has not always been conducive to the efficient and harmonious carrying on of the public business.

After the close of World War II, organized labor became an important factor in local politics, generally on the side of the Democratic party. The CIO (ILWU) Political Action Committee was largely responsible for Democratic successes in the 1946 election. The PAC was then discontinued, but in the next few years the ILWU sought to gain control of the Democratic party, although it continued to indorse a few Republican candidates. Support from organized labor has strengthened the Democratic party, but at the same time has been a cause of dissension within the party. In the elections of 1954, 1956, and 1958, the Democrats won and retained firm control of both houses of the territorial legislature.

The summary account which has just been given of the territory's political development may be supplemented with a brief review of some features of the successive gubernatorial administrations.

Governor Sanford B. Dole (1900–1903) and Governor George R. Carter (1903–1907) guided the territory through the period of adjustment to the new American pattern of government, including the formation of the county governments and some modification of the central administration. So many of the early territorial legislators were new at the game, full of weird ideas and a determination to have their own way, that the first two governors had hard work getting the lawmakers to deal seriously and realistically with matters of public business that were really important. But legislators acquired experience and learned to take a broader view of their duties as well as their privileges. Governor Carter got along with the legislature rather better than his predecessor.

Governor Walter F. Frear (1907–1913), in his inaugural address, described the seven preceding years as a time of adjustment and reconciliation; not all the problems had been solved, but a better spirit existed and it was possible to look ahead with optimism. This administration was characterized by careful management of the territory's fiscal affairs. It was a time of prosperity, making possible rather large expenditures for harbor improvements, road construction, and other public works. Frear gave special attention to the problem of homesteading and land settlement and did much to correct serious abuses that had crept into the application of the basic land act of 1895. He antagonized certain interests, but was completely successful in defending the policies of his administration from charges that were brought.

Governor Lucius E. Pinkham (1913–1918) was the first of the Democratic governors; he probably owed his appointment to the excellent record he had made as president of the Board of

Health. Since the first World War began only a few months after Pinkham's inauguration, the greater part of his administration was much concerned with "preparedness" and Hawaii's participation in the war. A conspicuous feature of the early years was the building up of the National Guard in the territory. Two other matters in which Pinkham was greatly interested were the development of a civic center for Honolulu and the Waikiki reclamation scheme, the latter being a sanitary measure for draining and filling a large area of swamp land back from the beach. He did much to promote these projects but actual construction work upon them started after the war in McCarthy's administration and was continued during the prosperous years of the Farrington regime.

Governor Charles J. McCarthy (1918–1921) came into office only a few months before the end of the war and therefore had the task of getting the territory back to a peacetime basis. He carried on the improvement projects bequeathed to him by his predecessor. McCarthy believed that Hawaii's progress during two decades as a territory and her record in the war demonstrated that the islands were ready for statehood. He therefore recommended to the legislature (1919) the adoption of a memorial to Congress on this subject. He was the first governor to give such support to the statehood movement.

A few months before Governor Wallace R. Farrington (1921–1929) stepped out of office, he summed up one phase of his administration in these words: "The conspicuous advance step of recent years has been to bring the machinery of public administration up to a more modern standard." This had been done by a reorganization of the accounting systems of the territory and the counties, establishment of a retirement system for public employees, and a scientific classification of personnel employed by the government. He advocated an equalization of taxes and a careful study of the whole tax system. Farrington's two terms coincided almost exactly with the "normalcy" era of Harding and Coolidge. Hawaii shared in the prosperity of that period, and the territorial and county governments were able to spend large sums for public improvements. One notable result was that Honolulu had its "face lifted" by a phenomenal program of public and private building, so that the island metropolis came to look like a modern American city. Farrington was intensely devoted to American ideals and sought to promote them by strengthening the school system and by other appropriate measures.

Governor Lawrence M. Judd (1929–1934) had hardly gotten well settled in the executive office when the stock market crash in New York gave warning of financial trouble ahead. As the depression settled over the islands, the governor had the unpleasant duty of initiating drastic cuts in salaries and other territorial spending. As a further consequence of the depression, this administration had to deal with the problem of widespread unemployment in the territory. Judd had other troubles. A crime of violence (the Massie case), greatly magnified by newspaper publicity, brought upon the territory and its people an avalanche of criticism, much of it entirely unjustified, and for a time there was serious danger that Hawaii, as a result of congressional action, might be subjected to a carpetbag regime. The governor, ably assisted by many citizens, put up a strong defense. The legislature in special and regular sessions enacted remedial laws, and the danger was averted.

Governor Joseph B. Poindexter's first term (1934–1938) fell in the depression years and followed the pattern of economy set by the preceding administration. It was in this period that the movement for statehood got well under way. A strong impetus was given to this movement by the realization of how completely Hawaii was under the control of Congress so long as her status continued to be that of a territory—a realization brought home forcibly to industrial and civic leaders of the territory by developments following the enactment of the discriminatory Jones-Costigan sugar control act in the spring of 1934. Progress of the statehood movement was interrupted by World War II, which struck the islands in the midst of Poindexter's second term (1938–1942) with the Japanese attack on the naval base at Pearl Harbor.

CHAPTER TWENTY

American Hawaii: The Land and the People

THE political and governmental developments just described were only part of the process of changing Hawaii into an American community. Before and after annexation, many persons both in Hawaii and on the mainland were very critical of certain conditions in the islands which differed noticeably from those in the states; among these were the racial composition of Hawaii's population, with its large proportion of oriental aliens, and the absence of a substantial farming middle class. Oriental aliens could not become American citizens. Their children born in the islands were American citizens by virtue of the Organic Act and the Constitution of the United States. Were they Americans in spirit or could they be made so?

Some critics of the Hawaiian scene seemed to think that Americanization was a process that would not work on people of oriental ancestry as it did on those of European origin. These critics thought that if the population of Hawaii was to be Americanized, this would have to be done by bringing into the islands a large number of American citizens from the mainland or people from Europe who would be eligible for naturalization. If this were done, it was assumed, many of the newcomers would acquire homesteads and thus augment the middle-class farm group. Immigration and homesteading were therefore thought of as instruments of Americanization.

Homesteading, as part of general land policy, has rather a long history in Hawaii. It should be pointed out, however, that homesteading as practiced in the islands is quite different from homesteading on the mainland. In continental United States this was a method by which immense areas of virgin land were brought into cultivation as farms supporting a large middle-class population group. In Hawaii there were no large areas of virgin land either suitable or available for homesteading on that large a scale. Hence the Hawaiian homestead is much smaller in area; also, the method of acquisition is different, and in a large class of cases the title obtained is a long-term inalienable leasehold rather than a fee-simple title.

The *kuleanas* granted to the common people of Hawaii about 1850 were really homesteads, though that name was not generally applied to them. Contemporaneously with the *kuleana* grant, the government lands were made available for purchase or lease, and it was made possible for those Hawaiians who did not have *kuleanas* to buy small plots of land from the government at a low price. Some took advantage of this opportunity. In course of time many of these early homesteads passed out of the hands of the Hawaiians by direct sale, by mortgages which the native owners were unable to pay off, or by failure of heirs. During the third quarter of the nineteenth century, as the population declined and the sugar industry developed, many *kuleanas* and other small holdings were absorbed into plantations, and large tracts of government land and crown land were sold or leased for long periods to plantation companies, cattle ranches, or the like. During this period and later, the trend was away from individual homesteads (small farms) and toward large-scale agricultural enterprises.

There were, however, a good many people who, while not directly opposing the growth of plantations, believed that there was room for small farms and who advocated homesteads as a means of building up a sturdy farm yeomanry. It was argued that the prospect of getting homesteads would be an inducement to a desirable class of immigrants. Homesteading, it was said, would lead to a more diversified and therefore less vulnerable agricultural economy. One of these advocates of homesteading was Sanford B. Dole, who, as a member of the legislature in 1884, had much to do with the enactment of a law "to facilitate the acquiring and settlement of homesteads."

The act of 1884 directed the minister of the interior to lay out portions of available and suitable government lands in lots of not over twenty acres and offer them for sale as homesteads. Persons taking the lots were allowed five years in which to comply with the conditions for obtaining fee-simple titles. This law, amended from time to time, remained in effect until 1895. Under it, nearly six hundred homestead lots were taken up, most of them by Hawaiians and Portuguese; but less than half were finally patented. A recent study of Hawaiian land policy says that "whatever the cause, bona fide settlers under the Homestead Act of 1884 and its amendments were few."

In 1895, President Dole in a message to the legislature of the Republic of Hawaii made this comment: "The Homestead Law of 1884 made a beginning and has furnished valuable experience, but it is inadequate to the work which is now demanded from social, material, and political standpoints." Upon his recommendation, the legislature enacted the comprehensive Land Act of 1895 which, with numerous amendments, has remained in effect to the present time. In this act several plans were provided for the sale or lease of government lands. General leases (for not more than twenty-one years) and cash sales at auction (not over one thousand acres in one piece) were methods ordinarily applied to sugar cane and grazing land in large tracts. Smaller areas of the homestead type might be acquired in three ways:

(1) By a "homestead lease" for a term of 999 years, granted after a probationary period of six years. This lease is inalienable, descending to heirs of the original lessee, and the only financial obligations are the payment of small initial fees and real property taxes. This type of homestead was devised for the native Hawaiians and was used almost exclusively by them.

(2) By a "right-of-purchase lease," a lease for twenty-one years with option to purchase after the end of three years.

(3) By a "cash freehold" agreement, really an installment pur-

chase extending over three years. There was a provision whereby six or more persons might form a "settlement association" and obtain homesteads in one block of land under the cash freehold plan.

Of these three methods, the right-of-purchase lease was the most popular. The comparatively little use made of the homestead lease by the Hawaiians was disappointing.

The Land Act of 1895 had had only a short trial when Hawaii was annexed to the United States. Under the terms of annexation, all the government lands of Hawaii, including the crown lands, became the property of the United States; however, the land laws of the United States were not to apply in the islands, and it was left to Congress to determine how the public lands should be administered. In the Organic Act, Congress directed that the land laws of Hawaii, except as otherwise provided, should remain in force and that the revenues derived from the public lands should be appropriated by the laws of the territory for the benefit of its inhabitants. But in this act, Congress imposed two restrictions on the management of the public lands: (1) that no lease of agricultural land should be made for a longer period than five years; (2) that no corporation—and hence no sugar plantation—should acquire and hold more than one thousand acres of land in Hawaii, but this should not affect vested rights.

The imposition of these restrictions was a result of the view held by many members of Congress that large-scale plantation agriculture as practiced in Hawaii was bad and should be made to give way to an agricultural economy based on small farms. Experience then and later tended to show that a small-farm economy was not best for Hawaii and was not practical. The only significant effect of the five-year limit on leases was to handicap the sugar plantations in their crop planning. When it became clear that the limitation produced no good result, Congress in 1908 raised the limit to fifteen years, but at the same time provided that all leased agricultural land should be subject to withdrawal from lease at any time that it was needed for homestead or public purposes. The thousand-acre restriction proved to be ineffective. It was regularly evaded in ways that had the tacit approval of the administration in Hawaii and the Interior Department in Washington, and was ultimately repealed (1921).

Annexation, as suggested above, gave fresh impetus to the homestead movement. Homesteading had the earnest support of the territorial governors before the first World War, though one of them (Carter) had little faith in it. By the early part of Frear's administration, certain abuses had become evident; for example, it was clearly apparent that many homesteads were taken up by persons whose only object was to get title and then sell out at a profit. Frear denounced this practice as "fake homesteading" and largely by his efforts the law was amended (1910) in a way which it was thought would discourage speculators and make things easier for genuine homesteaders.

Another amendment adopted at this time provided that on the petition of twenty-five or more persons it would be mandatory for the commissioner of public lands to open up agricultural land for homesteads at the place named in the petition. This, together with the amendment permitting the withdrawal, for homesteading purposes, of leased government land, opened the way for the homesteading of sugar cane lands. There had always been much complaint that the best agricultural land was not available for homesteading because it was leased to plantations. These amendments made it possible to homestead such land whenever twenty-five persons demanded it. The experiment was tried, but the first important case of homesteading sugar cane lands—the Waiakea homesteads on which, after considerable fumbling, sugar cane continued to be raised by the plantation company under agreements with the homesteaders—turned out so disastrously for all concerned that the practice was abandoned about 1921. The Waiakea difficulties, however, continued long after that date; the rising labor costs, impossibility of mechanization, and other conditions compelled the Waiakea Mill Company to go out of business in 1948. The land was converted to other uses, such as small truck farms, pasturage for livestock, growth of trees for lumber, a golf course, and residences for neighboring Hilo.

In 1921 a new plan of homesteading was inaugurated with the enactment by Congress of the Hawaiian Homes Commission Act. The idea behind this law was to get the Hawaiian and part-Hawaiian people out of the congested and too-often squalid city areas in which many of them were living, and to put them back on the land as homesteaders, and thereby better their condition and in time develop among them a class of independent citizen farmers. Foremost in promoting this "Hawaiian Rehabilitation Project" was Prince Kuhio, Hawaii's delegate to Congress, aided by many Hawaiian and non-Hawaiian community leaders. From earlier experience it was recognized that the people would need financial assistance and expert guidance if the enterprise was to succeed.

The project was placed under control of a commission; it is financed mainly by a revolving fund of one million dollars (later increased to two million) built up from rentals of public lands and water licenses. There was made available to the commission about 200,000 acres of government land, which did not include any sugar cane land; from this available land, portions are laid out in homestead lots of different sizes, which are leased for 99 years at a nominal rental to people of not less than one-half Hawaiian blood. An essential feature of the plan is selection of the homesteaders on the basis of their qualifications and fitness to succeed. The commission lends money to them and gives them technical and other help to enable them to get started.

Operations were at first confined to a small area of Molokai but have been gradually extended to other islands. The main agricultural homestead settlement developed by the Hawaiian Homes Commission is located at Hoolehua, Molokai. It was originally intended to be a diversified farming area, but has been given over to the production of pineapples under agreements with three pineapple companies. Diversified crops failed in this place because of the lack of water for irrigation. It is generally agreed that pineapples saved the Hoolehua homesteaders, but did so without making independent farmers of them. One of the most useful features of the rehabilitation scheme has been the opening of numerous small residential and subsistence homesteads in the vicinity of Honolulu and other towns where many of the Hawaiians have employment. At the end of 1956 there were more than 10,000 Hawaiians living in the various homestead communities, farm and residential, on the islands of Molokai, Hawaii, and Oahu. Since that date, a new homestead settlement has been established at Anahola on Kauai.

The rehabilitation project has had its ups and downs, and some moments of acute crisis; there have been many changes in the law and in the personnel of the commission, its organization, and its procedures. There can be no doubt that the project has accomplished much good, but it still has a long way to go before it brings to full realization the vision of its founders.

Included in the Hawaiian Homes Commission Act was an amendment of the territorial land law to permit the leasing of sugar cane lands without their being subject to withdrawal for homestead purposes. The homesteading of sugar cane lands was practically discontinued, and the policy was adopted of leasing such lands at annual rentals that would produce a substantial revenue for the territorial government.

Homesteading under the provisions of the Land Act of 1895 was greatly curtailed after the Hawaiian rehabilitation project was started. Between 1910 and 1921, twenty-two homestead tracts were opened, but only one was opened between 1921 and 1946. That homesteading under the acts of 1884 and 1895 had not proved a success was the considered judgment of the Land Laws Revision Commission created by the legislature of 1943. In its final report (December 31, 1946) the commission asserted that "the majority of homesteaders have proved themselves to be mere speculators or investors," and it said that the "only legitimate present demands for public lands are for pastoral lands . . . and for lots for homesites convenient to occupational locale." It recommended, among other things, "that all sales of public lands be discontinued except for residential purposes," and "that the public lands . . . not suitable for residential purposes be conserved and disposed of only upon lease."

In recent years there has been much talk about land monopoly in Hawaii. Attention has been focused upon this subject by the rapid growth of population and the acute housing shortage which developed during and after World War II. It has been highlighted by the outspoken language of Governor Ingram M. Stainback and others. The complaint is not new. As far back as 1890, W. R. Castle said, "One of the crying evils of Hawaii is its land ownership. Two immense estates are said to own over one third of the kingdom." Today, in 1960, the cry is still against a few estates which keep a tight hold on huge areas of land.

One may conclude that land policy or, more narrowly, homesteading, has not done much to promote Americanization. What about immigration?

It has been shown in earlier chapters that immigration, up to the time of annexation, was mainly a matter of supplying the labor needs of the sugar industry. In 1900 the territory had a population of 154,000 and the largest racial groups were: Japanese, 61,111; Hawaiian and part-Hawaiian, 39,656; Chinese, 25,767; Portuguese, about 18,000. In 1895 President Dole had said that "Asiatic immigration is mainly of a transitory character, experience showing that it cannot be relied on for permanent population." By 1900 it was obvious that Hawaii had a permanent oriental population group. After annexation, much stress was laid upon the importance of bringing in American settlers and Europeans who could become American citizens, in order to prevent the orientalizing of Hawaii.

Efforts to induce people from the United States mainland to settle on the public lands of Hawaii met with very limited success. The farming population was not much augmented, although every year a few business and professional men and mechanics have come, and many of these, as well as some tourists, have remained in the islands as permanent residents.

The legislature in 1905 created a Board of Immigration whose policy was "to bring into Hawaii such persons as would be capable of becoming American citizens," and which continued actively at work up to the first World War. The operations of the board were financed at first mainly by contributions from the sugar plantations and agencies, later by a special tax on incomes in the higher brackets. Many of the plantations co-operated by offering to furnish each immigrant family an acre of land and a house, to which they might in time acquire a permanent title.

Earlier experience had shown that Portugal and the Portuguese islands were the most prolific source of immigrants of the desired type. From there and from Spain, during the years 1906 to 1913, the board brought 12,891 immigrants (4,334 men, 3,169 women, and 5,388 children). This was good material for a non-oriental population. Unfortunately, the distant charms of the west coast of the United States lured many of these people away from the islands after a short time. The Board of Immigration also introduced 2,121 Russians, but few of these remained very long in Hawaii.

To supply their labor needs, the sugar plantations and the rising pineapple industry still found it necessary to rely mainly on orientals. Annexation stopped the immigration of Chinese, but Japanese continued to come in large numbers as a result of the operations of emigration companies in Japan. From 1900 to 1910, more than 77,000 arrived, but in the same period more than 75,000 departed either to Japan or to the United States mainland. Still the Japanese population increased by more than 18,000 as a result of births. During the same decade about 5,000 Koreans came to the islands and the greater part of them remained. The sugar planters introduced several thousand Puerto Ricans. In 1907 the inflow of Japanese laborers was slowed by the "Gentleman's Agreement," but Japanese "picture brides" continued to be admitted until the immigration act of 1924 excluded all orientals. By 1920 Japanese comprised 42.7 per cent of the population. Since then the number of Japanese has increased at a normal rate, but the percentage has dropped steadily; in 1957 it was down to 33.4 per cent.

In 1906 the Hawaiian Sugar Planters' Association made an experimental introduction of a few Filipino families. After the Japanese immigration was stopped in 1907, the sugar planters began the importation of Filipino laborers in large numbers. Many others came voluntarily. Because of the depression, the HSPA in 1932 discontinued the introduction of Filipinos until 1946, when a few thousand were brought in to relieve a temporary labor shortage. In all, about 125,000 Filipinos came to Hawaii. Enough of these have remained to give the territory a substantial Filipino population group, amounting in 1957 to more than 73,000.

From the foregoing account it appears that neither homesteading nor immigration have done what some persons expected of them as instruments of Americanization. Immigration, indeed, made the task more difficult. Yet all recent analyses by sociologists and congressional committees have agreed that Hawaii is, in all essential respects, an American community. The history of the territory and especially the behavior of its people in two wars have proved that those of oriental ancestry, as well as European, can become and have become good and loyal American citizens.

Powerful forces have been at work to bring about this result. By far the most important has been education, the work of the many public and private schools, which is described in a later chapter. But much has been done by other agencies, such as Christian churches, public libraries, Young Men's and Young Women's Christian Associations, Boy Scouts and Girl Scouts, clubs and social organizations of many kinds. Someone has remarked that athletic sports and contests have contributed to Americanism. In Hawaii these follow the traditional American pattern. Especially valuable are games played by teams, in which players of different racial origins pool their efforts and learn to respect each other for individual worth.

Deserving of special mention is the long campaign of education begun about 1920 by the Reverend Takie Okumura, a Japanese Christian minister, for the specific purpose of promoting the Americanization of the Japanese in the islands and the removal of causes of friction between them and others in the community. His earlier efforts were directed to the older Japanese, aliens who could never become American citizens but who had become permanent residents of Hawaii. In 1927 he organized the first of a series of conferences for the "new Americans"—young Americans of Japanese ancestry—in which delegates selected for their leadership qualities could meet community leaders in government, business, education, and religion, and hear and talk with them on subjects of special interest to these young Americans. The fifteenth of these conferences was held in the summer of 1941, when the threat of war hung darkly over the Pacific. The theme of the conference was "Our Present Patriotic Responsibilities." The next few years were to show how these young people and others in the same category interpreted this theme, and how completely they accepted and carried on their responsibilities as American citizens

CHAPTER TWENTY-ONE

Hawaii's Place in the Nation

HAWAII had a dual status. For over half a century as a territory it was preparing for the day when it would be admitted to the Union as a state. As a territory, moreover, it had certain rights and obligations to the nation as a whole. It was in this position, as a territory on the road to statehood, that the people of Hawaii usually thought of their island home. But Hawaii is also a defense outpost of the nation. This defense value was the decisive argument that finally brought annexation, and it is in this light that many, perhaps most, of the people of continental United States think of these Pacific islands.

Annexation removed whatever danger there may have been that Hawaii would fall into the possession of some other great power. Since there was at that time no serious threat to American security in the Pacific, little was done for several years about preparing the islands for their function as a fortress—little, that is, beyond acquiring land, making plans, and getting the necessary authorizations from Congress. In 1898 and 1899 the President by proclamation reserved several pieces of land in Honolulu and elsewhere on Oahu for use by the army and navy. These included certain lands adjacent to the harbor which were officially designated as "Naval Station, Honolulu," and the areas later occupied by the military establishments of Fort Shafter and Schofield Barracks. Subsequently other areas were appropriated. The intention was to concentrate all important military and naval installations on the island of Oahu.

The first troops of a permanent garrison were an infantry regiment and a battalion of engineers which arrived in August, 1898, and set up a temporary post, Camp McKinley, in the Waikiki area near Diamond Head. First of the permanent military establishments was Fort Shafter, located on the outskirts of Honolulu toward Pearl Harbor; some of its buildings were completed and occupied in 1907. Fort Shafter became the headquarters for the army forces in the territory. Plans developed for the army called for a series of Forts to guard Honolulu Harbor and Pearl Harbor, a centrally located garrison post to house a large mobile force capable of moving quickly to any point threatened by an invader, gun emplacements and observation posts strategically located for the defense of the coastline, and a network of roads enabling the defenders to reach all parts of the island.

Before World War I the main harbor defenses had been established and partially developed: to the east, Fort Armstrong at the entrance of Honolulu Harbor, Fort De Russy at Waikiki, and Fort Ruger at Diamond Head; to the west, guarding the entrance to Pearl Harbor, Fort Kamehameha ("the King's post") and Fort Weaver. In the same period, on the Leilehua plateau in the center of Oahu, was established the garrison post Schofield Barracks (first occupied in January, 1909), which ultimately became the largest in the United States. In the early years Hawaii was part of the Military Department of California, but in February, 1913, the Hawaiian Department of the army was created as an independent command subordinate only to the War Department.

When aviation demonstrated its value in the first World War, an army air force organization was developed in the Hawaiian Department. First flying field to be established was Luke Field on Ford Island in Pearl Harbor (a field later released to the navy). Second was Wheeler Field, adjacent to Schofield Barracks; third was Hickam Field next to Pearl Harbor, which is now Hickam Air Force Base, headquarters for the entire Pacific Air Force command. Of secondary importance is Bellows Field on the northeastern side of Oahu.

Although the United States ever since 1887 had held a right

to use Pearl Harbor, nothing was done about it until after annexation. Development of the naval base has proceeded along two lines: improvement of the entrance channel and anchorages within the locks; and construction of drydocks and shore installations. Under an appropriation made by Congress in 1900 an opening through the bar at the outer end of the channel was dredged to a depth of thirty feet and a width of two hundred feet. At later times the channel was still further deepened, widened, and straightened, and a vast quantity of mud and coral was dredged from the inside of the harbor. It was not until 1908 that creation of a naval base at Pearl Harbor was actually authorized by Congress. Construction of a drydock was begun in 1909. Faulty planning resulted in a disastrous collapse (February, 1913) when the work was far advanced. With new plans the project was resumed nearly two years later and was successfully completed in the summer of 1919. In the meantime, wharves, shops, and other necessary buildings had been constructed. This work was only the beginning. Between the wars, especially after 1931, and during World War II, naval facilities in and around Pearl Harbor were enormously expanded. Development of aviation has led to the establishment of three naval air stations on Oahu: one at Ford Island in Pearl Harbor; one at Barbers Point, now the major naval air base; and one at Kaneohe, which is now occupied by a Marine Corps integrated air-ground force.

At the outbreak of the first World War in 1914, Oahu's harbors became a refuge for several German naval and merchant ships; when the United States entered the war in 1917 these ships were seized, and some of them later performed service for our country. Aside from this small episode, Hawaii saw no hostile action, but the people of the islands contributed their full share financially and in personal service to the cause of our country and her allies.

Hawaii's participation in war work began long before the United States became one of the belligerents. In the fall of 1914 a War Relief Committee was formed; this and several similar groups were finally merged in the Hawaiian Chapter of the American Red Cross, which was organized after the United States entered the war. Hundreds of thousands of dollars were contributed directly for relief and Red Cross work, and huge quantities of surgical dressings, other hospital supplies, and clothing were shipped from Honolulu to the war areas; preparation of these articles gave work to many willing hands from all the races mingled in Hawaii's population. Many persons, both men and women, found opportunity for civilian war service at home in the diversified activities of the Red Cross, War Camp Community Service, Young Men's and Young Women's Christian Associations, Knights of Columbus, and other organizations. In war areas in Europe and in Siberia, many volunteers from Hawaii participated actively in Red Cross, ambulance, and relief work.

The entire population was called upon to do its part in food production and conservation, and the people responded willingly to appeals headlined by such expressions as "Food will win the war," "Grow your own food," "Hooverize" (a wartime synonym for economy in the use of food), "Eat more bananas." The island populace joined the rest of the nation in having "meatless" and "wheatless" days and in growing vegetables in school and home gardens. Hawaii had a Territorial Food Commission with an auxiliary and very active Women's Committee before the United States Food Administration came into existence. Some special food problems were created by actual or threatened shortages of fish, rice, and taro, staple foods for a large part of the local population.

On the financial side, the territory made an excellent record. Subscriptions of almost thirty million dollars were made in the five Liberty Loan campaigns, the quotas being oversubscribed in every case. The sale of what were sometimes called "baby bonds" —Thrift Stamps and War Savings Stamps—was promoted by a publicity campaign featuring many novel posters, songs, and slogans, with the organization of school children into a "thrift army." In this effort Hawaii made a record that was equalled by only one state on the mainland.

Hawaii contributed its quota of manpower to the armed forces. Before and after the United States entered the war, there were about two hundred volunteers for service in the British army. It has been estimated that about 9,600 men of these islands served in the army or navy of the United States during the war. A few hundred of these had enlisted in the regular army before the summer of 1918, a few hundred were volunteers for and graduates of officers' training camps held at Schofield Barracks in 1917 and 1918, but the bulk of them entered service either as members of the National Guard or as draftees inducted through the Selective Service System. The National Guard of Hawaii (two regiments) was called into federal service in the summer of 1918. The regiments were brought up to war strength by assigning to them the men of the territory inducted into the army through the Selective Service System. The two Guard regiments were not sent overseas, but were used to replace regular army units which were withdrawn from the territory. Hawaii was represented on the battlefields of Europe by those who volunteered, as mentioned above, and the territory's honor roll included the names of a substantial number who were killed in battle or died of wounds.

The accustomed routine of life in the islands was disturbed in many ways during these eventful years in which winning the war was the object of supreme importance. Transportation to and from the islands was seriously interfered with. Tourist traffic nearly ceased. The old Royal Hawaiian Hotel in Honolulu was converted into the Army and Navy Y.M.C.A. There was a strong anti-German feeling in the community, and alien-owned German economic interests in the islands were liquidated. Assets of the old firm of Hackfeld & Company were acquired by a new corporation, American Factors, Ltd. Prohibition of the liquor traffic came to the islands as a war measure by act of Congress about a year and a half before the Eighteenth Amendment went into force.

In the years following World War I, island people gave more attention to the relations between the territory and the nation. Some thoughtful citizens began to wonder how much longer Hawaii would have to go on under territorial status. They thought the territory was ready for statehood. While recognizing that local conditions might cause delay in attaining that goal, they were disturbed by the accumulating evidence that a great many people on the mainland, including members of Congress, looked upon the islands as a mere possession or colony of the United States instead of as an integral part of the nation only one step removed from statehood.

Hawaii was subject to all taxes and other general obligations imposed upon the states, and annually paid into the federal treasury millions of dollars, sums larger than those paid by many of the states; but the territory was excluded from the benefits of federal laws making appropriations to the states for good roads, education, child welfare, and other purposes. Governor Farrington brought this situation to the attention of the legislature in 1923 and declared, "A vigorous campaign should be conducted to restore territorial prestige and position in the federal scheme of appropriation and administration." The legislature responded by enacting what is called "Hawaii's Bill of Rights." This act formally asserted the territory's right to the same treatment from Congress as that received by the states, and it provided for a commission to go to Washington and assist the delegate in Congress to secure legislation that would include Hawaii "in all acts in aid of good roads, education, farm loans, maternity, home economics, training in agriculture, trade and industry, and other acts of a like nature, which apply to the states as a whole."

When the matter was thus presented to it formally and strongly, Congress recognized the justice of the territory's claim, and a law was promptly passed (1924) extending to Hawaii the benefits of the various appropriation acts of the kind mentioned that were then in force. But similar appropriation bills enacted at a later time had to be carefully watched to make sure that their benefits extended to the territory as well as to the states.

There was another point about which the people of the islands were much concerned. They had heard of "carpetbaggers" and they wanted none of those creatures holding office in the territory. When the law for the government of Hawaii was being enacted, the members of Congress seemed to be of the same mind. The Organic Act provided that the governor, secretary of the territory, territorial circuit judges, and department heads, whether appointed by the president or the governor, must be citizens of the territory and hence must have resided in the territory for at least a short period before appointment. This qualification did not apply to the federal district judge, district attorney, marshal, and other federal officers. But an influential member of the United States Senate stated that it would be "an utter impossibility for any presidential nominee for any territory to pass through the Senate and be confirmed unless the appointee is a resident of the territory." Other members appeared to agree with him. National platforms of both political parties repeatedly endorsed this principle.

In spite of these declarations, some non-citizens of Hawaii were appointed by the president and confirmed by the Senate to official positions within the territory. Irked by this experience, the citizens of Hawaii, through their legislature, appealed to Congress to remedy the evil by appropriate legislation. Congress gave friendly and favorable consideration to the appeal and in 1921 amended the Organic Act by making a residence of three years in the territory a prerequisite to appointment to any of the territorial and federal offices mentioned above, except that of secretary of the territory. The exception was probably due to an oversight.

After the legislation of 1921 and 1924 was passed, there appears to have been a fairly widespread feeling in the islands that the territory's status as an integral part of the nation had been recognized, and its relations with the federal government adjusted in a satisfactory manner. The principle of home rule seemed to have been accepted. There was sporadic talk about trying for statehood; the territorial legislature passed the usual resolutions on that subject and Hawaii's delegate in Congress dropped statehood bills into the legislative hopper; but most of the people appeared to be content with the existing scheme of government. They had been lulled into a false feeling of security, politically speaking, as events of the 1930's were to show.

Two entirely unrelated and dissimilar episodes pointed up for the people of Hawaii their utter dependence on the will of Congress in all matters relating to their form of government and details of administration. The first of these was a crime of violence—the Massie case, an assault by a group of Honolulu hoodlums on the wife of a young naval officer (September, 1931). In the trial of the young men indicted for the assault, there was so much uncertainty in the evidence that the jury was unable to agree on a verdict. While a second trial was pending, one of the defendants was seized and killed by a party composed of the young naval officer, his mother-in-law, and two sailors. The slayers were tried and found guilty of manslaughter; a sentence of ten years' imprisonment pronounced upon them was commuted by the governor to one hour.

In newspaper reports, the attack on the young navy wife, the lynching, and the resultant trials were broadcast to the nation with lurid and exaggerated, largely untruthful descriptions of local conditions, which gave the territory an enormous amount of the worst possible advertising. At the request of the United States Senate, an assistant United States attorney general, Seth W. Richardson, made an investigation of conditions in the territory, with special reference to the administration and enforcement of the criminal laws. The investigation failed to disclose evidence justifying the wild reports that had been circulated on the mainland, but it did reveal some laxity and inefficiency in the enforcement of criminal laws and some defects in the machinery for the administration of justice. Richardson recommended several changes in the existing laws and in the law-enforcement organization. He also recommended removal of the residence requirement for appointed officials of the territory. Bills to carry out these recommendations were introduced in Congress in April, 1932. Other bills were introduced looking to the establishment of a commission government in Hawaii in which the army and navy would have a voice.

Long before the occurrence of the Massie case, thoughtful citizens of the territory were aware of the defects and laxity described in the Richardson report. Governor Judd in 1930 appointed a Crime Commission which made many recommendations, some of them very similar to the recommendations in that report. The legislature of 1931 passed some remedial laws. In 1932 and 1933, under the pressure supplied by the agitation on the mainland and the bills pending in Congress, additional corrective laws were passed by the legislature.

None of the bills that had been introduced in Congress was enacted into law. After Franklin D. Roosevelt became president, one of his early acts was a request to Congress for authority to appoint someone other than a resident of Hawaii as governor of the territory. A bill for that purpose was introduced in the House of Representatives but it failed to pass. Home rule for Hawaii was saved for the time being, but the experience of these years was a lesson to the people of the territory.

A second episode which illustrated the inferior position of the territory was the Jones-Costigan sugar control act of 1934 and its application to Hawaii. The act provided that quotas should be set for the amount of sugar that could be marketed on the United States mainland by the various sugar-producing areas. The quotas for mainland beet and cane sugar were fixed by the act itself at figures somewhat higher than their average production in recent years, while Hawaii was placed in a group with foreign countries and island possessions of the United States, whose quotas were to be set by the secretary of agriculture. The quota thus set for Hawaii was about 8 per cent below its recent average. The law further provided that in case it was necessary to reduce still more the amount of sugar marketed, the reduction had to be made in the quotas assigned to the foreign and offshore producing areas; the latter areas were severely restricted in the amount of refined sugar they could market, while no such restriction applied to mainland producers. There were other features which discriminated against Hawaii both in the act and in the method of its administration by the secretary of agriculture.

Unable to prevent these acts of discrimination by arguments directed to Congress and the secretary of agriculture, the sugar industry of Hawaii brought a suit in the supreme court of the District of Columbia to test the validity of the Jones-Costigan Act and to prevent the secretary of agriculture from carrying out its provisions, on the ground that it violated the constitutional rights of the sugar producers of Hawaii. Involved in this court action were the status of Hawaii in the nation and the power of Congress to discriminate against the territory. Justice Jennings Bailey, before whom the case was argued, decided against the Hawaiian complainants and ordered the suit dismissed; he admitted that Hawaii was an integral part of the United States and an incorporated territory, but he declared that Congress had plenary power to legislate for and could discriminate against the territory if it saw fit to do so.

The Hawaiian sugar producers filed a notice of appeal, but before the appeal was perfected a compromise agreement was made with the secretary of agriculture under which Hawaii was given a higher quota and more equitable treatment in the administration of the act. The appeal was then dropped; thus Justice Bailey's decision stood on the records as a judicial determination of the power of Congress over the territories. Some people criticized the sugar industry for not carrying the case on up to the Supreme Court of the United States in order to get a final, authoritative decision on the questions involved in it. The president of the HSPA replied that the benefits gained by the com-

promise agreement "outweighed by far the expense and inter-
minable delays of litigation. Finally, as with all court cases, there
was the uncertainty of the outcome. A possible adverse decision
would not only have been seriously detrimental to the interests
of the stockholders but might even have jeopardized the rights
which this territory should in all equity continue to enjoy."

The developments growing out of the Massie case and the
Jones-Costigan Act made a profound impression on the people of
Hawaii. They were shocked to see the status of the territory, and
what they had supposed to be its rights, treated so cavalierly by
Congress, the national administration, and the court of the District of Columbia. Many who had before been indifferent or opposed to statehood were now converted to that cause. They concluded that only as a state would the islands be safe from the dan-
gers that had threatened them during these years.

CHAPTER TWENTY-TWO

Treasure in the Fields

THE story of Hawaiian agriculture in the twentieth century is one of relatively steady progress in the development of two great crops, sugar and pineapple. These industries had their ups and downs, but the most dramatic phase of their history is that which shows the application, under the spur of necessity, of scientific large-scale methods to create the utmost efficiency in production, protection, and distribution of these dominant crops.

In 1898, and at intervals thereafter, the cry of "crop diversification!" was raised. Hawaii has often been criticized for putting its agricultural future into only two baskets, sugar and pineapples. But there have been compelling reasons for this specialization. In the first place, cultivatable land in the islands runs to no more than 300,000 acres, or about 7 per cent of the total area. It is impossible on this limited land to raise both "money crops" and crops which furnish all the varied foods needed by the population. If the land is devoted to concentrated yields of sugar cane and pineapples, the people then have money to buy imported supplies from other food-raising regions. It is true that a wide variety of foods can be grown in the mild climate of the islands; diversified crops which have a wholesale value of more than $15,000,000 a year are now raised. But no staple crop has been found capable of taking its place alongside sugar and pineapples.

During the 1890's when the McKinley Tariff removed protection from Hawaiian exports, a flurry of experimentation in diversified farming went on. In 1893 a company was formed to grow sisal for making cordage; a variety of agave plant was developed which gave strands of a better quality than that raised in Yucatan, but labor costs were too high, and the towering poles of untended "century plants" in various corners of Oahu are reminders of the death of this infant industry. In the first decade of the twentieth century, rubber trees were introduced, and there were several vain attempts to compete with the rubber growers of the East Indies. Cotton growing was revived, but the quality was ruined by the pink boll worm. Rice had been raised for many years to supply the needs of the oriental population, but in spite of the aid of the United States Agricultural Experiment Station established in 1901 in Honolulu, the rice industry died out except in a few areas, mainly because skillful rice raisers could no longer be brought in from China, and because it was cheaper to import rice from Texas and California. Banana raising for export has always been a risky enterprise, owing to lack of dependable transport and reasonable shipping costs. Coffee raising, centered mainly at Kona on Hawaii, stabilized somewhat during the past half-century, but even this quality product was speculative and has always had to face, without tariff protection, the threat of a market flooded with foreign-grown coffee. (Coffee, however, is still Hawaii's third most important crop, with a value in 1958 of more than $7,000,000.) A good quality of tobacco was developed in Hawaii, but the growers did not have large enough reserves to survive the depression of the 1930's. Hawaiian honey was shipped before 1914 to candy manufacturers in Europe, but the First World War wiped out this market, and the present export value of honey is only $137,000. Such recently developed crops as the flavorsome macadamia nut have found a modest place in Hawaii's agriculture, but the question, "What basic crop other than sugar and pineapples can be grown economically in Hawaii?" has found no new answer.

Sugar and pineapple, then, are the dominant products of the island fields. Neither crop, it should be noted, is one that is suited to the small independent farmer. In fact, raising these two crops should not be called "farming" in any sense, for it requires large-scale operations under complex organization. It is true that fields can be cultivated by small holders under a contract, lease, or bonus system; but most of the problems of these two industries can be solved only by mass methods, under centralized management.

Sugar, for example, requires almost two years to mature. During this time it must be continually weeded, irrigated, and protected from a variety of insect enemies. The workers must be fed and sheltered close to the fields in which they work, and their routine must be planned to keep them steadily occupied during all seasons. Heavy equipment, such as tractors, trucks, and harvesting machines, must be kept busy most of the time. The crop, when ready, is an interlaced, heavy tangle of cane and leaves that must be harvested quickly. By road, flume, overhead cable, or railway, the cane must be transported from the field to the mill within twenty-four hours after cutting, or its precious sweet juice will drip to waste or ferment in the stalk. The mill must be designed with the best engineering skill, and operated twenty-four hours a day if it is to have the greatest efficiency. Maximum efficiency can be attained only in large mills, and large mills demand steady supplies of cane to keep their crushers fully supplied on schedule. The million-ton sugar crops of recent years could never have been produced in the face of rising costs unless the managers of the industry had evoked a scientific and technological revolution.

One force in that revolution was set going in 1895, when the Hawaiian Sugar Planters' Association was organized as successor to the old Planters' Labor and Supply Company. The most impressive activity of this co-operative association has been its Experiment Station, which began in the same year when a part-time chemist was hired to work on certain problems. From that small beginning has grown the Experiment Station of today, which costs the sugar companies two million dollars a year, but which brings benefits many times that amount in the way of scientific discoveries and methodology.

Early problems on which Experiment Station experts aided the industry were concerned with the proper selection and use of commercial fertilizers on the soil, and with the economical application of irrigation water to obtain the best results during the cane-growing season. In later years the Experiment Station collaborated not only with the plantations but with territorial and federal government officials in an effort to protect and extend the forests which are essential to conserve the natural water supply of the islands so necessary to the sugar industry. But the use of science in every phase of the sugar industry, from clearing the land to the final stages of mill extraction, from breeding new varieties to making war on insect pests, has been studied by the experts, with benefit to the whole group.

Irrigation is needed on most Hawaiian cane lands. To grow one pound of sugar requires no less than 4,000 pounds of water. Many great ditch systems have been constructed since the days of the Hamakua Ditch earlier described. To tap large bodies of underground water, plantation engineering crews have drilled many tunnels through mountain rock. The Olokele Ditch on Kauai is thirteen miles long, and eight miles of it is composed of tunnels. The Waiahole project, completed in 1916, collects water from streams on the windward side of Oahu and carries it through the Koolau range to the Oahu Sugar Plantation; it involved the cutting of more than eleven miles of tunnels. Since 1880, many artesian wells have been drilled to furnish irrigation water; the Ewa Plantation near Honolulu has more than sixty wells, which furnish more than a hundred million gallons of water a day. Great reservoirs have been built for storing irrigation water; the largest in the islands, the Wahiawa Reservoir on Oahu, has a capacity of two and a half billion gallons.

The most spectacular feature of the Experiment Station's work has been its battle to protect the cane against insect enemies and plant diseases. Many insects attack the sugar cane plant, and were they not checked would destroy the industry. One of the most successful means of fighting insect pests has been to seek the nat-

ural foes of the enemy species and to import these new insects
to wage war against the pests.

The native cane varieties had long adjusted themselves to survival of attacks by native insects. But late in the nineteenth century, in the days before plant quarantine was practiced, some new
and harmful insects arrived to disturb the old balance. A tiny
grasshopper was observed in the fields in 1900 and classified as
Perkinsiella saccharicida, or sugar cane leaf hopper, probably
brought in from Australia. It was not considered to be a danger,
but in the four years following, the fields were increasingly attacked by swarms of these hoppers, who left the fields blackened
and withered. In 1905, the cane loss from the leaf hopper reached
$3,000,000. If the enemy was not defeated, the industry would
be completely destroyed.

A Division of Entomology was quickly organized by the Experiment Station, and five scientists were put to work, seeking a
means of control. Two of the men went to Queensland in Australia, and after intensive search found a parasitic insect that laid
its eggs in the body of the leaf hopper. After a series of difficulties, these parasites were collected and brought to Hawaii, where
they were liberated in the fields with good results. Entomolo-
gists explored for parasites in Fiji, China, Formosa, and different
parts of Australia, and other foes of the leaf hopper were successfully imported. Within a few years, the devastating plague of
hoppers had been greatly diminished, but was still not fully controlled. *Cyrtorhinus,* an insect brought from Australia in 1920,
has proved to be the most effective enemy of the hopper to date.

Success with the leaf hopper encouraged the scientists to use
similar methods against other insects. A plant quarantine had been
set up in 1903, but some insects still continued to evade the bar-
riers, and others had been in Hawaii for many years. One of
these, the sugar cane borer, *Rhabdocnemis obscura,* had first appeared in the 1860's. The borer laid its eggs in holes drilled in
the stems of growing cane; the grubs which hatched out fed themselves by burrowing upward through the stalk, often completely

destroying the plant. In 1906 an HSPA entomologist set out on a journey which took him through China, the Malay States, Java, and the Dutch East Indies. At last he discovered on the remote island of Amboina a borer which was harassed by a parasitic fly, the New Guinea tachinid. After four years of disheartening effort, a cage filled with these delicate tachinids was brought alive to Honolulu, and ultimately the borer-eating young flies were able to reduce the depredations of the borer by about 90 per cent.

Another beetle, *Anomala*, became a pest about 1912. It laid its eggs underground near the roots of cane, and the grubs chewed the root system, making the cane yellow and stunted. After another search, an enemy was brought from the Philippines, the *Scolia* wasp, which stings the *Anomala* grub into paralysis and lays its eggs on the living body. Since the life cycle of the *Scolia* is about half that of *Anomala*, victory over the beetle was gained in about two years.

A creature that will devour almost any insect was imported in 1932. This was the large toad named *Bufo marinus*, originally a native of Central America. More than a hundred were shipped from Puerto Rico to Hawaii; their offspring have been settled in all the islands, and it is averred that all growers of plants have benefited by the giant appetites of these insectivorous toads.

One way of fighting plant diseases is to develop new varieties of cane that will resist infection, and produce high sugar content as well. Until about 1900, the most popular variety grown in Hawaii was that called "Lahaina," imported into Maui about 1854 from Tahiti. At the beginning of the present century this variety became, for some mysterious reason, affected with root rot. This was a major threat, but the HSPA scientists at once began to experiment in the art of breeding new varieties from the microscopically small seed of sugar cane (for generations the cane had been reproduced only by stalk cuttings). With the most painstaking precautions, pollen was gathered and crossed with West Indian varieties, and seed beds were started. The variety numbered "H 109" turned out to be the main survivor of the original 5,252 transplanted seedlings derived from plantings in 1905. This strain, as experiments by George F. Renton in 1912 on Ewa Plantation revealed, was resistant to the deadly "Lahaina disease," and also gave a sugar yield as high as 15 tons of sugar per acre. In 1917 the H 109 plantings had spread to 4,000 acres; by 1924 both Ewa and Waianae Plantations were planted completely in H 109, and other growers were rapidly replacing Lahaina with the new variety.

The development of H 109 was the first important achievement in the breeding of improved cane varieties in Hawaii. This variety, which was worth many millions of dollars to the Hawaiian sugar industry, reached its maximum extension about 1931, when it was planted on more than 117,000 acres. In later years it has been superseded by still better varieties. The cane census of December, 1946, showed H 109 growing on less than 2,000 acres, while a new variety known simply as 32-8560 was planted on more than 132,000 acres. In the 1950's, variety 37-1933 held the lead, while variety 44-3098 was rapidly expanding in second place. The development of new varieties of cane for different growing conditions is a very important part of Experiment Station activities. Hundreds of thousands of seedlings have been started, and from them only the most promising are retained for further trial. In the early days cane varieties were known by name (Lahaina, Rose Bamboo, Yellow Caledonia); later they were named with a letter or letters and a number (H 109, D 1135, POJ 2878); but in recent years they are simply given numbers, such as 32-8560 and 37-1933, the first part representing the year in which the seedling was started.

On other fronts, the success of the experimental method has been almost as striking. Application of soil chemistry to the lands of Hawaii is a laborious but highly valuable routine. The development of methods to keep down weeds by chemical and other means has been carried on. A mulch paper, laid on the ground between rows, was developed at Olaa Plantation, and later was adapted by pineapple growers with even better results.

Giant harvesting machines have been devised to reap the cane by mechanical means. The fields are usually burned over before harvesting, a drastic method of consuming the "trash" without damaging the juicy cane stalks. Then large cranes carrying steel claws pluck off the standing cane without harming the roots (it was discovered that "ratoons," or second-growth crops from the same planting, grew better when the cane was snatched by the machine than when it was cut by cane knives). A modification of the snatching method was developed at Waialua Plantation and called the "Waialua rake." This consists of a huge steel-pipe claw which is dragged back and forth across the field on cables operated by two tractors with drum attachments. Such a method does not discriminate greatly in the material it delivers in heaps to be loaded and taken to the mill, where much additional cleaning must be done. Such progress has been made in the development of machinery that today nearly all Hawaiian cane is harvested mechanically; and on most plantations huge, specially designed trucks have replaced older ways of moving cane to the mill.

Improvements in milling technology have also been marked. In 1905, extraction of total sugar content in the cane reached 96 per cent. The first twelve-roller mill was installed by the Oahu Sugar Company in 1907. The mass of material handled is great, because sugar cane may yield as much as a hundred tons per acre, and seven to twelve tons of cane are needed at the mill to produce one ton of sugar.

Nowhere in the world has science been applied to agriculture to a greater extent than in Hawaii, and the results are evident in the sugar production record. It is true that sugar has been protected by tariffs, but even so it could not have survived unless great savings had been made all the way along the line.

The production of sugar in Hawaii in 1895 was 150,000 tons. One planter stated that this was undoubtedly the largest crop that the islands could ever produce. But in 1905, it was 426,000 tons; in 1915 it was 600,000 tons; in 1932 the first million-ton crop was harvested.

After the acquisition by the United States in 1898 of colonial possessions, Hawaii had to meet competition from Puerto Rican and Philippine sugars, which gained free admission; moreover, Cuba was given tariff preferences. Nevertheless, the promise of new security under annexation caused lively stock trading. Shares and dividends were high. A stock exchange had been started as early as 1883, but had been discontinued after two years; now a new exchange was opened to handle trading in Hawaiian shares. These were boom days, in which great fortunes were made and some fortunes lost. A number of new plantations were founded between 1895 and 1905. In 1900 there were, on seven islands, fifty-six plantations, but this number has been reduced to twenty-seven on four islands by consolidation of some small ones and abandonment of unprofitable marginal plantations.

A group of Hawaiian sugar producers in 1904 obtained control of a sugar refinery at Crockett on San Francisco Bay. From this has grown the huge refinery of the California and Hawaiian Sugar Refining Corporation, owned by twenty-seven Hawaiian plantations. In this way the island sugar industry freed itself from dependence on other mainland refineries. A small amount of sugar is refined in the islands, but the bulk of the crop has always, since the Reciprocity Treaty went into effect, been shipped to the mainland for refining.

In 1913 a Democratic administration took over the White House, and fears that sugar would again be placed on the free list were realized when the Underwood Tariff was signed in October, 1913. The price of sugar raws dropped to 2.28 cents a pound, although there was no reduction in price to the consumer.

The First World War, however, caused a tremendous increase in demand for sugar, and the free sugar clause was repealed by Congress in April, 1916. As a result of this change, plantation wages were increased, and many companies distributed bonuses to workers and extra dividends to stockholders. On August 9, 1917, the price of sugar raws was 7.52 cents, half a cent higher than the highest price since 1889. Late in August, the federal government acted to stabilize the price; the Sugar Department of the Food Administration set the base price and controlled distribution. Plantation labor forces were reduced by the needs of the armed forces, and hundreds of schoolboys worked in the fields during the summer. The tremendous shortage of vessels for Pacific shipping during the war caused high freight rates, but sugar was given first priority, and the government did everything to keep it moving to market.

After the close of the war, the price of raw sugar soared to the fantastic price of 23.5 cents in 1920 when the price-setting Equalization Board was discontinued. Monthly bonuses to laborers went from 300 per cent to more than 500 per cent. This artificial condition could not last, but the corresponding slump did not hit until 1923. There were many causes for this deflation, and the challenge was met in various ways, all of which resulted in a tightening in the efficiency of production that was a benefit to the long-run development of the industry.

A blow to Hawaii's sugar industry was dealt by the Jones-Costigan sugar control act of 1934, an amendment to the Agricultural Adjustment Act. The basic purpose was to prevent overproduction of sugar, but through the power of congressmen from sugar states, specific minimum quotas were written into the bill for mainland beet sugar and cane sugar, while the American Territory of Hawaii was permitted to share with island possessions and foreign countries in what was left after the mainland quotas were filled. Hawaii was called upon to suffer the loss required by a 10 per cent reduction in sugar acreage.

Hawaii was properly recognized as a "domestic sugar producing area" in the Sugar Act of 1937, under which it operated during the years of World War II. Hawaiian cane sugar was allotted 25.25 per cent of the domestic national quota, which in turn was about 55 per cent of the estimated annual needs of the United States. The foreign importation was almost altogether drawn from the Philippines and Cuba. Although the administration of the act caused some complaints of injustice, the quota theory was approved in principle by the producers.

This theory was embodied in the Sugar Act of 1947, although quotas were therein set for the following five years on a fixed-tonnage basis rather than a percentage basis. Of the estimated domestic consumption of 7,500,000 tons of sugar a year, domestic beet and cane producers were allocated 4,268,000 tons. Hawaii, as a domestic producer, was allocated an annual quota of 1,052,000 tons, which amounts to about 14 per cent of the national needs. In order to fulfill this quota under post-war conditions of increased costs of production, it was necessary for the sugar industry to prove again that it could meet the challenge by using improved tools and more refined scientific methods.

Mechanization of methods of operations has made it possible to produce more sugar with fewer workers; but wages have gone up as the number of workers has gone down. In 1946, with 28,000 employees, the payroll was $37,500,000; in 1957, 17,000 employees received $56,000,000. Hourly-rated sugar workers in Hawaii receive the world's highest year-round agricultural wages. The plantation companies have 14,000 stockholders. Capital invested in industry is about $200,000,000. Both the state and federal governments receive a large part of their tax incomes in Hawaii from the sugar industry and its employees. If this great and basic industry should collapse, the disastrous effect would be felt not only in the islands but in continental United States.

The pineapple industry, Hawaii's second most important, was mainly developed in the present century. Fortunately, pineapples may be cultivated on soils not suited to sugar cane, for they do not need irrigation and can grow at higher elevations. During less than half a century, the value of the pineapple crop has risen from almost nothing to many millions of dollars a year.

The pineapple has been grown in Hawaii for more than a hundred years. Just who brought in the first plant is not known, but the Spaniard Marin experimented with it, and this fruit was sold to ships during the whaling days. During the 1880's several men believed that the fruit might be raised commercially, and about 1885 several varieties of pineapple were imported, among them the Smooth Cayenne variety, which is the one most suitable for canning and which is still grown almost exclusively in the islands. The leaders in this experiment were Captain John Kidwell and R. A. Jordan, and small plantations were set out in Manoa Valley and near Pearl Harbor. The main market in early days was for fresh pineapples, which were sent to the Pacific Coast. About 1891 the canning of pineapples was begun on a primitive scale, but difficulties soon caused abandonment. With annexation and removal of customs duties on fruit sent to the mainland, the pineapple industry received an impetus.

The modern industry dates from 1900, when some energetic farmers from Southern California formed a colony at Wahiawa, Oahu, and on homestead lands, under the leadership of Byron O. Clark, began raising a number of crops, including pineapples. The fruit was planted with a seven-foot space between rows so that the land could be cultivated by horse-drawn implements. An abandoned cannery, removed from Pearl Harbor and set up at Wahiawa, was the scene of the first attempts to preserve the fruit. A leader in the new industry was James D. Dole, who realized that its greatest future lay in improving canning operations on a large scale and shipping a quality product to mainland markets. In 1901 Dole organized the Hawaiian Pineapple Company and the first crop was canned in 1903; it ran to 1,893 cases. In 1906 the company erected a cannery at Iwilei in Honolulu, which has grown to be the largest fruit cannery in the world.

From Oahu the growing of pineapples spread to Maui, Hawaii, and Kauai. In 1912 the first million-case pack was shipped. In 1922 almost the entire island of Lanai was bought by the Hawaiian Pineapple Company, which proceeded to build a harbor, make a settlement for workers, and lay out a vast plantation. The lands of the Wahiawa colony had passed from the hands of the homesteaders into the possession of large corporations, and like the sugar industry, pineapples became a large-scale venture, from planting to packing and shipping.

The need for co-operation in the pineapple industry was demonstrated to be even more acute than the need in sugar; in fact, the pineapple growers learned much from observing the history of the sugar industry. The first occasion demonstrating this need arose in problems of distribution rather than production. In 1907 the United States suffered a financial panic; in the two years 1906–1908, the pineapple industry doubled its pack each year, and in February, 1909, found itself with about three fourths of the entire supply of the previous year on hand. The Hawaiian Pineapple Growers Association, which had been organized in May, 1908, spent $50,000 on a successful co-operative advertising campaign. Again in 1912 the industry was faced with a large carryover; a new organization was formed, the Association of Hawaiian Pineapple Packers, and an assessment of five cents a case was used to finance another advertising drive. Hawaii has always been able to grow more pineapples than the world market could normally absorb, and the industry has succeeded mainly by educating the public to greater consumption of this delicacy. At the present time, although the uses for pineapple are still increasing, expansion is limited somewhat by the prices of such competitive canned fruits as peaches, and canned juices such as grapefruit.

Co-operation in the application of science to the pineapple industry was begun in 1914, when the necessity for control of various pests and diseases became evident, and a contract was made whereby the staff of the HSPA Experiment Station undertook work on such problems. A member of the Station was sent to Central America in 1919 in search of new varieties. Early in the 1920's the wilt disease threatened the future of the industry, and in 1922, with the collaboration of the Territorial Board of Agriculture and Forestry, an explorer was sent to Central America in search of parasites that would prey upon various pineapple pests. Later this exploration was extended to Fiji, Haiti, the Philippines, and South Africa. An iron-sulphate spray was demonstrated in 1916 which permitted the growing of pineapples in certain areas where without this spray the plants were unable to obtain sufficient iron from the soil for normal growth. By 1924 tarred mulching paper was in general use to control weeds, to preserve moisture in the soil, and to retain warmth.

An experimental plot of one hundred acres was leased at Wahiawa in 1922, and from 1924 to 1926 an experiment station, forerunner of the present Pineapple Research Institute, was organized with headquarters at the University of Hawaii.

The returns from the use of mechanical methods in the pineapple industry have been almost as striking as those in sugar. Almost all the special machinery and technology used in the growing and packing of pineapples have been invented and tried out in Hawaii. An invention of 1913 was the Ginaca machine, which with more than human speed and accuracy removes the shell and core in a single operation, leaving a smooth, clean cylinder of tender fruit. An immense harvesting machine has lately been used, which passes down roads through the fields and loads the heavy, hand-picked fruit into trucks by means of moving belts.

During the First World War difficulty in obtaining shipping space for pineapple products was encountered, but cases continued to move with rapidity to wartime markets, and after the war there was a great expansion in planted acreage. Discovery by the scientists that the mealy bug was responsible for the transmission of wilt cut down losses, and opened up a still greater possibility of increasing the pack beyond world demands. Negotiations for voluntary reduction of pack were forced upon the competing growers during the depression of the 30's, when a major reorganization of the industry took place. In 1932 the Pineapple Producers Co-operative Association was formed, with the object of planning production for the benefit of the whole industry. This program extended to 1943. Today the Pineapple Research Institute, with a staff of about forty scientists working in collaboration with the University of Hawaii, continually studies problems concerned with the production of the fruit.

Nowadays about 65 per cent of the world's supply of pineapples is grown in the Hawaiian Islands. There are nine pineapple companies operating thirteen plantations, and nine canneries process the fruit. About 75,000 acres of land are tilled by the industry, which uses about 6,000 agricultural laborers and 4,000 manufacturing workers. During the harvesting season from June to September, an additional 11,000 persons are employed. Millions of dollars' worth of canned and fresh fruit, as well as canned pineapple juice, is annually shipped. Recently the industry has introduced fresh frozen pineapple to mainland markets. Valuable by-products include citric acid, pineapple bran for cattle fodder, calcium citrate, alcohol, and natural sugar reclaimed by a new ion-exchange process.

The growth of the sugar and pineapple industries in Hawaii has brought into existence and developed a number of other groups dependent upon these giant industries. These include banks, sugar factors, trust companies, and other financial organizations. Under the stimulus of building sugar machinery, the Honolulu Iron Works has grown to tremendous size and has installed sugar mills as far away as the Philippine Islands and Cuba. To supply island needs, a commercial fertilizer factory and a can factory have been established. The growth of transportation, by ship, barge, rail, and highway, has had to keep pace with the demands of the basic industries. Speedy communication methods, such as telephone, cable, and radio, have likewise been supported. The importance of sugar and pineapple is evident in the fields wherever one looks as he travels through the islands; the network of industrial activities based on sugar and pineapple runs through the whole fabric of modern Hawaiian life.

CHAPTER TWENTY-THREE

The March of Education and Culture

Hawaii has witnessed in the twentieth century a striking growth in school attendance from kindergarten through the university levels, and today it has a modern educational system fully equipped to train American citizens to take their proper part in world affairs. Religious freedom continues to be exercised in the Hawaiian tradition of tolerance, and the churches hold a high place in island life. Cultural assets of the community include libraries, museums, an art gallery, and theatrical societies. An all-year program of sports and other recreational activities makes Hawaii one of the nation's finest playgrounds.

A fifth of Hawaii's tax dollars are spent on public education. The schools have continued to develop in this century under a truly American pattern, and the people of the islands are proud of the record that has been achieved. A joint Congressional committee which held hearings on statehood in Hawaii in 1937 made the following statement: "The public schools of Hawaii are the foundation of good citizenship. As a part of their curriculum they inculcate the basic principles of democracy in the youth who pass through them. With so many children of alien parentage among them, a definite program of Americanism is necessary. Too much praise cannot be given to the schools of Hawaii for the splendid manner in which they have met this problem and in the great measure of success that has attended their efforts." A similar committee in 1946 stated that "illiteracy in the islands among native-born citizens is almost non-existent," and pointed out that standards of instruction in the schools are the same as on the mainland

and higher than those in many states. It also noted that "the University of Hawaii compares favorably with many state universities."

Establishment of a strong school system on the American pattern had begun long before annexation. Under such men as A. T. Atkinson, who became inspector general of schools in 1887, steady advancement was made toward the ideals of universal, compulsory, non-sectarian, and tax-supported education. By 1888 all English-language government schools were free to students, without payment of tuition. In the same year, teacher-training classes were begun; teachers' conventions were revived, and a summer meeting in 1890 was the forerunner of the present university summer sessions for teachers. For some time American textbooks had been used in the public schools, and already about 40 per cent of the teachers were Americans.

Further advances were made during the brief period of the Hawaiian Republic. Government subsidies to private schools, long granted under the monarchy, were ended. Education was restored to its early important place under a separate Department of Public Instruction. English was made the required language for instruction in all public schools. The need for professional training of teachers finally resulted in the establishment of the Honolulu Normal and Training School in 1896. Modern public high schools were inaugurated. The kindergarten movement in Hawaii also had its birth in these years.

Hawaii's schools had won to such a high standard that the commission appointed by President McKinley in 1898 to recommend legislation for the new territory had nothing but praise for the system, finding it perfectly suited to the needs of the island population. "The school system and its methods are peculiarly American," the commission reported. "There are few countries in which education is so universal as in Hawaii. . . . The present public school system in the Hawaiian Islands is such an admirable one that improvements in the system can only wisely be made as the Territory expands in population and intellectual growth. The committee therefore recommend that the present school system remain in force." This advice was heeded by the framers of the Organic Act.

The fundamental structure of public education in Hawaii has not materially changed since 1900. But an expansion of about 800 per cent in school enrollment has brought with it a tremendous concomitant growth in problems of teaching personnel, in need for expansion in buildings and facilities, and in financing of the growing system. Success in giving a democratic common basis under American ideals to generations of children of Hawaiian, Puerto Rican, Chinese, Japanese, Korean, Filipino, and varied *haole* ancestries has well demonstrated the soundness of the theories of education that were early worked out in practice in the schoolrooms of Hawaii.

Some important changes in the public education system were made in the 1920's, partly as a result of a survey conducted under the federal Office of Education in 1920. The most significant improvements were made in more extensive teacher training, specialized vocational education, broadened secondary schooling, provisions for more higher education, and control of foreign language schools.

The most striking change had to do with the training of teachers. The Normal School raised its admission requirement to accept only high school graduates, and the "collegiate diploma" was granted only after two years of Normal School work.

Classification of pupils in the grade schools was improved through the use of standard tests and study of individual abilities. Better school programs and courses were worked out by teachers and supervisors. With the assistance of federal funds, courses were begun in vocational agriculture, vocational shop, and vocational homemaking. Active health instruction programs were started in the schools with practical results, particularly in dental hygiene.

The first public "English Standard" schools opened their doors in the 1920's. These schools enrolled children of any ancestry provided they passed proficiency tests in the use of the English language. The purpose of this segregation was to prevent children with a good background in English from being exposed during school hours to the effects of "pidgin English," an island jargon which has grown up as a primitive means of communication, particularly between persons of different ancestries. Finally the English Standard schools came under attack as being undemocratic. The general improvement in English usage and progress in all the public schools has led to abandonment of the practice of singling out only a few schools as "English Standard."

Secondary education had been left, under the monarchy, to the various private schools (Lahainaluna did not become a high school in the modern sense until 1923). Not before 1895, when the Honolulu High School (now McKinley High School) was founded, did public education include the secondary grades. Expansion was slow. Hilo High School opened in 1905, Maui High School in 1913, and Kauai High School in 1914. These four, and the Normal School, were the only public secondary schools at the time of the federal survey in 1920. As a result of the survey's recommendations, junior high schools were set up, and by 1930 there were nine senior high schools and sixteen schools with junior high grades. Enrollment in the secondary grades increased more than 300 per cent in this decade, and expansion was rapid in the 1950's. Significant movements have been the bringing of senior high school facilities to rural areas, further development of vocational education, and experimentation in new courses, such as the "core curriculum." Today there are public high schools and intermediate (junior high) schools available to students in all parts of the state.

A unique problem which aroused criticism during the survey of 1920 was the group of foreign-language schools which had grown up in the territory. Side by side with the public schools was an entirely alien system dating back to the special conditions under the Republic, when the first Japanese language school was begun by the Reverend Takie Okumura, a Christian minister, to instruct the children of Japanese immigrants in their parents' tongue. These schools, which were held before and after public school hours, became a fixed institution and grew rapidly; by 1919 there were 163 Japanese language schools, with an enrollment of 20,000 and a corps of teachers numbering 450. (Chinese and Korean schools enrolled another 2,000 students in twenty schools with forty teachers.)

Critics of these schools remarked that teaching the Japanese language was not to be separated from teaching ideals of Japanese nationalism; and public school teachers felt that the long hours, divided attention, and oriental methods of instruction hindered the processes of learning under the American system. These language schools, unlike other private schools, were not subject to the supervision of the Department of Public Instruction. The federal survey recommended the abolition of all language schools except those for alien children who were denied American citizenship, and suggested that oriental languages be offered in the public schools as part of the regular curriculum. However, the legislature of Hawaii in 1920 rejected such a drastic move. An act to regulate the foreign language schools placed them under the Department of Public Instruction, and provided for the certification of teachers by that department. Under this law, 138 schools were issued provisional licenses; but eighteen schools refused to comply and began legal action to test the constitutionality of the law. When the Hawaii supreme court refused to enjoin the Department from carrying out the law, the case was appealed to the Ninth Appellate Court in San Francisco in 1926. Here the Hawaiian law was ruled unconstitutional, and this judgment was sustained by the Supreme Court of the United States in 1927. As a result, the Japanese schools, firmly entrenched, extended their plants, increased enrollments, and brought many new teachers from Japan.

The attack on Pearl Harbor on December 7, 1941, closed the doors of all language schools in Hawaii, and many people believed that they would never open again. A new law to control such schools was passed by the legislature in 1943. This was not questioned until late in 1946, when a small group of schools—Chinese language schools this time—again challenged the constitutionality of such control. The case was carried to the Ninth Appellate Court once more, and late in 1947 the law was judged to be unconstitutional. An appeal to the Supreme Court of the United States failed to change this decision.

Today, Hawaii is the only part of the United States which has a centrally controlled educational system; there are no local school boards or county systems with varying standards. The requirement for teaching certification in any public school in Hawaii is five years of completed college work. All teachers must have the same minimum of training, all are paid on the same base schedule no matter in what school or what grade they teach, and rural schools have teachers with as much training as those in city schools. Opportunities for attending high school are as good in plantation communities as in the cities.

The Hawaii Education Association, organized in 1921, has been an active force in promoting sound educational policies. The salary scale in the public schools is high; U.S. Office of Education figures for 1945 showed that only four states and the District of Columbia paid higher annual salaries for teachers than the rate for Hawaii. Sabbatical leaves are given to island teachers. There has been a lively program of teacher exchanges; between 1934 and 1941, three hundred teachers from Hawaii exchanged jobs for a year with chosen mainland teachers. Like all territorial employees, teachers benefit by the generous provisions of the Retirement Act passed in 1925. Many of the college students in Hawaii eagerly look forward to teaching as a career, but it has always been necessary to bring in teachers from outside to supplement the local supply, so that the stream of teachers bringing American ideals and methods to the islands remains unbroken after more than a century.

In 1959 there were 208 separate public schools in Hawaii, including kindergartens, special classes, and schools for the handicapped. Although the pupils, like the teachers, represent many ethnic groups, fewer than one-half of one per cent of the public school pupils are foreign born. Adult education, a function of the Department of Public Instruction, was brought to more than fourteen thousand persons in 1959 in evening classes throughout the islands.

Public higher education had its origin in this century, and Hawaii has its own university, which was founded under federal land-grant provisions and which corresponds to state universities on the mainland. This institution was organized in 1907 under the name of the College of Agriculture and Mechanic Arts; with John W. Gilmore as its first president, it opened September 14, 1908, with five students and a faculty of twelve. The name was changed in 1911 to the College of Hawaii. The college, temporarily located on Young Street in Honolulu, near Thomas Square, moved in 1912 to its present site at the mouth of Manoa Valley, three miles from the center of the city. In that year the main edifice was Hawaii Hall, now the center of a spreading campus containing a number of classroom buildings, laboratories, and athletic fields. The name was finally changed in 1920 to the University of Hawaii.

The university is open to all qualified persons regardless of sex, racial ancestry, or nationality, and its courses are fully accredited by the Association of American Universities. It is controlled by a Board of Regents appointed by the governor for four-year terms. The instructional organization (as of 1960) includes Colleges of Tropical Agriculture (including the Hawaiian Agricultural Experiment Station and the Co-operative Extension Service in Agriculture and Home Economics), Arts and Sciences, Business Administration, Education (formerly Teachers Colleges, formed in 1931 when the Territorial Normal School and the University School of Education were united), Engineering, General Studies (formerly Extension Division), and Nursing; Graduate School; and the Gregg M. Sinclair Library. The Legislative Reference Bureau is administered by the University, as are the Aquarium at Waikiki and the Harold L. Lyon Arboretum. The University has co-operative arrangements with the Pineapple Research Institute of Hawaii, Hawaiian Sugar Planter's Association, United States Bureau of Entomology (Fruit Fly Laboratory), United States Fish and Wild Life Service, and Bernice P. Bishop Museum, and performs many other kinds of public service. The faculty members, drawn from many mainland universities, are especially well qualified in such fields as the history and politics of the Pacific region, Pacific area studies, oriental languages and literatures, social science (particularly racial interrelations), volcanology, anthropology, the natural sciences of the Pacific basin, sugar technology, and tropical agriculture.

In the years since World War II, several private colleges have been established to share the burden of higher education with the University of Hawaii. Most important are Chaminade College of Honolulu (Catholic) and the Church College of Hawaii (Mormon). The former was founded (1955) by the Society of Mary (Marianists); it began as a junior college, was expanded in 1957 to a four-year college, and in 1960 was accredited by the Western College Association. The Church College, established near the Mormon Temple at Laie in 1955, has been accredited as a junior college by the Western College Association. Jackson College, established in 1949, is operated by the Hawaii Baptist Foundation. Manaolu College, opened on Maui in 1950, is a junior college with high standards. Honolulu Christian College (1953) provides education in an evangelical context.

Private schools below the college level have been important in Hawaii. In 1959 there were 95 such schools, covering all grades from kindergarten through high school. Some of these schools had their origins under denominational auspices, and many of them have had lengthy careers of service.

Punahou School is now more than a hundred years old. It is one of the largest and best known schools in Hawaii, and its curriculum covers both elementary and high school grades.

Two schools begun by the Anglican Church in the islands are Iolani School for boys and St. Andrew's Priory for girls. Iolani was started in 1872 by Bishop Willis; it was combined in 1887 with an earlier Episcopal school, St. Albans. The school accepts boys of all racial heritages, and Sun Yat Sen, who came to be the George Washington of modern China, gained a part of his education at Iolani. St. Andrew's Priory was founded in the reign of Kamehameha IV, under the sponsorship of Queen Emma; at the same time another girls' school, called St. Cross, was founded at Lahaina, Maui, and continued for many years to do valuable work. The program at St. Andrew's has always emphasized homemaking and other rounded activities designed to develop Christian character.

An extensive system of Catholic elementary and secondary schools has grown up in Hawaii since the days when Ahuimanu School was organized on Oahu in 1846 to fulfill a pledge extracted from Kamehameha III by Captain Mallet. Ahuimanu's functions as a boys' school were taken over by St. Louis College, organized in Honolulu in 1880 by the adventurous Father Larkin. An early announcement referred to it as "The College of St. Louis, an Hawaiian Commercial and Business Academy, offering classical, scientific and commercial courses." In 1882, the school moved to a site in Nuuanu Valley, where it was to remain for forty-six years. In the following year, to insure a stable teaching staff, the college was turned over to the Brothers of Mary, a teaching order which since that time has furnished the St. Louis faculty with instructors. A site of two hundred acres in the Kaimuki district was acquired in 1923, and in 1928 the new plant was occupied; an imposing group of structures now lies below the suburb of St. Louis Heights. The name of the school was changed to St. Louis High School when Chaminade College of Honolulu was established on the same campus.

High-school education for Catholic girls was begun in 1909, although for fifty years previous there had been opportunities for girls to obtain sectarian education on the elementary school level. The new school, Sacred Hearts Academy, opened in September, 1909. Rapid growth required the addition of new buildings in 1920 and 1926.

Other units in the system of parochial education in Hawaii include St. Mary's in Hilo, St. Anthony's on Maui, and several schools under the Maryknoll order.

Perhaps the most novel educational institution in the islands is the Kamehameha Schools, founded under the will of Bernice Pauahi (Mrs. Charles R. Bishop), heiress to the private lands of the Kamehameha family. It was her desire to provide for young people of Hawaiian ancestry "first and chiefly a good education in the common English branches, and also instruction in morals and in such useful knowledge as may tend to make good and industrious men and women." The school for boys opened in 1887, the school for girls in 1894. Attention has always been given to vocational studies. A mass of imposing concrete buildings crowning the heights overlooking downtown Honolulu marks the modern site of the schools. Mrs. Bishop's original endowment has grown under shrewd trusteeship until its present net worth is about fifteen million dollars. The large number of active "Kam" alumni who have become a part of Hawaii's modern life testifies to the value of Mrs. Bishop's educational legacy.

Another private institution, Mid-Pacific Institute, is the successor of two Protestant missionary schools which were merged early in the twentieth century. One of its predecessors was Kawaiahao Seminary, which grew out of a girls' school sponsored by the Hawaiian Mission Children's Society. Mills School (named for the founder of the American Board of Commissioners for Foreign Missions) was the other; it dated back to 1892, when Mr and Mrs. Francis Damon, former missionaries to China, began giving lessons in their Honolulu home to Chinese boys from rural districts of the islands. The school grew, and later absorbed two other similar ventures—the Japanese Boarding School and the Methodist Korean Boarding School. The present-day Mid-Pacific Institute for boys and girls occupies several large buildings adjacent to the University of Hawaii campus.

Freedom of religion continues to prevail in the Hawaiian tradition, and in the islands many faiths and sects worship side by side. There are about a hundred churches in the city and county of Honolulu alone, and these include many Christian denominations, as well as Jewish, Buddhist, and other oriental churches. One interesting institution which reflects Hawaii's interracial religious efforts is the Church of the Crossroads, which was founded to serve young people who had fallen away from Buddhism and Shintoism and had found no new affiliations. These young folk wanted to attend a Christian church where English was used, but were too shy to seek enrollment in one of the older churches with settled congregations. From its beginnings in 1923, the Church of the Crossroads has been a favorite place for such young people. The new buildings finished in 1935, with their charming blend of architectural reminders of all the great religions of the world, offer an ideal setting for worship and, in particular, for weddings.

Perhaps the most marked growth in church congregations during the present century has been in the Baptist Church and, particularly, the Mormon Church, whose rise has earlier been narrated. The war in the Pacific seriously affected the work of oriental religious groups in Hawaii. Many Japanese Buddhist and Shinto priests and teachers were interned, and activities of the shrines and temples were greatly curtailed. Since the war, there has been a marked revival. Formerly the Buddhist bishops were appointed from Japan; but late in 1945, sixty priests of the Honpa Hongwanji Buddhist sect met and for the first time elected a bishop to head their mission. The foremost authority on the subject remarks that since the war, the largest number of religious recruits from first-generation Japanese have been gained by "militant evangelistic groups such as the Southern Baptists, Seventh Day Adventists, and Mormons."

The old Kawaiahao Church continues to be the center of worship for the Hawaiian race, and services in both the Hawaiian language and English are still given there and in other churches.

Books are plentiful in the islands. The Library of Hawaii, established in 1913 as successor to an older subscription library, serves the island of Oahu through fifty-six distribution outlets, including the main building in Honolulu. During the 1920's, county libraries on the other islands were set up independent of the Library of Hawaii. Other collections of books on Hawaii are found in the University of Hawaii Library, the Carter Library of the Hawaiian Mission Children's Society, the Bishop Museum Library, and the collection of the Hawaiian Historical Society.

The Bernice Pauahi Bishop Museum of Polynesian Ethnology and Natural History, founded in 1889 by Charles Reed Bishop in memory of his wife, has become an internationally known research center for the collection and publication of knowledge concerning Polynesian life and environment. The museum is not only a headquarters for scientists, but houses the most important collection of Hawaiian and Polynesian artifacts to be found in the world. The museum is associated with Yale and the University of Hawaii in Pacific area research. Other museums and collections of interest to students of Hawaiian history include the Queen Emma Museum, the American Mission Home, oldest frame building still standing in the islands, and the Public Archives Building in the palace grounds.

Center of Hawaii's artistic activities is the Honolulu Academy of Arts, a gift to the community in 1922 from Mrs. C. M. Cooke and her family. This attractive building offers periodic exhibits and houses permanent collections of Hawaiian, Occidental, and Oriental art of many kinds. Its staff gives lectures and courses for children and adults, and provides for the exhibition of the work of local artists.

Social and recreational facilities in Hawaii are many. Numerous clubs and fraternal societies meet regularly. Outdoor living the year round makes the islands a vacationist's paradise. There are dozens of public playgrounds. Almost every known sport is offered, from swimming, surfing, and yachting along the shores to skiing, hiking, and hunting in the mountains. Facilities are available for golf, tennis, horseback riding, fishing, skating, football, boxing, wrestling, bowling, and dancing (including Hawaii's best known dance, the hula). Most of the people of the islands are music lovers; there are many choirs and choral societies, and a symphony orchestra. The Royal Hawaiian Band gives a weekly concert and plays on festive occasions. There are many motion-picture theaters throughout the islands, and Honolulu supports an active community theater and a University theater guild. Special community festivals are held on particular dates such as Kamehameha Day, Regatta Day, Lei Day, and Aloha Week.

CHAPTER TWENTY-FOUR

Hawaii in World War II

On the "day of infamy," December 7, 1941, the surprise Japanese attack upon the American military and naval power at Pearl Harbor and elsewhere on Oahu plunged the United States into World War II. From the ruins of that defeat a new Hawaii was born, dedicated to victory in the Pacific; and the slogan "Remember Pearl Harbor!" vitalized the mighty potential war-making forces of America in the long conflict against fascism throughout the globe.

Through a long series of mischances, the Hawaiian Islands lay completely open to the attack that no one in command could believe would come. The Japanese plan counted upon the well-known week-ending habit of the Americans and upon the routine that usually brought our ships into harbor over Sunday. The entire Pacific fleet—with the exception of two carriers, seven heavy cruisers, and attendant destroyers which fortunately were on task force duty west of Oahu—was moored in the harbor without barrage balloons or torpedo baffles. More than a third of the officers were ashore. There were no observation planes in the air. The army radar service was merely on a training basis. The only planes which could have acted on a warning were parked on the fields, unprepared for immediate flight. Most of the army's anti-aircraft weapons were not supplied with shells and would have required from one to four hours to get into action. The commanders of America's forces in the eastern Pacific were responsible for laying their forces open to the precise kind of attack that was theoretically most to be feared, and this on the very morning when a dispatch from Admiral Hart in Washington had warned them that war in the Pacific could be expected to break out within a few hours.

The Japanese action against Pearl Harbor and Oahu had been cunningly planned. As early as November 11, at least ten long-range submarines had departed from Japan to make rendezvous outside the harbor entrance. Five of them carried two-man midget submarines aboard. Vice Admiral Nagumo's main body left the Kuril Islands on November 25. It was made up of two battleships, two heavy cruisers, a light cruiser, nine destroyers, and six carriers with more than 360 aircraft on their decks. Their orders were to return to Japan if discovered more than two days before the scheduled attack; they could also be recalled if the diplomatic offensive carried on in Washington by Ambassadors Kurusu and Nomura turned out favorably for Japan. Otherwise, the air attack would be launched from the ships at a point 200 miles north of Oahu before daylight on December 7.

Unalerted, the islands lay open to the lightning attack on that Sunday dawn. The first plane dived over Pearl Harbor at 7:55 A.M., coming from the south in company with a dive-bomber unit that struck the army planes on Hickam Field and the navy PBY's on Ford Island. Another bomber unit came in from the north and smashed the unmanned army fighter planes ranked wing-to-wing on Wheeler Field near Schofield Barracks. Immediately behind the dive bombers at Pearl Harbor were 40 new-model torpedo bombers, which launched their heavy missiles at the ships moored like sitting ducks along Battleship Row. Fifty horizontal bombers came in their wake, and then came 45 fighter planes to meet any opposition that might get into the air, and to mop up the remains of any surviving installations on Oahu.

The attackers knew that a second wave of 171 aircraft was following in support an hour later; but most of the damage was done by the first wave. In the first fifteen minutes the Japanese wiped out or immobilized almost the entire air strength of Oahu. In that short period they had also done much to destroy their chief objective, the United States Pacific Fleet. Aerial torpedoes, launched with full knowledge of the mooring plan, exploded against the steel sides of the immobile battlewagons; bombs landed on the decks, magazines exploded, and several vessels rolled over amid the smoke of the wreckage. One or two ships managed to get under way, but the second wave of dive bombers at 8:50 A.M. went in to finish the kill.

The air attacks knocked out the Pacific Fleet and paralyzed American naval action in that ocean for many weeks to come, at a loss to the Japanese of only 29 aircraft, one fleet submarine, and five "suicide" submarines (one of them sunk outside the harbor by the U.S.S. *Ward* at 6:45 A.M. by the first shots fired in the Pacific war). The cost to America that morning was great. All eight of Admiral Kimmel's battleships were out of action. Two of them, the *Pennsylvania* and the *Maryland*, could be restored fairly quickly, and the *Tennessee* was to be repaired by the shipyard workers almost as soon. The *Oklahoma* and the *Arizona* were total losses. Three other ships were, through almost superhuman efforts, ultimately restored to sea service; it was nearly five months before the *Nevada* was patched up well enough to limp back to the mainland, and much longer until the *California* and the *West Virginia* were sent on their ways to restoration. Three cruisers—*Raleigh*, *Helena*, and *Honolulu* (this ship had first visited its namesake city only two years before)—suffered rather serious damage, and three destroyers were wrecked. The lives of 2,086 naval officers and men had been lost. Army losses reached 237 lives. Total casualties in killed, wounded, and missing from both services were placed at 3,435.

Everyone who lived through that Sunday morning in the islands has his story to tell of the disastrous blitz that changed Hawaii's destiny forever. The greatest defeat in American history aroused the fighting spirit of Americans to forge the greatest warpower the world has ever known. Hawaii, which at the time was already on a war defense basis, did her share in the winning of the global struggle on many fronts. Robert Shivers, head of the F.B.I. in Honolulu during the war, told a congressional committee: "It was not the civilian population who was confused. Nowhere under the sun could there have been a more intelligent response to the needs of the hour than was given by the population of these islands. . . . It is high time that the people of the United States should be told of Hawaii's contribution to this war, which is unequaled in the annals of our country."

Hawaii was immediately put on a war footing. A Major Disaster Council had been created on April 26, 1941, and in October of that year the Hawaii Defense Act, commonly called the M-Day Bill, giving the governor extended emergency powers and appropriations for civilian defense, had been passed by the legislature in special session. Now the emergency had arrived. Governor Poindexter at 11:30 A.M., in accordance with the M-Day Bill, proclaimed the existence of a defense period. At 3:30 that afternoon, at the instigation of the commanding general and under authority of the Organic Act, he issued a formal proclamation invoking martial law, suspending the privilege of the writ of habeas corpus, and requesting Lieutenant General Walter D. Short to exercise all the powers normally exercised by the governor of Hawaii. Civil government had ceased to exist.

Next day Short stated that he had assumed the post of military governor. Hawaii's military government set up offices in Iolani Palace and began issuing directives that affected every phase of Hawaii's wartime life.

Quickly and quietly, by prearranged plan, men from military intelligence groups and the F.B.I. moved to round up a number of Japanese suspects in Hawaii. Among those placed in protective custody were members of the consulate staff, as well as many of the 200 consular agents scattered throughout the islands. Crews of the sampan fishing fleets, manned mostly by men of Japanese ancestry, were detained. But the number of residents actually held on suspicion in Hawaii, in contrast with the drastic practice in West Coast defense areas, was only 1,440; and the number actually interned and sent to camps on the mainland was only about one per cent of the adult Japanese population in the islands.

Defense measures went into effect one after another. On December 7 a rigid nightly blackout was ordered (the first practice blackout of Oahu had been held in 1939). The Hawaii Territorial Guard was organized the same day. On December 8 the military governor ordered the closing of all schools, theaters, and saloons (the sale of liquor was restored in February on a controlled plan). Both public and private schools, he announced, were to be used as emergency evacuation centers, hospitals, first-aid stations, and military posts. Censorship of all mail, telephone calls, and cables was clamped down a few days later. On December 13, gasoline rationing was begun; motorists, except those in essential war jobs, were allowed only ten gallons a month. The complete rubber tire supply was later taken over by the authorities. Since on December 7 there was in the islands a stock of food sufficient to last the civilian population for no more than six weeks, it was soon necessary for an Office of Food Control to be set up to schedule the importation of needed supplies. Shortages were thereafter sporadic, and to check inflation an Office of Price Control was set up; later, a branch of the national Office of Price Administration was opened in the territory, and a rent control office was likewise established.

The story of Hawaii's civilians in the war is one of instant and unswerving voluntary participation for the common good. The achievement is greater when one recalls that the job was done despite many material shortages and an acute lack of manpower, and was done under crowded emergency conditions. From the outset, civilians met all their tasks to the best of their abilities.

Even while the bombs were dropping and radios were blaring "Take cover! Oahu is under attack! This is the real McCoy!", the civilian population avoided panic, refused to be stampeded by rumors, and mobilized for service. Civilian doctors and nurses rushed to aid the growing rows of casualties at Pearl Harbor and at the Honolulu emergency hospital. From the community blood bank, which had been started early in 1941, some 1,200 doses of life-giving plasma were drawn to help the victims of the attack.

Thereafter hundreds of citizens came to donate blood, and by the end of the first year of war, 15,850 persons had given blood for the victims of war.

Only a few scattered bombs, if any, fell on the city, although some damage was done by spent anti-aircraft shells from the defenders' guns. One explosion went off beside the governor's residence in Washington Place. Ironically, one part of the city where damage was greatest was a downtown section where many Japanese lived. Of the first 36 civilians killed by shrapnel and fire, 20 were of Japanese blood.

The citizenry rushed to help themselves and to help others. Householders dug bomb shelters. Schoolteachers and other volunteers drove to centers about the island to fingerprint all inhabitants and issue identification cards. Men who had joined the Police Reserves were now on patrol almost every night. Other men of the community began organizing the Businessmen's Military Training Corps, which had its first drill in February.

The Office of Civilian Defense had absorbed the Major Disaster Council but carried on its functions. Civilian hospital accommodations were expanded. About 6,500 citizens served as air-raid wardens; many others joined up as first-aid workers or ambulance drivers. Poison gas decontamination centers were set up at 35 locations on Oahu, and an alarm system was organized. Distribution of gas masks was begun by the OCD on January 2, 1942. Four hundred thousand masks were given to adults with instructions on their use, as well as 70,000 masks for children and 32,000 "bunny masks" for infants. A program for evacuation of civilians from dangerous sections was worked out, with 2,200 volunteer supervisors in charge; and 35 evacuation centers were set up and were provisioned with food and supplies from the Red Cross. An emergency feeding section was set up to feed volunteer workers and men of the Territorial Guard; the section served 300,000 meals in a single year. A war-garden program within a short time had 15,000 home gardens and many acres of plantation lands in food crops. The mass immunization of all residents of Oahu against smallpox and typhoid fever, ordered by the military governor on March 18, 1942, was begun on March 30 when 6,000 residents were given "shots" in a single day.

From the first days of the attack, preparations both civilian and military to withstand invasion went forward energetically. Gun emplacements and barbed-wire fences were erected, and the beaches were patrolled day and night. Acres of tough *kiawe* trees were uprooted to ensure a free zone of fire against landing parties. Buildings were hastily camouflaged with paint and nettings and improvised shrubbery.

Threats of combat still hovered over the islands in the early days. The news that came on Christmas Eve, 1941, that Wake Island had been captured after a heroic defense brought fear of invasion closer. Submarine warfare had begun on December 8. On December 30, Japanese submarines briefly shelled the ports of Hilo, Nawiliwili, and Kahului, although there were no casualties and damage was slight. On January 28, 1942, an army transport, the *Royal T. Frank,* was torpedoed in Hawaiian waters, with the loss of 29 lives. Air-raid alerts were frequent. Early on the morning of March 5 a lone plane mysteriously dropped four bombs on the wooded heights back of Roosevelt High School, without damage. As it turned out, the most exciting drama of civilian participation in the fight was the terrorizing of the "forbidden isle" of Niihau off the shores of Kauai, where a martial episode revealed that the fighting qualities of old Hawaii had not been lost.

On the privately-owned small island of Niihau, whose 150 inhabitants, living in pastoral quiet, had no radios and hence were unaware of the outbreak of war, a dazed Japanese aviator was forced down about 2:00 P.M. on December 7. His papers, maps, and gun were taken from him by Howard Kaleohano, who noted that there were bullet holes in the plane and suspected trouble. Kaleohano then buried the papers and waited for the arrival next day of the weekly sampan from Kauai. The launch did not arrive, and instructions on handling the prisoner were lacking.

During the next few days the aviator got in touch with the two

Japanese residents of Niihau—there were only two, one an alien and the other an island-born citizen—and somehow enlisted them in an attempt to get back the possibly incriminating papers. One of the recruits first threatened and then tried to bribe Kaleohano, without avail, to reveal the hiding place. The other, Harada, armed with a shotgun, on Friday helped the aviator to escape from his guard. The three Japanese then dismounted two machine guns from the plane, and turned them on the village. Kaleohano and five other cowboys got away, rode to the beach, and began a sixteen-hour haul across the channel to Kauai in a whaleboat.

Desperately seeking the papers, the three Japanese terrorized the peaceable people of Niihau all night and set fire to Kaleohano's house. Early next morning, a husky Hawaiian, Benjamin Kanahele, 51 years old, at the point of a gun was forced to make a pretended search for Kaleohano. The aviator, enraged, threatened Kanahele's wife and then shot Kanahele three times, in chest, hip, and thigh. The Hawaiian rose in his wrath. He seized the enemy by the body and smashed him against a stone wall, crushing his skull. Meanwhile, Kanahele's wife scuffled with Harada, who then committed suicide with his own gun. The attempt to take over one of the Hawaiian Islands by the enemy had been defeated barehanded. Admiring islanders who heard the story commented: "Never shoot a Hawaiian three times—he will get mad at you!" Later, Kanahele was decorated with the Medal of Merit, and Kaleohano with the Medal of Freedom.

The crucial days of the war in the minds of most of the people in Hawaii came early in June, 1942. Some of them knew that a big attack against the islands was brewing to the westward, but many who had no facts felt that something important was happening off there in the blue stretches of ocean. They were right. On June 4, the Battle of Midway Island began with a Japanese air attack at dawn. The men, ships, and planes of Admiral Chester W. Nimitz's command were ready, and in repeated assaults against the invading Japanese fleet inflicted a crushing defeat. At the end of the three-day battle, American ships and planes pursued the retreating enemy westward, and Japan's boldest blow directed against the eastern Pacific had been crushed and the people of Hawaii could breathe somewhat easier.

As a precaution against seizure and use of American currency by the enemy, however, a special issue of "Hawaii" bills replaced regular currency on June 25, 1942. Securities held in the territory were perforated for the same reason.

To present Hawaii's record in World War II would require a separate volume; here a few facts must suffice to show the extent of participation of her people.

Although registration under the Selective Service law began in the territory in 1940, few men in Hawaii were called up during the first year of the war, owing to the crucial shortage of manpower in this defense area. After the new call was made, Hawaii more than met her quota of manpower. A total of 32,197 territorial residents were inducted into the armed forces during the life of the Selective Service Act. An additional 4,580 residents entered the forces other than through selective service. As a congressional committee was to conclude in 1946, "People of all racial ancestries co-operated in preparing for and prosecuting the war." The percentages by racial groups of those inducted from Hawaii up to October, 1946, are, in round numbers: Japanese, 50 per cent; white, 15 per cent; Chinese, 10 per cent; part-Hawaiian, 9 per cent; Filipino, 9 per cent; Hawaiian, 3 per cent; all others, 4 per cent.

Many of the men of Hawaii had entered the armed forces, and Hawaii itself had become a bristling fortress. Hawaii was the staging area for many Pacific attacks, the headquarters for army and navy, and a giant training school for invasion landings, jungle combat, soldier survival, and gunnery (the isle of Kahoolawe, just south of Maui, was the most fiercely battered island in the Pacific, for it was the target grounds for all the naval artillery practice in these waters during the war, including full-scale rehearsals for Pacific invasion tactics). Hawaii was a supply area, a prisoner-of-war area, and a recuperation and recreation area dotted with many hospitals and rest camps. Among the hundreds of thousands of service men who passed through the islands, the civilian residents did what they could to build morale, by bringing amusement and relaxation to as many men as possible, considering the limitations and restrictions of the times.

Many homes in Hawaii were freely opened to American service men during the war years. As more thousands of men continued to arrive, however, it became impossible to entertain more than a fraction of these visitors. At the peak of military strength on Oahu, in July, 1944, a total of 254,000 army troops alone were stationed on that island—a number about equal to the population of Honolulu at the time; and during 1945, soldiers were arriving in the islands at the rate of 30,000 a month. To supplement the entertainment that men on leave could find at movies, USO and Special Services shows, shooting galleries, and bars, many civilians helped to put on camp performances by the Community Theater, visited convalescents, and opened the churches, libraries, concert halls, Academy of Arts, and other agencies to men from the armed forces. One example of friendliness was the Air Force Morale program, under which private homes in various island spots were given over to "tired flyers" who could recuperate in these restful surroundings.

Boy Scouts, Girl Scouts, Y.M.C.A., Y.W.C.A., schools, clubs, religious groups—all were busy on patriotic tasks. The women of the community flocked to find places in the Volunteer Special Services of the Hawaii Chapter of the American Red Cross, and gave their help in knitting, sewing, and making surgical dressings; in motor corps driving; in setting up canteens to feed service men; in acting as nurse's aides or "gray ladies" in island hospitals; in home-service assistance; and in various auxiliary capacities.

The people of Hawaii generously contributed financially as well. Hawaii heavily over-subscribed all seven war loans; total war bond sales reached $202,016,712.

Hawaii's main civilian job, in war as well as in peace, continued to be agricultural production. The government considered both sugar and pineapple to be essential crops. Between 20 and 30 per cent of the territory's pineapple production was taken by military and lend-lease agencies. Sugar plantations, in spite of losses in manpower and reduction in land and machines (most of their heavy equipment and drivers were lent to the U.S. Engineer Corps), kept production at a high level at a time when sugar was in great demand and was in fact rationed for war needs. In almost all high schools the week was reduced from five to four school days so that students could volunteer for work in the fields; and this student aid did enable the cultivation of sugar and pineapples to remain at a high level. Continued production of sugar was the wartime contribution of the people of all the main islands.

A series of war-born events that were to culminate in a vindication of the constitutional rights of Hawaii's citizens grew out of the "martial law" regime, particularly the situation under which army officers had taken over the judicial functions of the territory. Under the military governor, trial by jury or by civilian judges was suspended in every island courtroom, and although the federal district court was permitted to remain open, all other cases were routed to new courts set up under the direction of the provost marshal. Even traffic violations were considered to be the province of army judges, and citizens were haled before a major or a colonel who decided the case without a jury and without any right of appeal. Arbitrary judgments and punishments much in excess of those provided in civil statutes became common. In November, 1942, for instance, military judges examined 1,454 defendants; each and every one of them was pronounced guilty. Fines in excess of $2,000,000 were collected in the first two years of operation.

The vital right of American citizens, the writ of habeas corpus which protects them from detention unless they have been formally charged, had been suspended and remained suspended long after the imminent danger of invasion had passed. The legal battle to restore this right became a lengthy campaign.

The first challenge to the validity of this suspension was made in the Zimmerman case in February, 1942. Judge Delbert E. Metzger refused to issue a writ of habeas corpus in the case, but noted that the court was acting under duress in view of a military order. Before the case reached the Supreme Court of the United States, however, it was rendered moot because the army had meanwhile taken the prisoner to the mainland and had there unconditionally released him.

The legality of military rule in Hawaii was next challenged by a Honolulu attorney, Garner Anthony, in May, 1942, in an article written for a nationally read law journal. Anthony's arguments made him the standard-bearer of those who believed that Hawaii should not be governed as if it were a zone under military occupation.

Governor Poindexter's second four-year term expired in March, 1942, but he was not replaced until the inauguration on August 24, 1942, of Ingram M. Stainback. Upon this new executive, a native of Tennessee who had practiced law in the territory for almost 30 years, devolved the leadership of its government through the remainder of the war and into the following years of readjustment. One of his first acts was to appoint Garner Anthony as his attorney general, to begin the attempt to bring back civilian rule in the territory.

Governor Stainback and his attorney general went to Washington, D.C., in December, 1942, to urge the prompt restoration of civil rights to Hawaii. There they were vigorously aided by Joseph R. Farrington, who had been elected in November as Hawaii's delegate to Congress. Also in Washington at the time was General Emmons, the military governor, who soon thereafter, on his return to Hawaii, forecast on December 22 the early modification of martial law and restoration of a number of functions to the civil government. Action on this plan was announced by both Governor Stainback and General Emmons in the governor's office on February 8, 1943. These proclamations, which became effective on March 10, restored civil authority for many operations of the territorial and county governments, and also put under civil administration many bureaus such as price control, liquor control, and food control. But the military still retained the right to control shipping, the waterfront, public utilities, and communications; and the privilege of the writ of habeas corpus was still suspended.

It was expected that there would soon be a complete restoration of civil rights, and President Roosevelt directed General Emmons to "refrain from exercising authority over civil functions." However, month after month passed with no further modification of the practices of the military command in dealing with the civilians of Hawaii.

When the Glockner and Seifert cases came up in the federal court in June, 1943, Judge Metzger ordered the military authorities to produce the two men, then interned in a camp on Oahu. Lieutenant General Robert C. Richardson, who in the summer of 1943 had succeeded to the command of army forces in the Central Pacific Area, failed to bring the men into court. He then issued the notorious General Order No. 31 which threatened federal judges, lawyers, and others with fine and imprisonment if they attempted to file applications for the constitutional writ of habeas corpus. In the course of the proceedings, the general was fined $5,000 for contempt of court; later the fine was reduced to $100, and he was pardoned by President Roosevelt. The two prisoners, like Zimmerman, were released by the army, and again a judicial review of the case was forestalled.

In the Duncan case, Judge Metzger granted on April 13, 1944, a writ of habeas corpus and discharged the defendant from custody on the ground that martial law had legally ceased to exist after March 10, 1943. His decision was reversed by the Ninth Circuit Court in San Francisco; but the Hawaiian Bar Association protested against martial law, and in a series of other cases (notably the case of Harry E. White) and appeals, the question of the constitutionality of martial law in Hawaii was carried to the highest court in the land.

On December 7, 1945—four years to the day from the time

when martial law had been invoked amid the ruins of the Japanese attack—the Duncan and White cases were argued before the Supreme Court. The defenders of civil rights in Hawaii were vindicated on February 25, 1946, when the Supreme Court, by a six-to-two decision, repudiated the action of the army and held that the martial law imposed upon the territory had been unconstitutional. "Extraordinary measures in Hawaii, however necessary," ran the decision, "are not supportable on the mistaken premise that Hawaiian inhabitants are less entitled to constitutional protection than others." Under the assumption that Hawaii is an integral part of the United States, its people could not be denied their rights under the Constitution. The martial law cases will long stand as clarifications of the basic rights of American citizens everywhere.

The record of Hawaii's Japanese in World War II is a vivid argument for American democratic ideals. Fears of fifth-column activities and sabotage were completely unfounded. The congressional investigation of Hawaii's claim to statehood in 1946 concluded "that both army and navy intelligence authorities testified that not a single act of sabotage was committed by any resident of Hawaii before, during, or after the attack on Pearl Harbor, and that these same authorities commended the important patriotic service rendered, under the most critical conditions, in military intelligence and war work by all citizens of Hawaii, regardless of racial origin."

Far from thinking of sabotage, a number of persons in Hawaii's Japanese community gave active assistance in the conduct of the war. Its leaders formed various contact groups and emergency councils to supply liaison between that community and the military and civil authorities, and did much to maintain good morale among both alien and American-born Japanese in Hawaii. Many people of this racial stock served patriotically in different phases of war activities. No evidences of "bloc voting"—under which, for example, most of the racial group would plump for a political candidate of their own race—were uncovered. As a matter of fact, the

Japanese have always had much less than their numerical share of elected or appointed political officials. Moreover, to avoid embarrassing the territory in the eyes of the nation during the war, Japanese candidates voluntarily withdrew from politics for the duration. The 1943 legislature was the first in many years to have no man of Japanese ancestry sitting in either house.

The chief effect of the war upon the Japanese group in Hawaii was to draw them from their somewhat isolated position and to bring them strongly toward participation in the broader life of the island commonwealth. They won respect and self-respect at home, and took deserved pride in the valor of their American soldier sons, who won abroad the admiration of a world at war. The loyalty of Hawaii's *nisei* (American-born Japanese) was forever proved on the battlefield. A final count of Hawaii's war casualties shows that 80 per cent of those killed and 88 per cent of those wounded throughout the war were of Japanese ancestry.

Unfounded fears of the loyalty of Hawaii's *nisei* kept them out of military service for some months after the outbreak of war. Members of the Hawaiian Territorial Guard who were of Japanese ancestry were placed on inactive status on January 23, 1942. Undaunted, a group of 160 of these young men, most of them students at the University of Hawaii, volunteered for any duty that the army saw fit to give them. Their request was granted by Lieutenant General Delos C. Emmons, who had replaced General Short on December 17, 1941. He attached them to a regiment of engineers, and for a year these "Varsity Victory Volunteers," as they called themselves, worked willingly at various kinds of skilled and unskilled labor. When enrollment in the army was at last permitted them, most of these men immediately volunteered for active service.

Hawaii's two National Guard regiments, which had been made part of the federal defense forces in 1940, were called to active duty at the outbreak of hostilities. Later the 299th was inactivated, but the 298th went into training as an organic regiment with the 25th Division and later with the 24th Division. In the summer of

1942, about 1,300 American-Japanese draftees, who had taken all their basic training with the 298th and 299th, left for Camp McCoy, Wisconsin, to train as the 100th Infantry Battalion.

This famed *nisei* outfit, from the time its first contingents landed at Anzio in September, 1943, made a heroic record, especially in the fierce battles around Cassino and the crossings of the Rapido and Volturno Rivers during the Italian campaign. Within ten months it suffered over 300 killed and 650 wounded out of its total of 1,300 men, and thus won the name of "Purple Heart Battalion." By V-E Day the 442nd Regimental Combat Team, with which the 100th had been incorporated, was referred to by military observers as "probably the most decorated unit in United States military history." The A.J.A.'s (Americans of Japanese ancestry) from Hawaii and continental United States received more than 1,580 decorations, exclusive of 4,500 or more Purple Hearts to commemorate wounds received during 225 days of actual combat. In conferring a Distinguished Unit citation on the 100th Battalion, Lieutenant General Mark W. Clark, commanding general of the Fifth Army, said: "You have written a brilliant chapter in the history of the fighting men of America. You are always ready to close with the enemy, and you have always defeated him."

The decision of the War Department in January, 1943, to call for 1,500 volunteers from among the remaining A.J.A.'s in Hawaii was a mark of official confidence in the loyalty of these Americans, and the call was hailed as an opportunity. Within a month 9,507 island *nisei*—more than six times the quota—applied for enlistment; this number represented about one third of all the A.J.A.'s in the territory between the ages of 18 and 38. Two later calls in the same year for *nisei* volunteers to attend an army school for interpreters brought an additional 600 enlistments from Hawaii. During the later stages of the war, a large number of Hawaii's Japanese served in the Pacific theater, chiefly as interpreters, with every major unit in every engagement from Guadalcanal to Tokyo, and at risk of their lives repeatedly saved allied units from destruction by intercepting information on enemy movements. The spirit of "Go for broke"—the motto adopted by the fighting 442nd—was shared by all the more than 16,000 American-Japanese of Hawaii who served in our forces during World War II. Even the women of the Japanese group shared this martial spirit. When the privilege of enlisting in the WAC was extended to Hawaii in October, 1944, more than half the volunteers, or 26 out of 59 women inducted, were of Japanese ancestry.

To everyone in Hawaii and the rest of America, the year of triumph, 1945, came none too soon. News headlines were hopefully scanned. In the first few days of the new year, a great American task force landed on Okinawa, homeland of many of Hawaii's immigrants. In February the U.S. Marines landed on Iwo Jima and made it an American base close to Japan's home waters. On May 9 hostilities in Europe officially ended, and the spontaneous celebration of V-E Day in Hawaii was made more impressive by the thought that six million American service men would soon be released for action in the Pacific theater.

The end came soon after the world's first atomic bomb used in warfare was dropped on Hiroshima on August 5, followed by a second bomb four days later on Nagasaki. The unofficial jubilee that broke out on August 14 at the news of Japan's forthcoming surrender was the greatest celebration in Hawaii's history. On the occasion of the signing of the surrender terms in Tokyo Bay, the festivities were more formal but no less heartfelt during the three-day holiday from September 1 to 4. The worst war the world had ever seen was over; victory was won. Peace had been a dream; now it was at last a reality.

The effects of World War II upon Hawaii were many; some of these effects are still appearing three years after the end of the war. A new Hawaii has taken the place of the old.

From the time that an attack on Hawaii plunged the United States into the global conflict until the signing of the peace in Tokyo Bay, the people of the islands felt themselves to be in the forefront of the conflict. Hawaii was the main staging area for the long Pacific war. Hundreds of thousands of service men and women passed through Hawaii or trained there or manned its installations. Hawaii clearly recognized itself as part of an immense and powerful nation, made up of people from many states and communities. Numerous marriages between Hawaiian residents and Americans from other regions tightened the bonds of unity. The loyalty of the American-born Japanese of the islands was bloodily but triumphantly demonstrated at home and on the battlefields. Hawaii discovered that it was no longer merely an offshore tourist spot, but the hub of a vast wheel of expansion in the midst of the world's largest ocean, the advance post of the industrialized Occident in its march into the Pacific area. The insecurity of Hawaii's future status made most of its population turn toward the ideal of self-determination and statehood. The economic effects of the war, as will now be shown, were intense and indeed upsetting; but all in all, World War II brought one benefit—it revealed Hawaii to itself in all its strength, and made clear forever that Hawaii's future was an integral part of America's future.

CHAPTER TWENTY-FIVE

Toward Economic Democracy

Hawaii's business world has passed, within living memory, from outright feudalism through a period of strong paternalism, and is now achieving, through a number of causes—not the least of which was World War II—a status of economic democracy close to that found in continental United States. The paternalistic rule was on the whole benevolent and administered with some regard for Hawaii's best future, and without the careful guidance and hard work of earlier business leaders, the bread-and-butter industries of the islands could hardly have survived. Strong labor organizations, whose rise was long delayed in Hawaii, have achieved great power within the past few years, and there are many signs that a new spirit of liberalism and co-operation will bring economic stability and opportunity to the striving, polyracial wage-earners of the "50th state."

It would not be true to say that the business domination of the early island families has wholly disappeared. The "Big Five," which according to whispered rumors have been the sinister, monopolistic bogie pulling the strings of Hawaii's economy, still survive. These five corporations act in the capacity of factors or agents for all but three of the sugar companies operating in Hawaii, and have substantial stock holdings in these companies. Together, the Big Five control about 96 per cent of island sugar production. Largest of these agencies is American Factors, Ltd., which was formed in 1918 to take over the business of the German firm of H. Hackfeld & Company, and which in 1958 represented six plantations responsible for 28.7 per cent of the total

sugar produced. The others are C. Brewer & Company, Ltd., with
23.0 per cent; Alexander & Baldwin, with 19.4 per cent; Castle
& Cooke, Ltd., with 14.2 per cent; and Theo. H. Davies & Company, Ltd., with 9.8 per cent. The agency system is less used in
the pineapple industry, although some of the Big Five have an
interest in that industry. The Big Five have holdings in other important enterprises such as public utilities, docks, shipping companies, banks, hotels, department stores, and affiliated concerns.
Power is held not only through direct stock ownership but through
financing and supply contracts, through holding companies,
through complicated land-leasing systems, through control over
transportation agencies, through personal inter-family relationships, through trusteeships, and through a web of interlocking
directorates. A congressional investigating committee in 1946 concluded that "the Big Five dominates a great portion of Hawaii's
economy, but this economic dominance has not prevented the
establishment of many and varied businesses. There are good prospects for small business in Hawaii. Further the influence of the
Big Five has not prevented the enactment of progressive legislation in the field of labor, education, health, and welfare."

For decades this strongly integrated, island-owned financial
bloc was predominant; but in recent times its control has been
weakened. During the 1930's an economic middle class began to
emerge in Hawaii, and some descendants of immigrant laborers
became American business men. New Deal labor legislation and
anti-monopoly programs made themselves felt. For instance, the
Matson Navigation Company, Ltd., affiliated with the Big Five,
by 1929 had virtually monopolized all freight and passenger shipping touching Hawaii with the exception of some customers of
the Dollar Line. An agreement was made with Dollar to give
Matson half the income from Dollar's Hawaii business. On August 7, 1938, a report of the U.S. Maritime Commission ruled this
agreement unfair and invalid. Soon afterward the commission
itself took over the Dollar Line, renamed it American President
Lines, and hopefully attempted to give Matson more effective

competition in the Pacific trade. As another instance, previously, Matson had in 1935 invested half a million dollars in the Pan-American Airways route across the Pacific. This agreement was not approved by the Civil Aeronautics Board, and thereafter Congress passed a law prohibiting steamship companies from owning airlines. At present the bustling post-war air business between Hawaii and the mainland is shared by Pan-American, United, and Northwest Airlines as scheduled carriers.

The extension of some large mainland businesses to Hawaii also began in the 1930's, and residents who disliked monopolies were pleased when S. H. Kress & Company invaded Honolulu and in competition with Big Five outlets started a large five-and-ten cent store. Then Sears, Roebuck & Company set up a mail-order office and by 1940 opened a large retail store on a par with its mainland branches. The post-war business scene has revealed many opportunities for new concerns to start without large capitalization and without the protection of the Big Five.

Even before the outbreak of World War II, the defense construction industry, which was supported by government contracts and owed little allegiance to the Big Five, became one of Hawaii's chief employers. In fact, in 1943 the tax-base figure on construction exceeded that for both the sugar and pineapple industries put together. Much of this work was financed by big mainland firms, and their managers and workmen brought in not only new capital but new methods that disturbed the old scheme of island life. The effect of these continued to be felt, although defense construction work came to an end after the close of the war.

World War II did, of course, bring much business to the islands, but it was not restricted to a few established firms. Government building contracts were scrutinized and were subject to government accounting and wage controls. Price controls under OPA and other laws prevented wide profiteering. Millions of dollars were spent in the territory by the visiting throngs of service men that filled the streets of Honolulu on leave days, but though bank deposits more than trebled in Honolulu between 1941 and 1946, much of this fresh money went into the hands of small purveyors of food and entertainment. Many non-*haole* businesses reaped fortunes from catering to the needs of wartime visitors. The enterprise of oriental business men was strengthened by the local practice of forming a *hui,* the Hawaiian name for an informal syndicate which enables Chinese or Japanese members to take quick advantage of a business opportunity by raising contributions of group capital within a few hours, for mutual sharing of profits.

The greatest challenge to Big Five predominance of recent years was the rise of organized labor in Hawaii.

The growth of a strong labor movement in the islands is a very recent development. This is not surprising. Most of the laborers brought to work in the fields before annexation were under contract to work for a term of years. They lived in unfamiliar surroundings and in competition with men of other races, and they were easily exploited. Many laborers did not renew their contracts, but instead returned home or drifted away from the plantations. After 1890, however, large numbers of immigrants began to settle permanently and make their homes in the islands. From that time, disputes became more frequent in the fields. The Labor Commission of the Republic of Hawaii as long ago as 1895 issued a warning against "agitators, evil disposed, thriftless and dangerous persons, inciters to strikes and disputes." For many years after that time, the Hawaiian tradition was against the erection of militant labor organizations.

Reasons why the mainland labor pattern did not early invade Hawaii are not far to seek. Employers there have been strongly opposed to unionization and have used various means to influence public opinion against it. Many persons honestly felt that the employers of Hawaii were so enlightened that unions were unnecessary; and employers sometimes forestalled labor demands by voluntarily raising wages and improving conditions. Charges of actual intimidation or coercion of employees seem seldom to have foundation, but undoubtedly the trespass law which permits plantation owners to bar unwanted persons from their property has been used to keep organizers out of some plantation villages. Again, most workers, both alien and Hawaiian-born, have come from a background where unions were little known. The middle-class public likewise has been unfamiliar with unions and has associated them with violence and strikes such as those which on one or two bitterly memorable occasions cut the shipping lifeline to the mainland. Local strikes were often considered to be evidences of merely racial rebelliousness.

The drawing of racial lines in labor activities has, indeed, been one of the chief causes of lack of labor solidarity. Early in the century, the policy of denying to orientals membership in the skilled trades unions smashed all hopes for effective organization, for a "one-nationality" union arouses prejudice and may be crippled by competing workers from another national or racial group, who will work for lower wages or even act as strikebreakers. Discrimination has been charged; it was once a common saying in Hawaii that there are three kinds of payment for the same kind of work—what *haoles* pay *haoles*, what *haoles* pay orientals, and what orientals pay orientals. Racial loyalties have conflicted with labor-group loyalties, although racial antagonism in Hawaii has never been acute. Language difficulties and differences in culture and outlook have further divided allegiances to working-class ideals.

Lack of highly competent leaders was one important cause for the relative lag in unionization in Hawaii. Except for a very few men, the labor leaders of Hawaii have been untrained in either the techniques or the traditions of unionism. Many leaders suffered from lack of confidence or overconfidence, or were too anxious to obtain quick results and therefore resorted to drastic methods. As in other places, a few proved to be rascals, and gave a black eye to the entire movement. Since unionism is a form of politics, the personal ambitions of various leaders sometimes conflicted with those of union rivals; moreover, much energy was wasted in jurisdictional quarrels such as the perennial disputes between the A.F. of L. and the C.I.O.

An interesting factor here is that many union leaders came to Hawaii from west-coast maritime unions; these men enjoyed prestige because of their militancy and their independence (they could not be blacklisted out of a local job) and because of the historical fact that strong union activity in Hawaii began on the Honolulu waterfront after the 1934 strike in San Francisco—a strike which had been given little support in the islands. During 1935 and 1936 about 500 striking seamen were ashore in Honolulu, and developed strong sentiment for unionism among local stevedores (who joined the strike) and other workers. This maritime leadership—the International Longshoremen's and Warehousemen's Union is still Hawaii's most militant union— has brought a number of results. Men from the maritime unions have been among the most energetic in organizing Hawaii, but their prominence has called forth denunciation of "mainland agitators." The use of violence comes more readily to men of the sea and the waterfront. Again, much of the inter-union friction in Hawaii has reflected the rivalry of men like Harry Bridges of the west coast C.I.O. waterfront workers and Harry Lundeberg, head of the Sailors' Union of the Pacific.

In the following account, attention will be given first to the activities of urban unions, which can best be considered separately from unions of plantation workers.

Unionism came to the islands in the days of the monarchy, for it is recorded that a charter to Typographical Union No. 37 of Honolulu was issued on August 9, 1884. But such organizations were made up chiefly of Americans who came from the mainland bringing their unions with them. Not until annexation was there any formal affiliation with national organizations, and before 1910 there were not enough unions even to form a central labor council. During World War I there was little activity. A wave of small strikes took place in 1919 and 1920, but not until 1935, when three maritime unions (the Sailors' Union of the Pacific, the

Marine Cooks and Stewards, and the Marine Firemen and Water-tenders) under the protection of national labor laws opened hiring halls in Honolulu, did the unions first obtain contracts from shipowners. After the strike of 1936, the longshoremen were organized under the C.I.O. On May 26, 1938, a number of maritime unions centered at Hilo presented demands to the Inter-Island steamship company which resulted in a strike that grew in intensity, until on August 1 an attempt to unload a steamship in that port resulted in a mass demonstration by strikers who were fired upon by police. Fifty persons were wounded—twenty of them were hospitalized—and the strike was ended on August 15.

The outbreak of war in Europe in 1939 made clear the necessity for strengthening national defenses in the Pacific, and the needs for construction and other skilled trades workers could not be met by the local supply, even though plantation labor was drawn upon by army and navy agencies. To meet this need, thousands of "defense workers" were brought to Hawaii from the mainland. Wages were high, and were further raised by upgrading generally. The crisis after December 7, 1941, brought an even more intense demand for civilian workers, and during the war the population of the territory (exclusive of those in the armed forces) rose from 419,000 to 502,000. The urgent pressure of war duties, combined with an early curfew and a blackout, made it impossible for labor organizations to function. The membership of unions in Hawaii had grown from about 500 in 1935 to about 10,000 just before the Pearl Harbor attack, but after that date the active list dropped to less than 4,000.

Moreover, the military government, which had taken over immediately after the blitz and had installed a strict martial rule, issued orders which froze both wage rates and labor mobility. General Order No. 38, issued December 20, froze wage rates as of December 7, forced all workers who had left their jobs since that date to return to their former employers, and stated that "men employed hereafter must report to the job for which they are ordered by the Military Government." These first attempts to establish a rigid labor control were amplified in General Order No. 91 of March 31, 1942, which effectively held the worker to his employer until the employer was willing to release him. The worker had no right of appeal, and the employer, if he wished, could give a release "with prejudice" that barred the worker from further defense jobs until the prejudice was removed. Men who failed to report for work as ordered, or who were absent from work without a release, could be given fines up to $200, imprisonment of not more than two months, or both, and were ordered, under threat of arrest by the military police, to appear within forty-eight hours before a "labor control board." On January 1, 1942, an agreement between the army and the plantations provided that the United States Engineers could requisition labor and equipment from the plantations.

All these emergency controls were at first accepted by labor with little protest, but as the war zone moved westward, resentment rose more and more bitterly. Workers who felt that they had been held in servitude at frozen wage levels voiced their objections along with other citizens who felt that military government of American territory and martial rule over Americans who were working patriotically for the national cause was unconstitutional— as the Supreme Court later judged it to be. Charges were made that the military government and army officers had shown an unfriendly attitude toward labor, had used intimidation to prevent unionization, and had lowered worker morale by failure to use non-military procedures in dealing with grievances.

The end of the war brought, in line with the mainland pattern, a wave of strikes resulting from rising living costs and the freedom of unions to fight for further gains in the post-war world. The elimination of wartime controls in Hawaii undoubtedly made much easier the lot of the post-war labor organizer, and the inevitable march of unionization was accompanied by a bitterness on both sides that promised many an explosion. During 1946, Hawaiian unions were either striking or threatening to strike during every month of the year. Anger was aroused by the fear that waterfront strikes on both United States seaboards, similar to the ninety-day strike of 1936, would close the ports and throw island economy into privations and food shortages worse than those suffered during the war. There were a number of strikes on the waterfront and others against the Rapid Transit Company, various trucking companies, and a tuna-packing company. The International Longshoremen's and Warehousemen's Union, a maritime union, had taken the lead also in almost complete unionization of sugar workers under the C.I.O.

Plantation labor disturbances have been more severe in their effects upon Hawaiian economy and the rise of unionization than have non-plantation strikes.

Major plantation strikes have occurred in the islands in 1909, 1920, 1924, 1937, 1946, and 1958. Minor strikes have been many. Attempts at organizing field workers have been restricted by the same causes that held back industrial unionization; in particular, the fact that strikes were often carried on by individual racial groups has led to failure in the past. Misunderstandings arose during the first importation of Japanese laborers, and thereafter, since the Japanese were less free to leave the plantations for other work and felt that their future lay in settling down at the field tasks, their attempts to find better conditions took the form of strikes. Wages and conditions were improved after annexation, but two minor plantation strikes occurred in 1902, two in 1903, and ten in 1904-1905, all among the Japanese. None of these strikes was aimed at union recognition. Not only this group but the whole body of laborers improved their lot as a result of these strikes.

In 1905 there was an effort on the island of Maui to call a sympathetic strike on the larger plantations when the Lahaina strikers were faced with a display of armed force, and planters raised wages two dollars a month as a result of this attempt.

In 1906 about 1,700 Japanese laborers struck at Waipahu, shutting down both mill and field work for eight days. The men acted in an orderly way, and each contributed to a strike fund. Demands included discharge of the plantation physician, increased wages for cane loaders and cutters, reinstatement of two discharged employees, and various service regulations. Intimidation was used through the bringing of armed police from Honolulu and through threats of eviction. Strikebreakers, both Chinese and Hawaiians, were used at higher rates of pay, and newspaper editors called for the importation of workers of other nationalities to break Japanese solidarity. The strike was settled when some of the minor demands were granted.

In May, 1909, a larger strike was called and about 7,000 Japanese left their jobs on Oahu plantations and stayed out until the strike was broken in August. The strikers demanded higher wages for day hands in the field, stating that planters were offering one-third more pay to Caucasians in similar jobs. The strikers refrained from violence except toward strikebreakers of their own nationality. Enough strikebreakers of other nationalities, chiefly Hawaiians and Portuguese, were employed at $1.50 a day to carry on mill operations; at the end of the strike these were discharged and the Japanese reinstated at lower wages. The strike ended through the financial weakness of the strikers, but afterward their conditions were improved and their wages raised. One result of the strike was the marked increase in labor importations. Filipino immigration began on a large scale in 1910; Portuguese and Russians were also imported.

During the following decade, plantation managements made many improvements in housing and in building hospitals, schools, churches, and playgrounds, and carried on welfare work among their employees. Financial incentives in the form of a turnout bonus were supplied, and a profit-sharing bonus was put into effect in 1912, revised in 1916 and 1917 to include contract cultivators. Toward the end of World War I, high prices and curtailment of war bonuses again brought unrest.

In 1919 a Federation of Japanese Labor in Hawaii was formed, which submitted to the HSPA on December 4 a list of demands to increase wages, revise the bonus system, install an eight-hour working day with double pay for overtime, and make certain welfare improvements. Similar demands were submitted on the same day by the newly organized Filipino Laborers' Association. The demands were flatly rejected and members of the two organizations went on strike on six Oahu plantations. The strike policy was to hit strategic Oahu and refrain from striking on other islands, so that employed workers there could give their aid to striking members of their organizations.

Management responded by evicting about 12,000 strikers. About half of these came to Honolulu, which was in the throes of an influenza epidemic; and it was estimated that 1,200 members of strikers' families died of this disease. Strike destruction, including the burning of cane, came for the first time to Hawaii's fields. Large losses resulted from the interruption of planting and harvesting schedules, and it was stated that the strike cost the planters $12,000,000.

The Filipinos returned to their jobs on February 10 under instructions from their organizer, Pablo Manlapit, and thereafter acted as strikebreakers along with Hawaiians, Portuguese, Chinese, Koreans, and Puerto Ricans. The Japanese began to weaken toward the end of June, and their leaders called off the strike at the end of July, about seven months after it began. Workers did achieve certain gains, however; a new wage and bonus schedule was adopted which abolished the race differential, increased the minimum wage by 30 per cent, and raised the bonus.

Thereafter employers placed more reliance upon Filipinos as a labor source, but by 1922 under the leadership of Manlapit this group claimed a membership of 13,000 in a "higher wage movement," and on April 1, 1924, when their demands for a $2 wage for an eight-hour day were rejected, the Filipinos struck. This strike lasted for eight months and 23 out of the 45 sugar plantations were involved in the drama. Oahu and Hawaii were badly hit, but the greatest episode of violence occurred on September 9 at Hanapepe, Kauai, where strikers held two Filipino strikebreakers as prisoners in their camp. The prisoners were surrendered to the police, but while they were being escorted away, a dispute arose which resulted in the killing of four policemen and sixteen strikers, and the wounding of many others. The National Guard was called out to suppress the riot. Seventy-six of the participants were tried for their acts, and sixty were given four-year prison sentences. The Filipino commissioner urged the strikers to return to work, and after three more months they went back.

During the thirteen years after the 1924 strike the plantation front was quiet. It was then broken by another strike of Filipino laborers on the island of Maui. The men were out between April 20 and June 21, 1937, and at its peak the strike involved some 3,500 Filipinos on three plantations; Japanese workers and members of the Maritime Union gave some financial support, and the strikers were aided by C.I.O. organizers. Slight wage raises were obtained. Strikes on the pineapple plantations in the same year (1937) involved altogether about 1,800 men. Additional minor strikes took place from time to time up to 1939, but they were quickly ended and gained little.

The first vote to be taken by an island plantation organization under the National Labor Relations Act was held at Kalaheo, Kauai, under an agreement signed May 20, 1939, by the company manager and union officers. A C.I.O. local was voted as exclusive representative for collective bargaining.

During World War II there was almost no union activity in the fields, but after the end of that war the C.I.O. took the lead in capitalizing upon the resentment of laborers against wartime repressions. The unions attacked in particular the "perquisite system" whereby the plantations had for generations furnished free housing, water, medical, and recreational facilities. This "paternalism," they said, had to go. To their surprise, the Hawaiian Pineapple Company, largest employer in the islands, agreed. The company turned its hundreds of homes over to a new housing authority from which the employees could rent for cash. It also offered a pay boost averaging fifteen cents an hour, more than the estimated cost of the perquisites.

The C.I.O. negotiators then challenged the sugar planters, and called out 28,000 workers on thirty-three plantations late in 1946. The strike, which was the most destructive in Hawaiian history, lasted from September 1 to November 14, 1946, during which time mills were silent and the irrigation ditches untended, while cane withered and died in the fields. The strike cost the people of the territory about $20,000,000; workers sacrificed, it was estimated, $8,250,000 in lost wages, and 183,000 tons of potential sugar vanished, at a time when the American nation was undergoing strict sugar rationing. The agreement that ended the strike abolished the perquisite system, and the plantations agreed to pay $10,500,000 a year in wage increases to its employees in lieu of these facilities. Minimum pay rates were set at 70.5 cents an hour, with an additional cost to the sugar industry estimated between $10,000,000 and $17,000,000. Workers thereafter received an average daily wage above $7.11. One plantation near Pearl Harbor was liquidated by its owners during the strike. An important result was the great impetus given to mechanization of plantation work. Increases in labor costs and labor interruptions, it is clear, can reach a point where machines must be widely used if the industry is to survive.

In 1947, two years after V–J Day, there were 47 organizations in the territory affiliated with the American Federation of Labor, 18 with the C.I.O. (including five I.L.W.U. locals), 4 independent unions, and 5 government employee's organizations. Total membership claimed by the unions, exclusive of government employees, was 55,000 to 60,000.

The need for employers to organize among themselves and preserve a united front against forthcoming labor drives was realized in 1943 with the founding of the Hawaii Employers Council. From a charter membership of 24 firms, the roster grew to 173 by the first annual meeting. In February, 1958, the Council had 223 employer-members, large and small, throughout the territory. Members represented the majority of Hawaii's businesses of every type, employing more than 54,300 wage earners. The goals of the Council were stated as follows: "To promote better understanding of the problems of industry; to re-emphasize the unity of purpose that exists among all levels of business—worker, foreman, management; to re-establish equal responsibility, one to the other, of the employee and management; to promote the observance of obligations, as well as rights, by employee leaders in industry; to provide (through industrial stability) maximum job opportunities in Hawaii's industry; to develop sound and workable policies and practices which will help bring industrial peace; to safeguard the public's right to free access to the goods and services provided for their use by Hawaii's industry; to prevent unnecessary strikes and disruptions of Hawaii's economic services; to provide community leadership in friendly solutions of the problems of industry; and to promote, in every way possible, the welfare and well-being of all of Hawaii's people."

The most notable political field of union activity since the end of the war has been the attempt to put solid union support behind friendly candidates. This was first tried in 1946 by the ILWU with its Political Action Committee. Its success in that year and its subsequent attempt to take control of Democratic party were mentioned in an earlier chapter. At that period the ILWU was a member of the CIO. Charges that the ILWU was Communist-dominated led to its expulsion from the CIO in 1950. The Communist issue implicated ILWU leaders in Hawaii as well as on the mainland and weakened its political influence. A six-month long dock strike in 1949 also reacted against the ILWU, which was unable to prevent enactment of the "dock-seizure law" by the legislature in that year. The ILWU tried but failed to get control of the constitutional convention of 1950, and signally failed in the effort to prevent adoption of the state constitution. In 1952 conservatives gained control of the Democratic party convention. After noting this fact, one historian of the Hawaiian labor movement adds: "Although the ILWU may not control the Democratic party in Hawaii, it must not be counted out politically by any means." Undoubtedly it was an important factor in Democratic victories in 1954, 1956, and 1958. Both the

ILWU and the re-united AFL–CIO give support to some Republican candidates who are especially friendly to the labor movement.

Many laws beneficial to labor are in existence in Hawaii. At the time the Organic Act was passed a number of federal laws were made applicable to the territory. Much of the labor and social-insurance legislation passed by Congress in recent years extended to Hawaii, such as the National Labor Relations Act, the Railway Labor Act, the Federal Employers' Liability Act, the Social Security Act, the Fair Labor Standards Act, the Walsh-Healy Act, and the Maritime Labor Relations Act. The legislature of Hawaii has passed a number of laws affecting labor, including a child-labor law, wage and hours laws, and social-insurance legislation, and a "Little Wagner Act" extending collective bargaining to agricultural workers. The legislature in 1939 set up a Department of Labor and Industrial Relations to administer all labor laws, to mediate in disputes, and set up appeal boards to consider claims for workmen's compensation.

As Hawaii's economy approaches a more democratic basis, signs are evident that the old racial walls of cleavage are being broken down. Intermixture through interracial marriage was greatly accelerated during and after World War II; and today about one third of all marriages in Hawaii are across the conventionally designated racial lines. Members of certain racial groups were able to better their economic position during the period of labor scarcity, and to embark on new business enterprises of their own. Young people of varied racial backgrounds have taken advantage of their opportunities under the American democratic pattern of life, by preparing themselves to compete for better jobs and to create new services in the growing metropolitan community. They have entered into the political life of Hawaii, giving new vigor to both parties and winning positions in the legislature and in the judicial and administrative branches of the government. And they are making places for themselves in the island professional, business, and social world.

One observer of the Hawaiian scene, Economist James H. Shoemaker, wrote in 1946: "Underlying all other Hawaiian problems is that of the adjustment of its economic and political structure to the rapidly changing character of its population. As late as 1920 the majority of the adult residents of the territory were immigrant aliens—largely oriental peasants or coolies with characteristic narrowness of outlook, lack of education, and low standards of living. Their children were many and were American-born citizens, educated in American schools to American standards and ideals. Those who were between one and 25 years of age then are 27 to 52 now, whereas those who were 35 to 55 years of age then are over 61 or deceased today. The key to an understanding of post-war Hawaii is a full realization of the extent and the implications of this change—that is, an appreciation of the fact that the sons and daughters or the grandsons and granddaughters of Chinese, Japanese, and Koreans are as capable, as educated, as ambitious, as democratic, as patriotic, and as thoroughly American as are the descendants of, for example, Germans now living in the American middle west. They are Americans by law, by training, by demonstrated ability, by the bravery of their sons in the armed forces, and by their proven patriotism at home. Numerous arguments, such as the volume of tax payments, industrial development, trade figures and the like are advanced in support of American statehood for Hawaii, but this basic fact overshadows all others."

CHAPTER TWENTY-SIX

The Winning of Statehood

THE growing feeling in the islands that Hawaii should be admitted to the sisterhood of states focused national attention on the Pacific territory. But the final triumph of statehood was not to be achieved without great effort and many disappointments. The various congressional investigations and public discussions carried on after 1934, however, not only demonstrated that statehood for Hawaii was a national issue but also developed a factual picture of the territory which showed it to be qualified for full membership in the American Union.

Statehood for Hawaii had first been proposed as early as 1849 by a Lowville, New York, newspaper. Statehood was a critical point in the abortive annexation negotiations of 1854, when the Hawaiian negotiators would not agree to any lesser status. This earlier talk of statehood had been forgotten by most islanders and the circumstances in Hawaii had changed greatly when annexation again became a practical question following the revolution of 1893. Contrary to statements frequently made is the fact that the commissioners who negotiated the uncompleted treaties of 1893 and 1897 did not ask for statehood. They requested that Hawaii be made an integral part of the United States, and the form of government which they suggested was that of a territory.

The question of statehood figured, however, in the congressional debates on the annexation resolution. Several members reminded their colleagues that Congress had no power to acquire territory except with a view to its admission as a state or states. Later, in the debate preceding the enactment of the Organic Act, it was both asserted and denied that the creation of a territorial government for the islands would carry with it a presumption of ultimate statehood.

Sentiment for statehood developed very early among the people and their legislators in the new territory. In 1903 the legislature petitioned Congress for admission of the islands as a state, and many subsequent legislatures adopted similar resolutions. Right after the close of World War I, in November, 1918, Hawaii's delegate in Congress, Prince Jonah Kuhio Kalanianaole, issued a public statement in which he cited Hawaii's record of service in the war effort, described elsewhere in this volume, as proof "of the Americanization of our people." "It is," he said, "the psychological moment to bring forward Hawaii's claim to statehood. . . . I shall introduce a bill (in Congress) . . . proposing to admit Hawaii to the Union of the States." He did so on February 11, 1919. It was the first of a long succession of bills on the subject. A few days later, Governor Charles J. McCarthy included in his message to the territorial legislature a recommendation that it adopt a resolution "memorializing Congress to pass an Act giving Statehood to Hawaii." Such a resolution was passed. The statehood bill introduced by Delegate Kalanianaole was referred to the House Committee on Territories but nothing further was done with it. A similar bill introduced by the delegate in the next Congress received the same treatment. At that time, not only in Washington but even in Hawaii, support for the statehood idea was rather weak. Political activities and legislation for some years centered on the Hawaiian Homes Commission Act and Hawaii's "Bill of Rights."

By 1930 Delegate Victor S. K. Houston, in Congress since 1927, had become convinced of the necessity for statehood if Hawaii was to be sure of fair and equal treatment in national legislation. He therefore urged the legislature to take appropriate action and on December 9, 1931, he introduced in the national House of Representatives a statehood bill in the usual form of an enabling act. Houston's plea for statehood was drowned in the uproar caused by the Massie case. His bill died in committee.

The year 1935 really marks a turning point in the history of the statehood movement both in Hawaii and in Washington. Until about that time, public opinion in the islands had not been strongly united in its favor, many influential business leaders and other citizens being either distinctly opposed to the idea or lukewarm on the subject. As has been shown earlier, however, developments growing out of the Massie case and the Jones-Costigan sugar control act converted a great many island people to the cause of statehood. They now saw that many people on the mainland—not excluding Congressmen—looked upon Hawaii as a mere possession rather than an incorporated territory only one stage removed from statehood. Hawaii was subject to all taxes and other general contributions imposed on the states, and annually paid into the Federal treasury many millions of dollars, sums larger than those paid by several of the states; but despite the acceptance of Hawaii's "Bill of Rights" by Congress, the territory was still excluded from many benefits granted to the states in various appropriation acts. It would be possible for Congress at one stroke to take away what it had granted in the Organic Act. The rights of the citizens of Hawaii would never be fully protected until legislators elected by them could sit and vote in the halls of Congress.

In 1935, likewise, Congress began to take notice of Hawaii's plea for statehood. Although the Massie case had turned a glaring spotlight on the islands, the net long-term result was that mainland people obtained a truer picture of all conditions in the territory. President Roosevelt visited Hawaii in 1934—the first President to do so— and although he did not commit himself on the subject of statehood, his administration thereafter was more friendly than it had been in the first months of the New Deal.

Delegate Samuel Wilder King introduced in January, 1935, a bill to enable the people of Hawaii to form a state government. He succeeded in getting the House Committee on Territories to appoint a sub-committee to conduct an investigation in the islands —the first of a series of such visits and hearings. The sub-committee, headed by Representative Eugene B. Crowe of Indiana, reported that it "found the Territory of Hawaii to be a modern unit of the American Commonwealth, with a political, social, and economic structure of the highest type." Three members of the five-man sub-committee felt, however, that considerable further study was necessary before action could be taken on the bill.

Two years later, another visiting Congressional committee, made up of senators and representatives, held hearings in the territory. This group reported that Hawaii had "fulfilled every requirement for statehood heretofore exacted of territories," and that it was entitled to "a sympathetic consideration of its plea for statehood," but recommended that the subject be deferred for further study and suggested that a plebiscite be held to determine whether the people of Hawaii really wanted statehood. Accordingly, the question "Do you favor statehood for Hawaii?" appeared on the ballot in the general election of 1940. Although this was an unfavorable time for such a plebiscite, because of growing tension between the United States and the Japanese Empire, the citizens of Hawaii voted more than two to one for statehood.

During the years 1941 to 1945, the people of Hawaii wholeheartedly united with the rest of the nation to prosecute World War II to victory. After this there could no longer be any doubt that those of Oriental ancestry in the islands were completely loyal to the United States even under great stress. During a Congressional investigation in 1946, both Army and Navy intelligence officers testified that "not a single act of sabotage was committed by any resident of Hawaii before, during, or after the attack on Pearl Harbor." The magnificent record of Hawaii's Americans of Japanese ancestry as combat soldiers in the United States Army during World War II and the Korean conflict deprived the foes of statehood of one of their favorite arguments.

In the years following World War II, developments in Hawaii and in the mainland portion of the United States provided a new and somewhat different frame of reference for the statehood campaign. Of great importance was the extraordinarily rapid progress of labor organization in the territory described in an earlier chapter. Two effects of this movement are to be noted, one favorable, the other unfavorable to the cause of statehood. On the one hand, it brought Hawaii closer to the mainland standard of unionization and labor-management relations. On the other hand, because the labor organizing campaign was led by the aggressive International Longshoremen's and Warehousemen's Union, which was widely believed to be Communist dominated, it raised the Communist issue as an anti-statehood argument which was exploited to the limit by such congressional leaders as Senator Hugh Butler of Nebraska and Representative John R. Pillion of New York. As early as May, 1947, Butler wrote that statehood would have no chance of success in the Senate "until Harry Bridges (head of the I.L.W.U.) stops running the government of Hawaii and Alaska." It could not be denied that there were Communists in the territory, but their number, the scope of their activities, and the extent of the menace which they represented were grossly exaggerated by some who used this argument against statehood. The people of Hawaii took steps to expose and counteract Communist machinations by means of an official "Commission on Subversive Activities" created by the legislature in 1949 and the unofficial "Hawaii Residents' Association" (Imua), which carried on a continuous campaign of education. But Communism continued to be a stock argument in the mouths of the opponents of statehood for Hawaii.

A different sort of element in the new picture of Hawaii that came into view after World War II was the greatly improved means of transportation by airplanes, bringing the islands within a few hours' flying time of other parts of the United States and destroying the old argument that Hawaii was too far away from the rest of the nation. Coupled with this was the continuous growth and diversification of Hawaii's industries, which provided a solid economic base for the territory. Worthy of mention in this connection are the decision of the Standard Oil Company to build a large refinery in the territory, and the extensive operations of industrialist Henry J. Kaiser. One of the rapidly growing industries was tourism, which had an extra value in making Hawaii known to more and more of the citizens of all parts of the nation. Most of the thousands of tourists who visited the islands became enthusiastic supporters of Hawaii's claim to statehood and their views were reflected in the Gallup and other public opinion polls which from year to year showed a large and growing majority of the nation's population to be in favor of statehood for the island territory. Sooner or later the politicians in Washington would have to respect this immense volume of public opinion.

A third phase of the new frame of reference after World War II consisted of changes in the political complexion of the national Congress and the territorial legislature. The managers of the statehood campaign tried to keep it on a non-partisan or bi-partisan basis, but when the control of Congress shifted from one party to the other, especially the change from Republican to Democratic in the later 1950's, and when the Democrats in the same period gained control of the territorial legislature and in the 1956 and 1958 elections also won the delegateship to Congress, these developments inevitably introduced complications, perplexities, and some confusion into the struggle for statehood.

Finally, it is to be observed that the vigorous efforts of the people of Alaska to achieve statehood for that far-northern territory had a profound influence on sub-tropical Hawaii's aspirations. Although it was recognized by all that Alaska's qualifications for statehood were much inferior to Hawaii's, the interesting circumstance that Alaska was traditionally Democratic while Hawaii was traditionally Republican afforded much opportunity for the maneuvering and horse-trading so dear to politicians. The Republican to Democratic shift in the later 1950's greatly improved Alaska's chances but for a time at least cast a shadow over Hawaii's hopes, and in the denouement made Hawaii the Fiftieth State instead of the Forty-ninth, which the island territory had long expected to be.

It was under these changed and changing conditions that, after the end of World War II, Delegate Joseph R. Farrington, who had succeeded Samuel W. King when the latter went back into the Navy during the conflict, worked to get favorable action on the statehood bills which he introduced periodically in Congress. A sub-committee of the House Committee on Territories, headed by Representative Henry D. Larcade, Jr., of Louisiana, held hearings on such a bill in Honolulu in January, 1946. After its return to Washington, the Larcade sub-committee reported that the people of Hawaii had "demonstrated beyond question not only their loyalty and patriotism but also their desire to assume the responsibilities of statehood." It said, "The Territory of Hawaii now meets the necessary requirements for statehood," and it recommended "that the Committee on Territories give immediate consideration to legislation to admit Hawaii to statehood."

President Truman in his message to Congress on January 21, 1946, urged the admission of Hawaii as a state. He was the first president to do so. Strong support had already come from Secretary of the Interior Harold L. Ickes. Encouraged by these developments, Delegate Farrington began pressing for a formal hearing on the statehood bill by the Committee on Territories. Because of the pre-occupation of Congress with post-war problems, however, no further action was taken on the statehood bill in 1946.

On the opening day of the Eightieth Congress in January, 1947, Delegate Farrington introduced a statehood bill drawn up by the Citizens' Statehood Committee in Hawaii. On the same day identical bills were filed by five Republicans and three Democrats, designed to make Hawaii the Forty-ninth State. The Farrington bill, H.R. 49, was referred to the Committee on Public Lands, and hearings were begun on March 7. Statements received from both the War Department and the Navy Department gave the official view that the granting of statehood to Hawaii would in no manner be detrimental to the defense of the nation. The committee agreed fully, after a study of all the evidence, that the admission of Hawaii as a state would add an informed and experienced element in national deliberations, both on defense and on relations with the Orient.

On the basis of all previous evidence and the new hearings, the Public Lands Committee unanimously approved the bill on March 19. The Rules Committee on May 15 passed it to the floor of the House of Representatives, and on June 30, 1947, the bill came up for debate and final vote. Discussion ran to less than four hours. The measure was passed on that day by a vote of 196 to 133, and thus was sent on to the Senate for consideration by that body.

In the meantime the territorial legislature in 1947 set up the Hawaii Statehood Commission, replacing an earlier Hawaii Equal Rights Commission and the Citizens' Statehood Committee. The new commission was given adequate funds and authority to maintain offices both in Honolulu and in Washington and to carry on an aggressive campaign of education on the mainland. It cooperated effectively with the territory's delegate to Congress.

In the Senate, the statehood bill (H.R. 49) was referred to the Committee on Public Lands (later entitled the Committee on Interior and Insular Affairs), and by it to the sub-committee on Territories and Insular Affairs. The sub-committee was unable to make an early visit to the islands, but its chairman, Senator Guy Gordon of Oregon, was directed to make an investigation of the territorial government and report back as soon as possible so that that bill might receive further consideration during the second session of the Eightieth Congress. Senator Cordon visited the territory in January, 1948, and with the assistance of Judge Carl E. Wimberly, also of Oregon, conducted an intensive investigation for about three weeks, inquiring especially about recent developments that might have a bearing on Hawaii's fitness for statehood. A particular effort was made to get the views of opponents of statehood. As a result of his investigation and study, Senator Cordon became an earnest advocate of early and favorable action on H.R. 49. His report, which was released on March 19, closed with these words:

THE WINNING OF STATEHOOD

"Hawaii has met the requirements for statehood. It is the chairman's opinion that the territory has served a satisfactory pupilage in the limited self-government permitted by the Organic Act. It is able and ready to accept the social, political, and economic responsibilities of state government as well as the advantages.

"As a state, it could more effectively manage its own affairs and contribute to the welfare of the nation. As a nation, the United States, by granting statehood to Hawaii at this juncture in history, could demonstrate to the world that it means what it says and practices what it urges when advocating true democracy for all peoples."

After receiving Senator Cordon's report, the Committee on Interior and Insular Affairs directed the sub-committee to hold a further hearing on H.R. 49 on April 15. At that time, strong statements were presented in favor of statehood, and no witnesses opposed the bill.

Advocates of statehood hoped that Senator Cordon's report and the record of the April 15 hearing, when added to the results of previous investigations and hearings, would be accepted as a full presentation of the case for final action. But Senator Hugh Butler and a majority of the committee thought otherwise. They held that on a subject of such importance, all members of the committee should have the opportunity, by visiting the territory, to resolve any doubts that might have been raised in their minds. Hence the committee, on May 8, voted (seven to five) "that we do not take action . . . at this time," and instructed Chairman Butler to arrange for members to visit Hawaii "to study the matter on the ground."

This vote was generally interpreted as practically removing any chance of getting a vote on statehood in the Senate during the Eightieth Congress, but one final effort was made. Senator William F. Knowland of California introduced a resolution to discharge the Committee on Interior and Insular Affairs from further consideration of H.R. 49 and place the bill directly before the Senate.

The Senate, however, declined to repudiate its committee by this unusual procedure, and the Knowland resolution was defeated. No further action was taken in this final session of the Eightieth Congress.

As it turned out, Senator Butler was the only member who took advantage of the committee's authorization to visit the islands. Under his direction, a committee investigator spent two months in Hawaii during the summer and fall of 1948. Butler followed with a staff member at the end of October and conducted an investigation by means of confidential interviews with a large number of local residents. He held no public hearings. In his report, dated June 21, 1949, he recorded his "deep conviction that international revolutionary communism at present has a firm grip on the economic, political, and social life of the Territory of Hawaii," and he recommended that "statehood for Hawaii be deferred indefinitely, until communism in the Territory may be brought under effective control," and to accomplish the latter result, he recommended that the territorial government and the United States Department of Justice take immediate and positive action.

Communism thus became a major issue in Hawaii's fight for statehood as a result of Senator Butler's investigation and report and of other developments which can be noted only briefly. In 1948 two suspected Communists were dismissed from their positions as public school teachers in the territory. In 1949 the I.L.W.U. staged a very damaging dock strike of six months' duration, to cope with which the legislature passed the "dock seizure law" mentioned in an earlier chapter. The 1949 legislature likewise created the Commission on Subversive Activities, and requested the United States House of Representatives' Committee on Un-American Activities to conduct an investigation in Hawaii. This was done by a sub-committee in April, 1950, and a mass of testimony was taken regarding activities of the Communist party and of individual Communists in the territory. Thirty-nine of the witnesses called (the "reluctant 39") refused on constitutional grounds to answer many of the questions put to them. In⟨a subsequent report, however, the committee said: "The evidence shows that as of 1951 the people of Hawaii have successfully cast communistic influence out of all phases of their political, social, cultural, and educational activities. The only sphere in which communism plays a part of any significance is in the I.L.W.U., an international labor organization which has headquarters in San Francisco." In 1950 the I.L.W.U. had been expelled from the CIO because it was held to be Communist-dominated. In 1951 seven alleged Communists in Hawaii were arrested by the F.B.I., indicted by a federal grand jury on charges of violating the Smith Act, and after a trial which lasted eight months all were found guilty. The verdict was later reversed by the circuit court of appeals in San Francisco on the basis of an interpretation of the Smith Act by the United States Supreme Court.

In view of the repeated failure of statehood to win approval from Congress, it was decided to try a procedure which had been used successfully by fifteen other territories in their quest for statehood, namely, to draft a state constitution and then ask Congress to approve it as the basis for admission to statehood. The 1949 legislature therefore passed an act providing for the holding of a constitutional convention. Delegates, sixty-three in number, were elected in the fall of 1949 and the convention opened in Iolani Palace on April 4, 1950. After three and a half months of earnest work, the constitution draft was completed and was signed by all but one of the delegates. The legislature, called into special session, approved the draft without change and provided for its submission to the voters in the general election on November 7, 1950. At that time the constitution received a three to one vote of approval by the electorate, despite a vigorous campaign against it by the I.L.W.U. This constitution has been commended by many leading authorities on government as a practical reflection of the best modern thinking in political science.

In the Eighty-first Congress (1949–50), a statehood bill, again numbered H.R. 49, received prompt attention from the House

Committee on Public Lands and was favorably reported by the committee on March 8, 1949. Nearly a year elapsed before the bill came to a vote in the House; it was then passed on March 7, 1950, by a vote of 262 to 110. In the Senate, the bill went to the Committee on Interior and Insular Affairs and was favorably reported on June 29, 1950. Both this bill and one for Alaska statehood were strongly endorsed by President Truman, who wrote to the committee chairman: "I know of few better ways in which we can demonstrate to the world our deep faith in democracy and the principle of self-government than by admitting Alaska and Hawaii to the Union, as the forty-ninth and fiftieth states"—prophetic words! But the Korean conflict intervened and neither of the statehood bills (Alaska and Hawaii) could be brought to a vote in the Senate during the remaining months of this Congress.

In the Eighty-second Congress (1951–52), bills to grant statehood to both Alaska and Hawaii for the first time reached the floor of the Senate with the strong backing of the Committee on Interior and Insular Affairs. Regarding Hawaii the committee said: "(1) The admission of Hawaii into the Union as a State is in the best interest of the Nation and the Territory. (2) The Territory meets all of the traditional requirements for statehood, and, as a State, would make valuable contributions to the Nation and to the world. . . ." But neither bill came to a vote in either house during this Congress.

In the Eighty-third Congress (1953–54), Hawaii came tantalizingly close to victory. The Republicans were now in control of the White House and the House of Representatives as a result of their victory in the 1952 election; in the Senate the two parties were nearly even. It must be remembered, however, that sentiment in Congress on the question of statehood for the two territories did not divide strictly on party lines. In this Congress the scheme of tying Hawaii and Alaska together in one bill was resorted to. Dr. Charles H. Hunter, the leading authority on the history of the statehood movement, explains that "the Republicans,

following the President's lead of immediate statehood for Hawaii
but deferment for Alaska, would not accept a statehood bill
combining both territories. The Democrats would not accept separate bills that considered Alaska and Hawaii each on its own
merits. The Democratic leaders freely admitted that if the
Hawaii bill could be brought to a vote alone it would pass. However, members of both parties who favored Alaska said that only
by tying Alaska to the Hawaii bill could they be sure that the
former would receive consideration."

The action taken can be briefly stated. Statehood bills for both
territories were introduced at the beginning of the first session in
January, 1953. After a bitter fight and a nearly successful attempt
to tie the two territories in one bill, the House Committee on
Interior and Insular Affairs on March 3 reported favorably on the
Hawaii bill. On March 10 the House passed it by a vote of 274
to 138 and sent it on to the Senate, where no action was taken in
the first session. Early in the second session, on January 27, 1954,
after a hard fight in the Senate committee, the Hawaii bill was
reported favorably by the committee, and a few days later the
Alaska bill was given a similar report. On March 11, the Senate
voted, 46 to 43, to amend the Hawaii bill by attaching Alaska to
it, and in that form the bill was passed by the Senate on April 1
by a vote of 57 to 28, and thus sent back to the House of Representatives. This in effect killed the measure; no further action
on the bill was possible because of various adverse conditions,
including President Eisenhower's known opposition to immediate
statehood for Alaska.

Along through this period, it was urged by certain leaders that
Hawaii be given not statehood but a commonwealth status similar
to that of Puerto Rico. Another anti-statehood idea was to let
Hawaii as a territory elect its own governor. These proposals received little support in Congress and even less in the territory,
though the Democrats in Hawaii did toy with the idea of an
elected governor.

On June 19, 1954, Delegate Farrington died while alone in his
Washington office, a martyr, some people said, to the cause of

statehood. At a special election on July 31, his widow, Mrs. Elizabeth P. Farrington, nationally prominent among Republican women, was elected to succeed him and she was re-elected in the general election in November of that year. Changes in the governorship of Hawaii may be noted. After Eisenhower became President he appointed (February 28, 1953) Samuel Wilder King, who had worked long and hard for statehood, to succeed Democrat Oren E. Long as governor. Four years later (July 26, 1957), President Eisenhower, who was trying to bring forward younger Republican leaders, appointed William F. Quinn to succeed King. Quinn had previously demonstrated considerable political campaigning ability.

The results of the elections in November, 1954, which gave the Democrats control of Congress and of the Hawaiian legislature, made it extremely unlikely that any statehood legislation would be enacted in the Eighty-fourth Congress. But a combination Alaska-Hawaii bill was introduced in each house. In the lower house the bill came to the floor for consideration under a rule that permitted no amendments. On May 10, 1955, the House voted, 218 to 170, to send the bill back to the committee. New single bills for each territory were introduced but all died in committee.

The Democratic trend continued to be strong in the election of 1956, despite the re-election of President Eisenhower. In Hawaii the Democrats strengthened their hold on the legislature and their candidate John A. Burns defeated Mrs. Farrington for the delegateship in Congress. Party leaders in Hawaii and on the mainland believed the island territory was safely Democratic for a long time to come and they had a vision of a solid Democratic representation in the national Congress from the State of Hawaii. After Delegate Burns arrived in Washington, he and his Alaskan counterpart agreed that the statehood bills should be kept separate and they pledged mutual assistance in the struggle for statehood. President Eisenhower in his budget message at the opening of the Eighty-fifth Congress in January, 1957, again urged statehood for Hawaii and for the first time gave a similar endorsement to

Alaska with certain reservations in the interest of national defense because of Alaska's proximity to Russian territory. Public opinion polls continued to show overwhelming popular support for statehood for both territories, and many leading newspapers chided Congress for the long delay in this matter.

In the light of later developments, it appears that under the circumstances just mentioned the Democratic leadership in Congress decided that both territories should be admitted promptly to statehood; Hawaii, however, would not be admitted until after Alaska was safely in the fold. Delegate Burns went along with this program, despite the fact that it might mean a year's delay for the island territory. Nothing could be done in the first session of the Eighty-fifth Congress, but in the second session (1958), statehood for Alaska was pushed through with surprising ease; the bill was passed (208 to 166) by the House on May 28 and by the Senate on June 30 by a vote of 64 to 20, and was signed by President Eisenhower. Republicans then made a strong effort to get favorable action on the Hawaii bill in the closing weeks of the session, but the Democratic leaders, including Delegate Burns, said the time was too short in view of other important legislation that required the attention of Congress. Hawaii had to wait.

In 1958 the national and territorial elections were again headlined by Democratic victories. Delegate Burns was re-elected by a substantial margin despite strong opposition. The Democrats retained control of both branches of the legislature, which for the first time was elected under the terms of a re-apportionment act passed by Congress in 1956. Under this act, which incorporated the plan prescribed in the constitution adopted in 1950 for the State of Hawaii, the legislature was increased in size to 76 members, 25 in the senate and 51 in the house of representatives. Under this plan the island of Oahu elects a majority of the house members, while the senate continues to be controlled by the neighbor islands.

Action on Hawaiian statehood finally came with dramatic swiftness early in the first session of the Eighty-sixth Congress. Bills were introduced in both houses. One numbered S. 50, introduced by Senator James E. Murray, chairman of the Senate Committee on Interior and Insular Affairs, had fifty-six co-signers, giving assurance that it would pass. This bill was approved by the committee on March 3, 1959, reported to the Senate on March 6, debated on March 11, and passed on that day by a vote of 76 to 15. Meanwhile, a similar bill reached the floor of the House of Representatives on March 11; for this bill the House substituted S. 50, which had just come from the Senate, and passed it on March 12 by a vote of 323 to 89. President Eisenhower signed it on March 18.

The statehood act set forth the procedures necessary before Hawaii could be proclaimed a state by the President; it accepted, ratified, and confirmed the state constitution which had been adopted by the voters of the territory in 1950; it directed the governor of the territory to issue a proclamation calling elections (primary and general) for the election of two senators and one representative in Congress and the state officers (governor, lieutenant governor, and members of the legislature) required by the state constitution; and it called for a plebiscite to be held on three propositions which were, in substance: (1) Do you favor statehood now? (2) Do you approve the state boundaries as set forth in the statehood act (which differed slightly from those in the state constitution)? (3) Do you approve certain designated land provisions of the statehood act? Approval of each of these propositions by a majority of the voters was a necessary prerequisite to statehood.

Governor Quinn by proclamation designated June 27 as the day for the primary and July 28 for the general election. He also directed that the plebiscite on the above-mentioned propositions should be held in connection with the primary election. In the plebiscite, the voters approved each of the three propositions by a vote of about 17 to 1. In the primary election, John A. Burns and Mitsuyuki Kido were selected as the Democratic candidates for governor and lieutenant governor respectively; William F. Quinn and James K. Kealoha became the Republican standard bearers. For the United States Senate the Democrats nominated Frank F. Fasi and Oren E. Long; the Republicans named Hiram L. Fong and Wilfred C. Tsukiyama. For representative in Congress the Democrats chose Daniel K. Inouye to oppose Republican Charles H. Silva.

The voting in the primary pointed to the probability of a Democratic sweep in the general election. But the Republicans conducted a vigorous, well organized, and well managed campaign which paid off on July 28. Quinn and Kealoha were elected governor and lieutenant governor. Republican Fong and Democrat Long were elected to the United States Senate. Democrat Inouye easily defeated his Republican opponent for Hawaii's one seat in the House of Representatives. The Democrats gained control of the state house of representatives by the same margin as in the 1958 territorial election; but the Republicans obtained a 14 to 11 majority in the state senate. With the governorship and a majority of the senate, the Republicans were in position to carry out the organization of the state government.

The results of the plebiscite and of the elections having been certified to Washington, President Eisenhower on August 21, 1959, signed the proclamation declaring Hawaii to be a state. A few minutes later, in Honolulu, Quinn and Kealoha were sworn in as the first governor and lieutenant governor of the State of Hawaii. The long struggle had finally come to a successful conclusion and Hawaii, as the "Aloha State," entered upon a new phase of her history.

PAU

Appendices

1. *Native Monarchs*

Name	Birth	Accession	Death
Kamehameha I	c. 1758	1795	May 8, 1819
Kamehameha II (Liholiho)	1797	May 20, 1819	July 14, 1824
Kamehameha III (Kauikeaouli)	March 17, 1814	June 6, 1825	Dec. 15, 1854
Kamehameha IV (Alexander Liholiho)	Feb. 9, 1834	Dec. 15, 1854	Nov. 30, 1863
Kamehameha V (Lot Kamehameha)	Dec. 11, 1830	Nov. 30, 1863	Dec. 11, 1872
William C. Lunalilo	Jan. 31, 1835	Jan. 8, 1873	Feb. 3, 1874
David Kalakaua	Nov. 16, 1836	Feb. 12, 1874	Jan. 20, 1891
Liliuokalani	Sept. 2, 1838	Jan. 29, 1891	Nov. 11, 1917

Liliuokalani was deposed and the Hawaiian Kingdom came to an end on January 17, 1893.

2. *President of Provisional Government*

	Term Began	Term Ended
Sanford B. Dole	Jan. 17, 1893	July 4, 1894

3. *President of Republic of Hawaii*

	Term Began	Term Ended
Sanford B. Dole	July 4, 1894	June 14, 1900

Hawaii was annexed August 12, 1898, but the territorial government was not established until June 14, 1900.

4. *Governors of Territory of Hawaii*

Name	Appointed by President	Term Began	Term Ended
Sanford B. Dole	McKinley	June 14, 1900	Nov. 23, 1903
George R. Carter	T. Roosevelt	Nov. 23, 1903	Aug. 15, 1907
Walter F. Frear	T. Roosevelt	Aug. 15, 1907	Nov. 29, 1913
Lucius E. Pinkham	Wilson	Nov. 29, 1913	June 22, 1918
Charles J. McCarthy	Wilson	June 22, 1918	July 5, 1921
Wallace R. Farrington	Harding	July 5, 1921	July 5, 1925
(second term)	Coolidge	July 5, 1925	July 5, 1929
Lawrence M. Judd	Hoover	July 5, 1929	March 1, 1934
Joseph B. Poindexter	F. D. Roosevelt	March 1, 1934	April 2, 1938
(second term)	F. D. Roosevelt	April 2, 1938	Aug. 24, 1942
Ingram M. Stainback	F. D. Roosevelt	Aug. 24, 1942	Aug. 24, 1946
(second term)	Truman	Aug. 24, 1946	April 30, 1951
Oren E. Long	Truman	April 30, 1951	Feb. 28, 1953
Samuel Wilder King	Eisenhower	Feb. 28, 1953	Sept. 2, 1957
William F. Quinn	Eisenhower	Sept. 2, 1957	Aug. 21, 1959

Hawaii became the Fiftieth State on August 21, 1959, when President Eisenhower proclaimed the inauguration of a slate of state officials elected on July 28, headed by William F. Quinn, Republican, as governor.

POPULATION OF HAWAII
1. *Population Before Annexation*

Year	Hawaiian and Part-Hawaiian	Foreigners		Total
1832				130,313
1836				108,579
1853	71,019	2,119		73,138
1860	67,084	2,716		69,800
1866	58,765	4,194		62,959

Year	Hawaiian and Part-Hawaiian	Born in Hawaii of Non-Hawaiian Ancestors	Foreign-Born	Total
1872	51,531	849	4,517	56,897
1878	47,508	947	9,530	57,985
1884	44,232	2,040	34,306	80,578
1890	40,622	7,495	41,873	89,990
1896	39,504	12,844	56,672	109,020

2. Population After Annexation

| Year | Citizens | | Foreign-Born | Total* |
	By Birth	Naturalized		
1900	62,022	1,199	90,780	154,001
1910	123,537	2,562**	65,810**	191,909
1920	170,571	4,157	81,184	255,912
1930	294,539	5,260	68,537	368,336
1940	365,164	5,553	52,613	423,330
1950	423,153	10,171	66,445	499,769
1960***	Details not available			609,096

* Figures include army and navy personnel stationed in Hawaii.
** Male population only.
*** Estimated.

3. Population by Geographical Area
(Source: Department of Health, State of Hawaii, Jan. 1, 1960)

	Population	Per Cent of Total
City of Honolulu	326,445	53.6
City and County of Honolulu (exclusive of City of Honolulu)	148,423	24.4
County of Maui (includes islands of Maui, Molokai—except Kalawao—, Lanai, and Kahoolawe, which is uninhabited)	44,246	7.3
County of Hawaii (exclusive of city of Hilo)	36,112	6.0
City of Hilo	25,764	4.2
County of Kauai (includes island of Niihau)	27,841	4.5
County of Kalawao (peninsula on Molokai)	265	0.0
Total	609,096	100.0

4. Population by Racial Antecedents
(Source: U.S. Census, 1950)

	Total	Per Cent of Total
Hawaiian	86,090	17.2
Caucasian	114,793	23.0
Chinese	32,376	6.5
Filipino	61,062	12.2
Japanese	184,598	36.9
Others	20,850	4.2
Total	499,769	100.0

After 1950 racial data were not kept because the intermixture of groups made it impossible to list individuals even according to race of father.

Areas of Main Islands (sq. mi.)

Oahu	604
Hawaii	4,030
Maui	728
Kauai	555
Molokai	260
Lanai	141
Niihau	72
Kahoolawe	45
Total	6,435

Domestic Products Exported

Year	Total Imports	Total Exports	Domestic Produce Exported
1844	$ 350,347	$ 169,641	$ 109,587
1850	1,035,058	783,052	536,522
1860	1,223,749	807,459	480,526
1870	1,930,227	2,144,942	1,514,425
1880	3,673,268	4,968,455	4,889,194
1890	6,962,201	13,142,829	13,023,304
1899	16,069,577	22,628,742	22,324,865
1905	14,718,483	36,174,526	36,126,797
1915	26,416,031	62,464,759	62,195,586
1925	81,802,547	105,599,819	105,504,292
1935	84,552,884	100,033,996	93,431,000
1945	240,845,927	84,417,471	84,417,471
1955	419,483,000	270,335,000	264,413,000

Index

The Hawaiian language was first put into the English alphabet by the missionaries after 1820. It consists of five vowels and seven consonants (*h, k, l, m, n, p* and *w*). In all words, every letter is sounded. Every syllable ends in a vowel, and many syllables contain only vowels. No two consonants appear without vowels between them.

Consonants have about the same values as in English, except that the letter *w* in the middle of a word is usually pronounced *v* when preceded by *a, e,* or *i* and followed by a short vowel.

Each vowel has a long and a short sound, but to distinguish them requires a trained ear. The vowels are pronounced as in Italian or Spanish, as follows:

> *a* as in *father;*
> *e* as in *obey;*
> *i* as in *marine* (like *ee* in *meet*);
> *o* as in *note;*
> *u* as in *rule* (like *oo* in *too*).

There are no true diphthongs, but the following vowel combinations are sounded about as indicated:

> *ai*
> *ae* } like *ai* in *aisle* or like *i* in *line;*
>
> *au*
> *ao* } like *ow* in *cow;*
>
> *ei* like *ay* in *day.*

The accent commonly falls on the next to the last syllable; some words are unaccented. In the Index all Hawaiian words have been divided into syllables and the accents indicated. The inverted comma (') is used in a few words to mark the "glottal stop," which is a sign that a *k* sound found in other Polynesian dialects has disappeared in Hawaiian. Where this mark appears, the accent falls on the preceding vowel.

A

186–187, 189; language schools, 244–245; books, 246; in World War II, 261

Cholera, 29, 190

Choris, Louis, 37

Christianity, 29, 40, 43–46, 76

Chronicle, San Francisco, 159

Church of the Crossroads, 250

Churches: 76–78, 89, 212, 240, 261; first Protestant, 45, 46; first Catholic, 61; membership, Protestant, 76–77; Congregational, 77, 134; Mormon, 78–79, 133–134, 250; Anglican, 105–107, 131–132; Methodist, 134, 293; and education, 247–249; since annexation, 249–250; in Honolulu, 250

C.I.O. *See* Congress for Industrial Organization

Citizens' Statehood Committee, 291, 292

Citizenship, under Organic Act, 195

Citric acid, 239

City and County of Honolulu, 197, 199

City of Joseph, 79

Civil Aeronautics Board, 273

Civil Code, 101

Civil War in U. S., 89, 95, 114, 115, 118, 119, 123, 131

Civil wars, 23–24, 30, 49

Civilian defense, 258

Civilian record in World War II, 257–270

Clark, Byron O., 236

Clark, Gen. Mark W., 268

Clementine, ship, 59

Clerke, Capt., 15, 16, 18

Cleveland, Grover, 160, 161, 178–179, 183

Cleveland, Richard J., 35

Clothing, in ancient Hawaii, 9

Clubs, 136, 251, 262

Coan, Rev. Titus, 76

Coconut, 8, 9, 11, 28, 41

Coffee growing, 87, 92, 94, 121, 226

Coins: from Mexico, 88; Kalakaua, 167

College of Agriculture and Mechanic Arts, 246

Committee of Safety, 177–178

College of Hawaii, 246

College of St. Louis, 248

Colnett, Capt. James, 32

Columbia, ship, 25, 32

Columbia River, 35, 88

Comète, ship, 56

Commerce, growth of (table), 300

Communications, 97–101, 157–159, 239, 257, 265

Congregational churches, 78, 134

Congress. *See* U. S. Congress

Congress for Industrial Organization (C.I.O.), 276–277, 279, 282–284; Political Action Committee, 199, 284

Connecticut, 43, 98

Constellation, ship, 67–68

Constitution, steamship, 98

Constitution of 1840, 49, 54, 63, 76

Constitution of 1852, 75, 105, 111, 112, 114, 139

Constitution of 1864, 108, 112–113, 138, 139, 163, 171, 173, 177

Constitution of 1887, 171–172, 174, 176

Constitution of Republic of Hawaii, 183–184

Consuls: foreign, in Honolulu, 50, 59, 60, 62, 63, 65, 68, 69, 72, 73, 74, 85, 89; Hawaiian, in Japan, 111

Contract labor, 97, 129–130, 186, 274

Cook, Capt. James, 13–19, 23, 30, 32, 50, 92, 166

Cooke, Amos Starr, 82, 107, 140

Cooke, Mrs. C. M., 251

Cordon, Guy, 292–294

Cotton growing, 94–95, 226

County government, 197–198, 200, 201

Cowboys, 96

Crime Commission, 222

Crimean War, 114

Crockett (Calif.), 233

Crop diversification, 225

Crowe, Eugene B., 289

Crowell, Capt., 32

Crown lands, 71, 167, 204, 206

Cuba, 233, 234, 239